Praise from Those Who Served

"No Marine knows more about Con Thien than Captain Jim Coan. He writes with the authority of an expert eyewitness to the Marines' epic struggle to hold on to the Hill of Angels from July 1967 to August 1968 despite the NVA's best attempts to seize this key piece of dominant terrain just south of the DMZ in Vietnam."
—Colonel Donald L. Price, USMC (Ret.) with 3 tours in Vietnam and author of *The First Marine Captured in Vietnam*

"Con Thien certainly has been re-created here. I have read few personal narratives from the Marine war in Vietnam that get as close to the sheer sacrifice and misery that I have always suspected to be their lot."
—Philip D. Beidler, US Army Vietnam War veteran and author of *Beautiful War: Studies in a Dreadful Fascination*, *The Victory Album: Reflections on the Good Life after the Good War*, and *American Wars, American Peace: Notes from a Son of the Empire*

"This is a terrific life episode of an individual Marine tank platoon leader. You will feel what it was like to be 'in the barrel,' as Con Thien was known by those who served there; it was an NVA artillery magnet. I will never forget when my tank made the turnoff to go up to the legendary base and the trepidations I experienced, as did Jim. A must-read and a great companion to his first book, *Con Thien: The Hill of Angels*."
—Robert E. Peavey, Vietnam War veteran of Con Thien and author of *Praying for Slack: A Marine Corps Tank Commander in Vietnam*

"Jim Coan writes his first-person narrative about his eight months at Con Thien as a US Marine tank platoon leader with such graphic detail that the reader seems almost able to crawl into his skin and experience the personal hardships and the persistent deep-seated fear of uncontrollable carnage and instant death that gripped the inhabitants of the artillery-scarred, red clay bulls-eye known as the Hill of Angels."
—John Wear, president of the USMC Vietnam Tankers Association and former member of the First Platoon, Alpha Company, 1968

"How can a book about war evoke any thought or concept of beauty? Jim Coan's personal memoir of the Vietnam War, *Time in the Barrel*, is one brilliant illustration. His account of his experiences as a platoon commander with the Third Tank Battalion—focused on thirty-four days at Con Thien over September and October of 1967—is heartfelt, it is factual, and it provides a personal and historical perspective on the lives of those Marines and corpsmen who served at the base during the month-long siege. Jim Coan's memoir is timeless in its ability to transcend events and places and is universal in its importance to the twentieth-century American military experience."
—Al Claiborne, Vietnam War veteran and chair of the Norman Lane Jr. Memorial Project

"An old adage states, 'War is long periods of boredom punctuated by moments of sheer terror.' This was not true of Con Thien in late 1967. It was twenty-four hours a day of living with the nagging fear of death from a random artillery round, punctuated by the terror of an hour or more of intense daily bombardment: up to a thousand rockets and artillery rounds each day. Jim Coan ably describes the experience of a novice—and quickly disillusioned—junior officer sent to lead a veteran tank platoon in the final month of the siege. He does not shy away from graphically describing the surreal mixture of living with the omnipresent rain, rats, and water rationing, the minutiae required for the day-to-day operation of a tank platoon, deadly combat, the risk posed by mines that might dismember a tank and its crew, and even random death from natural events like floods. If you want an unvarnished account of what life was really like during the siege, this is it."

—Oscar E. "Ed" Gilbert, Marine Corps artilleryman, NCO instructor in the Marine Corps Reserve, and author of *Marine Corps Tank Battles in Vietnam* and *Tanks in Hell: A Marine Corps Tank Company on Tarawa*

TIME IN THE BARREL

TIME IN THE BARREL

A Marine's Account of the Battle for Con Thien

JAMES P. COAN

THE UNIVERSITY OF ALABAMA PRESS
Tuscaloosa

The University of Alabama Press
Tuscaloosa, Alabama 35487-0380
uapress.ua.edu

Typeface: Scala Pro and American Typewriter

Cover image: Leathernecks of the Ninth Marines wait out a North Vietnamese Army
rocket-and-artillery attack against the outpost at Con Thien in late 1967; courtesy of the
United States Marine Corps History Division/Department of Defense (A193030)
Cover design: David Nees

Cataloging-in-Publication data is available from the Library of Congress.
ISBN: 978-0-8173-1999-1
E-ISBN: 978-0-8173-9205-5

To my Marine and corpsmen brothers who sacrificed all of their tomorrows while serving their "time in the barrel" at Con Thien.

When you go home
Tell them for us and say,
For your tomorrow
We gave our today.

—Message found outside the American cemetery at Iwo Jima

Contents

Photographs follow page 113.

Preface

From August 1967 through July 1968, I was a tank platoon leader with Alpha Company, Third Tank Battalion, Third Marine Division. My tour in Vietnam was served operating from fire support bases in Northern I Corps just below the Demilitarized Zone (DMZ) dividing North from South Vietnam. For eight of those months, my five-tank platoon was assigned to defend a US Marine firebase called Con Thien while attached to various Marine infantry battalions spending their "time in the barrel" (as in the phrase "like shootin' fish in a barrel").

The North Vietnamese Army (NVA) knew the strategic importance of Con Thien; they wanted desperately to drive us Marines off of there, but we were not about to be evicted. Our mission was to hold Con Thien at all costs. We would hold Con Thien, but many of us paid the full price.

I have a deeply personal perspective about that red clay bulls-eye known as the "Hill of Angels," having survived the siege of Con Thien in the fall of 1967. Hundreds of rounds of incoming rockets, mortars, and artillery pounded our beleaguered outpost daily. Monsoon downpours turned the red laterite clay soil into a morass of oozing mud, flooded bunkers and trenches, and made Con Thien a living hell. As our casualty list grew into the hundreds, the news media latched onto our ordeal, referring to it as a "little Dien Bien Phu." But we Marines knew otherwise.

Within these pages, I've attempted to describe the battle for Con Thien as I experienced it from the perspective of a novice second lieutenant assuming his first combat command. My position as a tank platoon leader required me to work alongside the infantry (affectionately called "grunts") in their trenches and bunkers yet make contact daily with their battalion commander and his staff. Also, by virtue of having my five tanks dispersed around the firebase perimeter, I had to traipse all over Con Thien every day. It was an ideal way to observe everything that happened on "The Hill," and it was also a good way to get killed.

I kept a diary while in Vietnam, recording my perceptions, fears, and frustrations—all those personal things one hopes to look back on someday (see appendix B herein). In the years following my return to "the world" from Vietnam, I was plagued by a nagging depression; something precious was lost to me on Con Thien's muddy slopes. I started writing to pass the lonely evenings, expanding on the entries in my diary. This writing exercise evolved into a form of self-therapy. Putting my thoughts in writing eased the burden of sadness carried inside me as an ever-present shadow on my soul. The faces of my dead friends gradually faded, and the bad dreams—most of them—went away.

Several more years passed before I resurrected my collection of Con Thien anecdotes and reread them. My dear wife, Sandra, deciphered my handwritten notes and typed them for me, all the while encouraging me to write a book about my experiences at Con Thien. I remain forever grateful for her support and encouragement. Now, the story of the siege of Con Thien can be brought to light and not be buried forever in the dusty backroom archives of some military history research facility.

The Marines and corpsmen portrayed in this book are real people, not dramatized caricatures, and not creatures of fantasy imagined in some time-distorted imagination. Direct conversational quotations have been added to provide continuity and give the reader a personal insight into the characters portrayed; thus, the dialogue in the text is as accurate as I could recall in order to honestly and accurately express what was said by the accredited speakers. I felt obligated to mention these men by their real names and describe fairly and accurately what happened to me and to them, both pleasant and not so pleasant. People make mistakes; others are less than brave . . . sometimes. Marines are human, not robots, and I chose to describe our ordeal at Con Thien with real people, not robots or stereotypical Marines. I hesitated to criticize or second-guess decisions made in the confusion of combat by exhausted Marines operating under profound stress. In a few instances, I chose not to mention a Marine by his real name if his behavior or attitude was such that he would not be pleased to read about himself in my book.

Throughout this narrative, I share my most personal thoughts, fears, and frustrations because, to fully grasp the enormity of the fierce struggle for Con Thien, that story needs telling through the perspective of personal experience.

Despite any impediments to official accuracy inherent in this writing style, it does allow for the reader to share vicariously the ultimate experience of combat.

This is a story of courage under fire by young Americans being led by career noncommissioned officers (NCOs) and officers from an earlier generation. All of them were well aware that most civilians back home were neutral at best, and that some were openly hostile to their cause. Still they carried out orders, called their officers "Sir," and gave their best efforts to be good Marines, even at the risk of sacrificing all of their tomorrows.

James H. Webb Jr., a highly decorated Marine officer who served in Vietnam as a rifle platoon leader, company commander, and later as secretary of the navy, captured that sentiment best when he wrote:

When I remember those days and the very young men who spent them with me, I am continually amazed, for these were mostly recent civilians barely out of high school, called up from the cities and farms to do their year in Hell and then return. Visions haunt me every day, not of the nightmares of war, but of the steady consistency with which my Marines faced their responsibilities, and of how uncomplaining most of them were in the face of constant danger. The salty, battle-hardened 20-year-olds teaching green 19-year-olds the intricate lessons of that hostile battlefield. The unerring skill of the young squad leaders as we moved through unfamiliar villages and weed-choked trails in the black of night. The quick certainty with which they moved when coming under enemy fire. Their sudden tenderness when a fellow Marine was wounded and needed help. Their willingness to risk their lives to save other Marines in peril. . . . I am alive today because of their quiet, unaffected heroism.[1]

Acknowledgments

I would first like to thank my wife, Sandra, for all of her help with this book project. Many years earlier, she undertook the task of deciphering my Vietnam journal notes and converting them into readable text on her Smith-Corona typewriter. Then, she retyped them into manuscript form on our first computer. Fortunately, she is a highly proficient proofreader and that additional help was invaluable.

An always-ready resource for this book project was John Wear, president of the USMC Vietnam Tankers Association and a former flame tank commander who served with me at Con Thien. He researched his archives and came up with several photos that he shared with me. The vice president of the Vietnam Tankers Association, First Sergeant Rick Lewis, USMC (Ret.), was at his local VFW when he came across a photo of one of my former crewmen at Con Thien, Sergeant Rex Davis, who is deceased. Lewis was able to locate the Davis family and obtain a photo album put together by the daughter of Rex Davis and forward it to me. Major Robert Simon, US Army (Ret.), was a decorated helicopter pilot in Vietnam, and he tutored me on how to fly a helicopter as well as how one is flown in battle formations. A former Marine fixed-wing fighter pilot in Vietnam, David Thompson, mentored me on the details of carrying out close air support missions in support of Marines on the ground. Many thanks also to Sergeant Major Billy McLain, US Army (Ret.), who shared with me what it was really like to be a combat engineer in Vietnam. Geoff McCloud, Mike Ligon, and Daniel Shaw are Marines who attend our Monday morning coffee group in a local café, and they were totally supportive of this book effort.

Through my involvement with the USMC Vietnam Tankers Association, I've been able to reconnect with several tankers mentioned in this book, including Tom Barry, William Brignon, Albert Trevail, and Ken "Piggy" Bores. They were all extremely helpful in clearing up any questions about our time in the barrel. Others in that organization whom I want to thank are Richard Carey and Lieutenant Colonel Raymond Stewart, USMC (Ret.), who made it their mission in life to record the complete history of USMC tankers in Vietnam.

I'm forever indebted to the outstanding staff at the University of Alabama Press, starting with editor in chief Daniel Waterman and managing editor Jon Berry. I also want to thank Dawn Hall and Kelly Finefrock-Creed for all of their expert help and advice in making this book project become a reality.

Maps

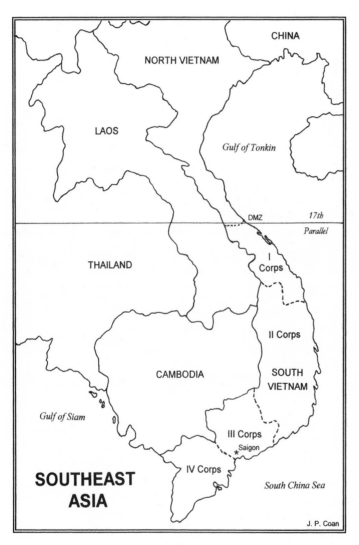

CHINA

NORTH VIETNAM

LAOS

Gulf of Tonkin

DMZ   *17th*
             Parallel

THAILAND   I
                          Corps

                       II Corps

CAMBODIA   SOUTH
                     VIETNAM

Gulf of Siam

                   III Corps
                   Saigon
         IV Corps

**SOUTHEAST
ASIA**   *South China Sea*

Southeast Asia

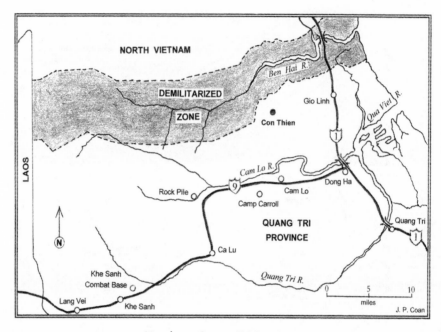

Northern Quang Tri Province

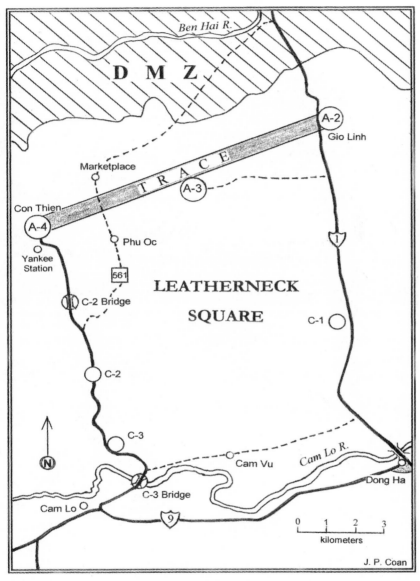

Leatherneck Square

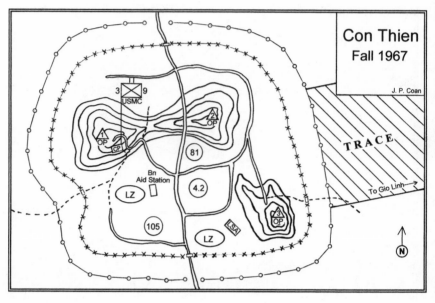

Con Thien, Fall 1967

TIME IN THE BARREL

INTRODUCTION

In July 1954, a conference was underway in Geneva, Switzerland, to negotiate a Korean War settlement. In attendance were the Big Four (the United States, Great Britain, the Soviet Union, and France) plus representatives from Communist China, and North and South Vietnam. When word of the French Army's disaster at Dien Bien Phu reached them, their focus shifted. France's colonial rule in Vietnam was ending, and it was crucial that top priority be given to resolving the Vietnam situation.

The Geneva Accords, issued on July 21, called for dividing Vietnam at the 17th parallel (referred to as a "provisional military demarcation line") with a five-mile-wide Demilitarized Zone (DMZ) as a buffer. The other major component of this agreement was that elections would be held in two years that would, in theory, finally allow the people of Vietnam to determine their own fate, whether to live under Ho Chi Minh and the Communists or Ngo Dinh Diem's American-backed government. But, President Diem had no intentions of following through on the election part of the "agreement." Unforeseen at the time, the Geneva Accords laid the groundwork for many more years of bloody conflict in Vietnam.

The DMZ generally followed the broad, winding Ben Hai River west from its mouth at the South China Sea for 30 miles until reaching the river's tributaries in the mountains, then followed the 17th parallel to the Laotian border. Where the Ben Hai empties into the sea is a barren expanse of sand dunes and occasional swamps. Inland a dozen miles from the coast, the lowland terrain becomes increasingly verdant and alive with rice fields, orchards, and occasional hamlets bordering the river.

One and a half miles below the eastern DMZ border, US military maps of the area indicated a prominent terrain feature 158 meters in elevation labeled "Nui Con Thien," which in English loosely translated means "a small mountain with heavenly beings." Early French missionaries believed there was something angelic about this little isolated hill mass rising up incongruously out of the relatively level surrounding countryside, thus the origin of the term "Hill of Angels."

The DMZ eventually evolved into anything but "demilitarized." The North Vietnamese began infiltrating troops and equipment across the DMZ into South Vietnam through Quang Tri Province, which abuts the southern DMZ border. By early 1966, as the number of infiltrators from the north increased exponentially each year, a group of far-removed Washington whiz kids and Pentagon planners devised a barrier system of firebase strong points to be situated below the DMZ, connected by a cleared swath of land sewn with barbed wire, mines, and anti-infiltration devices. The plan was called the Strong Point Obstacle System (SPOS). When presented to the then secretary of defense Robert S. McNamara, he indicated that he favored the plan so much so that he convinced General Westmoreland to make implementation of the barrier plan a top priority. Labeled "McNamara's Wall" by a cynical press, this "Maginot Line" concept was supposed to deter Ho Chi Minh's army from infiltrating across the DMZ into South Vietnam. Con Thien was a key component of that much-maligned barrier plan and a linchpin in the defense of the entire border region.

Why Con Thien?

Con Thien was a key piece of real estate. Anyone setting foot on any of Con Thien's three hillocks would realize that they had an unobstructed view for miles in every direction—an artillery forward observer's paradise. To the east, one could see along the cleared "trace" out to Gio Linh, another US firebase 6 miles away. And, beyond Gio Linh, one could observe American warships cruising in the South China Sea. An observer could see throughout the southeast portion of the DMZ, even across the Ben Hai River to the north. To the south was an unobstructed view of the sprawling Marine Corps military base at Dong Ha, 10 miles away, as well as the Marine firebases at Cam Lo and Camp Carroll along Route 9. The French Army had realized the importance of Nui Con Thien long before the arrival of the Americans, as they had constructed a concrete and steel fort on the highest of the three knolls that make up Con Thien.

The South Vietnamese Army (ARVN) moved onto Con Thien in early 1966, building bunkers and laying out deadly minefields (unmarked) on all the northern facing slopes of the three hillocks. The South Vietnamese and their American allies had observed the rules of the Geneva agreement for many years and kept their ground forces out of the DMZ, but in May 1966, the NVA's 324B Division attacked both ARVN firebases below the DMZ, Con Thien and Gio Linh. Those attacks were not successful, but from that time forward, the allied hands-off policy changed. Four US Marine infantry battalions and a sizeable force of ARVN invaded the southern portion of the DMZ during Operation Hastings in 1966, temporarily clearing the enemy forces out.

The "Trace"

In February 1967, Camp Con Thien was established by US Army Special Forces Detachment A-110. Navy Construction Battalion 4 (Seabees) soon joined them and built roads, bunkers, and connecting trenches, cleared an aircraft landing strip, and put in barbed wire obstacles. It was now officially an American base. A battery of US Army 175mm artillery pieces was emplaced at both Con Thien and Gio Linh to interdict enemy activities far up into North Vietnam. This proved to be too much of a threat for the NVA, and they retaliated by repeatedly shelling both bases. The big guns were then pulled back 10 miles to the Marine base at Camp Carroll, south of Route 9.

Assuming responsibility for both the security and construction of the Strong Point Obstacle System rankled Marine brass. They did not have the resources to do both adequately, and they loudly voiced that objection to General Westmoreland and Secretary McNamara, but their complaints fell on deaf ears. They were ordered to make do with the resources at hand, one way or the other.

The US Marines quietly commenced work on the barrier plan in early April 1967. Marines from the Eleventh Engineer Battalion, supported by tanks from the Third Tank Battalion, and a platoon of army M-42 "dusters," were tasked with completing a bulldozed "trace" 200 meters wide (later enlarged to 600 meters) for 6 miles that would connect Con Thien with the other key terrain feature to the east, Gio Linh. The First Battalion, Fourth Marines, assumed responsibility for all "trace" and firebase security, and the Marines were there to stay. The North Vietnamese Army saw this as a significant threat. Soon, the Marines along the barrier system came under heavy enemy fire. It was an especially harrowing task for the engineers. Completely exposed while working out in the open with their ground-clearing equipment, they endured snipers, mines, mortars, and incoming artillery from the DMZ, which inflicted a heavy toll on them.

3

Apparently, no one on General Westmoreland's staff or at the Pentagon had anticipated how strongly the North Vietnamese would strike back in an attempt to disrupt McNamara's pet project. The barrier plan was a profound threat to their entire future war of liberation in the northern provinces.

The North Vietnamese Up the Ante

The French Army's defeat by the Communist Viet Minh at Dien Bien Phu occurred on May 8, 1954. The night of May 8, 1967, the thirteenth anniversary of that pivotal battle, the NVA launched a massive ground attack on Con Thien.

At 0250, a green flare shot skyward from the tree line outside the southern perimeter. Almost immediately, sounding like hundreds of kettle drums beating in the distance, the booming of many mortars and artillery pieces firing could be heard all over Con Thien. Within seconds, the ground shook as hundreds of incoming rounds of artillery blasted the battered slopes and valleys.

NVA soldiers, led by highly trained "sappers" (engineer troops) employed Bangalore torpedoes to blast huge gaps in the northern perimeter wire. Once they had penetrated the wire, they tossed C-4 satchel charges at the bunkers housing the Green Berets and Navy Seabees. Three of the NVA attackers had flamethrowers and used them to roast several defenders crouched down in their bunkers. After they had overrun that initial defense line, the attackers headed toward what they thought were ARVN troops, but, unbeknownst to them, the ARVN troops had recently been replaced by two companies of the First Battalion, Fourth Marine Regiment, three tanks from Alpha Company, Third Tank Battalion, and a platoon of Marine engineers.

The NVA attacking force continued south, and might have overrun Con Thien, but they ran into a stalwart bunch of Marine infantry, engineers, and tankers who fought back so fiercely that they were able to prevent further penetration.

Three tanks on the northern perimeter from Alpha Company, Third Tank Battalion, led by Gunnery Sergeant Barnett G. Person, fought valiantly to stem the NVA charge. Sergeant David Danner, the tank platoon maintenance man, was asleep in the tank gunner's seat when an antitank rocket penetrated his tank's turret and exploded, severely burning him. Danner got all of the injured crewmen to an aid station. Refusing treatment of his painful wounds, he reentered the smoldering tank to retrieve its .30-caliber machine gun and several boxes of ammunition; then he poured a withering volume of fire into the ranks of the attacking enemy. At one point, Danner stopped firing long enough to rescue a seriously wounded Marine he saw lying in the open and carry him to an aid station bunker. Danner would not allow himself to be treated for his wounds until the attack was over that morning.

The tank commander of the second tank, Corporal Charles Thatcher, also painfully wounded in the back and neck by shrapnel as he pulled an injured crewman out of the tank turret, reentered his smoking tank and fired off all of the tank's machine-gun ammunition, inflicting heavy casualties on the attackers. With all of his ammunition exhausted, he climbed down from his disabled tank and retrieved a rifle from a dead Marine. Observing an enemy RPG (antitank rocket) team about to fire at his tank, Thatcher gunned them down before they could unleash their antitank rocket.

Gunnery Sergeant Barnett G. Person was the tank platoon sergeant. He advanced his tank to the main point of attack where his other two tanks lay immobilized. While several NVA soldiers crawled atop his tank attempting to disable it with satchel charges, Person kept his 90mm tank cannon blasting out beehive and canister antipersonnel rounds; his two machine guns sprayed thousands of bullets into the ranks of the determined enemy. His tank would be the only one still operable when daylight came.

Out of twelve crewmen on the three tanks, only one survived the battle unscathed. Three tankers were dead. Surviving their wounds, Corporal Charles D. Thatcher and Sergeant David Danner would receive the Navy Cross for their heroism that night. Gunnery Sergeant Person would be awarded the Silver Star for his bravery.

As the morning sun rose in the smoke-shrouded sky, vengeful Marines attacked isolated pockets of NVA and shot them down as they tried to escape. With the perimeter sealed off, making escape impossible, it was either surrender or die—most chose to die. After the battle, our engineers buried over two hundred NVA dead in a common grave outside Con Thien's northern perimeter.

That May 8 battle for Con Thien was a devastating defeat that would affect General Giap's future war planning for North Vietnam. He learned that he would not be able to attack and overrun the US Marines dug in at those barrier system strongpoints. Their tenacity and overwhelming air and artillery support were too difficult to overcome.

In response to that NVA surprise attack, The III Marine Amphibious Force launched a major retaliatory attack involving over 10,000 Marines and ARVN in an operation named Hickory, which was intended to once again clear the NVA out of the southern DMZ area between Con Thien and Gio Linh. Twenty tanks from Alpha and Bravo Companies participated. A major objective of Hickory was the removal of all civilians from their homes to create a free-fire zone from south of the Ben Hai to Route 9. All of those inhabitants were relocated to a government resettlement center at Cam Lo off of Route 9. Despite living in a battle zone, a surprising number of civilians had to be forced off of their ancestral lands.

Operation Hickory was only a temporary setback for General Giap's North Vietnamese Army; in due time, they would be back in force. The First Battalion, Ninth Marines (1/9), learned this tragically on July 2 during Operation Buffalo. In an infamous day-long battle known as the "Marketplace Massacre," an outnumbered Bravo Company came under heavy attack by a regiment of NVA that included shelling from artillery positions in the DMZ. A platoon of tanks responded from Con Thien and was able to retrieve all the wounded they could find. Only twenty-six Bravo Company Marines were able to walk out unaided. Sadly, the bodies of thirty-four Marines and corpsmen baked in the fierce summer heat for several days until they could be retrieved when reinforcements arrived. Operation Buffalo, which began as a disaster for 1/9, ended on July 14 as a total defeat for the Ninetieth NVA Regiment, which lost a reported 1,290 dead. Marine losses were 159 killed in action (KIA) and 345 wounded.[1]

The remainder of that scorching hot summer of 1967, intermittent firefights and ambushes transpired along and below the DMZ, but nothing of the magnitude previously experienced. Then, in concert with South Vietnam's September 3 Election Day, the NVA bombarded Con Thien, Gio Linh, and Dong Ha with their long-range 130mm and 152mm artillery ensconced in the DMZ. North Vietnam's General Giap had been ordered to take the offensive and neutralize Con Thien. From that day forth for the next six weeks, Con Thien was under siege, facing daily mortar, artillery, and rocket attacks. And the SPOS barrier-building folly would continue.

1.
THE FIRST DAY

That terrible Autumn day had been a long one, but the late afternoon seemed even longer. The sun seemed almost to go backwards in the sky. I thought that night would never come.
—Lieutenant James A. Graham, Confederate States of America, referring to the September 17, 1862, battle at Antietam

The date was September 10, 1967. I was a twenty-five-year-old US Marine second lieutenant waiting nervously in my commanding officer's jeep while he made some last-minute arrangements in his office.

This was the all-important day I had been striving for since I joined the Marine Corps eleven months earlier—the day I took command of a Marine tank platoon. But the platoon operated out of Con Thien, not exactly a desirable place to call home. People reacted strangely when I mentioned going to Con Thien, especially those who'd been there already. I felt something ominous about the fading grins, the serious, searching stares. And I didn't like the way they wished me "good luck," as if I was going to need it—lots of it. A heavy, gray, overcast sky did nothing to ease my apprehension over what was destined to happen to me in the days and weeks to follow.

The plan that morning was for the captain to chauffeur me from Alpha Company Headquarters at Dong Ha to a rendezvous point called Charlie-Two (C-2), 4 miles south of Con Thien. There, I would officially relieve Second Lieutenant Tom Barry, the present platoon leader of First Platoon, Alpha Company, Third Tank Battalion. My platoon's mission was to provide direct support to the US Marines defending Con Thien, a vital outpost only 1.5 miles south of the Demilitarized Zone dividing North Vietnam from South Vietnam.

Lieutenant Barry had preceded me by only nine days. He received two Purple Hearts for superficial shrapnel wounds from enemy mortar fire at Con Thien in a week. If wounded a third time, he would be rotated automatically "out of country" to Okinawa. I was chosen to replace Lieutenant Barry before he bought another "Heart," or maybe "bought it" all together.

Some priority scuttlebutt was circulating around Third Tank Battalion

Headquarters in Phu Bai that a major operation involving several US Marine regiments was scheduled. The operation was going to commence the middle of September and would involve all Marine elements, including tanks, in a massive sweep of the eastern sector of the DMZ—certain to be a bloody encounter.

I recalled my meeting with Lieutenant Colonel Chaplin, the Third Tank Battalion commanding officer, when he informed me that I was going up to Con Thien to take over Barry's platoon. It was right after the colonel's evening briefing. A blazing August sun was descending upon the barren horizon when he invited me to follow him into his quarters. The colonel and the battalion executive officer shared a plywood "hootch" with screened doors and windows to keep out invading insects. He gestured toward a battered camp chair, and I sat down expectantly, knowing something was up, something big.

I respected the colonel. He was a wise man, not impressed with his own importance, and a genuine person who appreciated a good joke, no matter who told it. He was serious this evening, however, as he sagged heavily into a wooden folding chair behind his field desk. "Lieutenant Coan, we're going to have to replace Mister Barry on Con Thien. He's been wounded twice; one more time and he leaves us. You're flying up tomorrow to Dong Ha. From there, you go on to Con Thien and assume command of First Platoon."

I exhaled deeply, then blurted out, "That's great news, sir!" Exhilarated by the prospect of my first command, yet not wanting to appear overly excited, I decided against saying more.

"Okay, but remember, you are no good to us dead. Stay down in that turret and don't be sightseeing when the shelling starts up there. You'll have a good man for a platoon sergeant, Gunny Hopkins. He's forgotten more about tanks than you know, so don't think you have all the answers . . . you don't. And wear that blasted flak jacket at all times, in or out of your tank, and make your men do it, too! Tankers have a way, sometimes, of believing they are made of steel, like their tanks. And, oh, yes . . ." His voice trailed off briefly as he stared at his desktop, obviously searching for the correct words; then, he continued on in a lowered tone: "Make certain you have the facts straight on your casualties, then call them in immediately. We can't afford mistakes in casualty reporting; it affects the entire system, not to mention the next of kin who receive conflicting reports on their loved ones. And, Jim, lieutenants aren't made out of steel, either. Good luck to you."

My life was going to take an interesting turn in the next few days, to say the least. Mentally and emotionally I was in good shape, prepared to handle anything thrown my way, but I couldn't shake the butterflies in my stomach. Pinpointing a specific reason behind the misgivings would have helped me relax more, but it was an elusive quest. Was I afraid of dying? No, no more so than in times past when I considered my ultimate mortal destiny. And I knew intuitively I would be okay under fire; I had no reason to think otherwise. But Con Thien, with its evil reputation, that *was* troubling me. Danger was lurking up there, and the manner in which I found it would be a totally new experience, and the not knowing what to expect was worse, by far, than knowing.

Dong Ha

My captain, a slender, blond-haired officer who, although in his mid-twenties like me, would have to show ID to prove he was over twenty-one, strode purposefully over to the jeep. I detected a hint of arrogance in his voice as he asked cheerily, "Ready to shove off, Lieutenant?"

"Yes, sir. I'm all ready to go, Captain," I responded carefully, determined not to give away how anxious I was feeling.

"Very well, then. Let's go find that diesel fuel truck at Charlie Two and meet Tom Barry." He retrieved a camouflage-covered steel helmet from the jeep floor, placed it securely on his head, and easily swung his long legs into the jeep. He wore a faded, battered USMC flak jacket, which was peculiar; he could have had his pick of any new ones from Alpha Company's supply.

The captain drove his own vehicle. Most company commanders used an enlisted man as their jeep driver. I thought this was an indicator of his style, loose and informal, but there was something detached and aloof about the man. I wasn't sure if we were going to work together well or not. Time would tell.

Our little jeep maneuvered effortlessly onto the main dirt road leading through the compound, and we headed north in the direction of Dong Ha's main gate. The captain recounted the disaster that had occurred a few weeks earlier, when forty-one enemy artillery rounds, fired from the DMZ, landed inside the perimeter of Dong Ha Combat Base and touched off a series of earthshaking explosions that rocked the base for over four hours. Stockpiles of ammunition, thousands of gallons of fuel, and tons of badly needed supplies had literally gone up in smoke. In fact, an ominous, black cloud of smoke from the exploding dumps billowed up over 12,000 feet and was observed as far south as Third Tank Battalion Headquarters at Phu Bai.[1]

Luxuriant green fields, rice paddies, and groves of shade trees thrived on both banks of the placid Cam Lo River paralleling our route westward toward Camp Carroll. An occasional water buffalo wandered through the open fields with a bare-chested peasant boy sitting astride the beast's back. Dong Ha Mountain rose majestically skyward to our right front a few miles distant, completing the peaceful panorama before us. This was beautiful scenery, right out of the pages of a travel agency brochure on Southeast Asia. Neither the captain nor I appeared to desire more conversation. We sat in silence, respecting each other's mood, watching the verdant countryside pass by.

Fate Is a Four-Letter Word

Americans were getting killed in this "little" war at the rate of several hundred per week. Officers like me were especially vulnerable because one couldn't lead men into combat by hiding in a safe place until the danger passed. Only one month "in country," and the number of my friends killed or badly wounded was beginning to mount.

I was profoundly saddened on two separate occasions earlier in the month by news of tragedy befalling two friends of mine: Lieutenant Tom Dineen, his wife pregnant, was a Basic School graduate with me who requested an infantry assignment and was subsequently killed in Vietnam by a booby trap; Lieutenant Ed "Duke" Jory, father of a newborn infant, went to an amtrac (amphibious tractor) battalion and was machine-gunned to death while leading a patrol. Some other lieutenants with whom I had attended tank school were also casualties. Steve Fitzgerald was shot through the back and critically wounded by an NVA sniper as he leaned out of his tank commander's cupola while attempting to break up an ambush on Route 9 near Ca Lu; he was medevaced out of country. Jim Georgaklis was wounded twice during the same battle by NVA mortar fire. And Tom Barry—two Purple Hearts in nine days at Con Thien.

Would Con Thien be my last experience as a mortal being on this earth? Was I doomed already, my fate sealed, living out my role in this tragic war drama until that chosen moment arrived when an enemy projectile with my name on it ripped into my body and snuffed out my life? It could happen. That it very well could happen was impressed upon me so vividly in the Alpha Company office back in Dong Ha. Nailed over the doorway outside the office was a hand-painted, wooden plaque with the heading: "Alpha Company Honor Roll." Beneath the bold, black letters of the heading were the neatly aligned names of each honored individual, his rank, and date of death in Vietnam. It seemed like a crude gesture to me, very unnecessary and very detrimental to one's morale; besides, one out of every four names on the "Honor Roll" was a lieutenant. I didn't need any reminders of how the odds were stacked.

An incident occurred at Third Tank Battalion in Phu Bai a few nights prior to my departure for Alpha Company Headquarters in Dong Ha that probably accounted more than anything for my pessimistic outlook. A short round from a friendly South Vietnamese artillery unit near Phu Bai landed directly on a plywood hut filled with sleeping Seabees in the compound adjacent to ours, 100 meters away. We heard the explosion and rushed blindly for the bunkers outside our hootch. After the all clear signal was given, several medevac helicopters landed with their deafening rotor noise and flashing red lights to haul away casualties. Few of us slept much that night.

The next morning, two other officers and I decided, mainly out of morbid curiosity, that we ought to go over to the Seabee area and see what had happened. The artillery round (75mm) had detonated instantly on contact with a tin roof on one hut, hurling thousands of steel and tin splinters throughout the length and breadth of the building. Few of the unsuspecting Seabees escaped without injury, as evidenced by brilliant red splotches on the bed linen and pillows. The rumor we heard was that two men were killed outright; several others were in critical condition. Those Seabees had no way of knowing that the cots they chose to sleep in several weeks earlier probably determined whether they lived or died in that split-second nightmare of flying shrapnel. It was just an unfortunate accident—wars are full of them—but we all left there with the very sobering knowledge that men really are subject to the whims of fate.

I began thinking that day, if a tragedy such as that could happen by accident in this war, sooner or later it might be my turn to face sudden death. An uncomfortable, nagging doubt began to fester in my subconscious that a showdown with fate might turn out badly for me.

O

Our jeep made a right-hand turn onto a dirt road and I was quickly jarred back to reality. "This is the Con Thien turnoff, Lieutenant. We still have several more miles yet." I nodded my head toward the captain to show I understood and took note of the village spread out before us. "That's part of Cam Lo Village," the captain continued. "Many of those villagers were evacuated from the DMZ and Leatherneck Square during Operation Hickory that ended this spring. This road we're riding on is Con Thien's MSR—main supply route—and any attempt to overrun Con Thien will most definitely require severing this main supply artery."

We passed slowly through the village. A few scrawny, barefoot peasant women in black silk pajamas and white conical hats jogged alongside the road. Each woman balanced a 15-foot pole on her right shoulder. Hanging from each end of the poles were heavy baskets full of goods that I surmised were going to market. They did not even give us a second look. Apparently, the novelty of Marine Corps vehicles had worn off long ago. My heart skipped a few beats at the realization we were getting closer.

Once past the outskirts of the village, we crossed the Cam Lo bridge, then the jeep accelerated. We were in open country—a free-fire zone all the way to Con Thien. Any people we observed on foot from then on were either American military or North Vietnamese (NVA). The free-fire zone extended from Cam Lo north to the DMZ, 9 miles away, and throughout the DMZ and Leatherneck Square. This was made possible by the removal of an estimated 13,000 civilians from the area by truck, amtrac, and helicopter during Operation Hickory in the spring of 1967.[2]

We passed clusters of Seabees and engineers working feverishly with graders and bulldozers on the road; they were also clearing the undergrowth alongside the road as an ambush deterrent. Marine riflemen slouched around on the hillsides providing security. This was soft duty for these "grunts" because they were south of the artillery fire-support base, C-2, and little enemy contact had been made lately this far south.

The gently rolling, shrub- and grass-covered terrain was not unlike that found in parts of California, except that we were traveling north on the MSR, which delineated the far western edge of Leatherneck Square, the scene of many bloody confrontations between US Marines and NVA forces the previous spring and summer.

14

I removed a waterproofed map case from the trouser pocket of my utilities and unfolded a map of the area. Located about 2,000 meters below the southern boundary of the DMZ was a horizontal control point with the number 158 beside it (158 meters or 474 feet in elevation). The Vietnamese words "Nui Con Thién" printed above the control point marked the outpost my tank platoon was assigned to help defend. Loosely translated, "Nui Con Thién" meant a small mountain leading to heaven. To Marines zeroed in on the hill's shell-cratered slopes, Con Thien was probably something much less than angelic.

As we approached the welcome gates of C-2, I noticed puffs of white smoke belching skyward every few seconds from within the enclave. A 105mm artillery battery was carrying out a fire mission in support of Con Thien.

The artillery firebase was protected by miles of interlaced, barbed concertina wire strung out around the perimeter. Outside of this wire obstacle was a minefield containing thousands of deadly antipersonnel mines primed to mangle any NVA trespassers. I learned a few days prior to leaving Battalion that C-2's minefield had claimed the lives of two engineers and a few stray cattle since its installation; no NVA were yet victims of that minefield.

We passed a flak-vested sentry at the south gate and proceeded along a dirt road winding through the artillery firebase toward our rendezvous point near the north gate. Numerous 105mm howitzer barrels aimed skyward in the same direction we were headed—north toward Con Thien.

"There's the truck, sir." I pointed to our right front, just inside the northern perimeter fence. A forest green, USMC diesel fuel truck sat in the open by itself. Two men slouched in the truck cab reading comic books. They sat upright as our jeep rolled to a halt nearby, and one man walked over to the captain's side of the jeep.

"Did we miss Barry's tanks?" asked the captain, his voice verging on anger if we had.

"No, suh," the man drawled. "We been here an hour and they ain't showed yet."

"Okay, great. Stay where you are, then. They'll be here pretty soon." His instructions completed, the captain spun off back down the dirt road, leaving the man enveloped in a blanket of dust. We parked adjacent to an imposing bunker near the road. "Stay here and keep an eye out for the tanks, Lieutenant.

I've got some business to square away." He sprang from the jeep and disappeared down into the bunker entrance.

I sat pensively in the jeep, watching Marines come and go. I was acutely aware of my freshly laundered utilities and shined jungle boots—unmistakably an uninitiated rookie in a combat zone. The sharp blast of howitzers firing periodically startled me as I tried to relax. Soon, I was lost in thought.

Looking Back

My presence in Vietnam was no whim of fate, nor was it an unwelcome development. I had volunteered for this, both eyes wide open, knowing full well I was probably headed for a war zone in Vietnam someday. Not exactly an adventurer by nature, I still longed for a chance to prove myself, to be a warrior, to become initiated into that unique fraternity of combat veterans. It was an adventure, yes, but much more than that. This adventure had deep roots set down many years before.

Growing up in Tucson, Arizona, I was plagued by allergies and more than my share of childhood diseases. I idolized an older stepbrother who had served as a Marine machine gunner in the Solomon Islands during World War II. Some of my most treasured belongings came from his sea bag after he returned home: a faded khaki garrison cap and a white bath towel, frayed at the edges, with U.S. MARINE CORPS spelled out in bright red letters. *The Sands of Iwo Jima* and *Flying Leathernecks* were classic John Wayne war movies. I sat through them enthralled, totally absorbed in the action. The bookshelf behind my bed held dozens of paperbacks, almost all with a military theme. Plastic models of fighter planes and bombers sat on every dresser and desk in my bedroom, and colored pencil tracings of war machinery were taped to the walls. I was obsessed with things military.

Then, along came Tony into my life—the class bully. Fourth grade was a nightmare of fear, tension, insecurity, and humiliation. I didn't know how to fight, and he knew it. When I arrived at the bicycle racks in the morning, he and his little band of followers met me, goading me into a fight, taunting me. I was easy prey, totally unprepared for what was happening. It was good sport for him; he never tired of the intimidation tactics. I learned later on in life that the best way to rid yourself of a bully was to fight back, even if you lost, but that lesson came too late to resolve this situation.

Tony eventually transferred to a different school, so we never had the one-on-one showdown that I knew would happen one day. But, with each passing year, a growing resolve solidified within: never again would anyone intimidate me or bully me, because I would defend myself with a vengeance. I took boxing lessons at the YMCA, climbed rope, did five different kinds of push-ups— anything that would build me up, make me strong. I was going to be ready next time—was I ever going to be ready.

Sports, particularly football, became another obsession. From age thirteen on, I lifted weights on a regular schedule, swam competitively, and ran track, but football was my passion. It was the rough contact. Each jarring block or tackle satisfied something basic to my psyche. Then, one of life's small tragedies struck in my senior year of high school. I was going to be the starter at right end. After the first two days of practice, my brand-new football shoes had rubbed raw, oozing, nickel-sized craters into both sides of my heels. The pain was wicked; I was hobbling through practices, wincing with each step. No matter what the trainer attempted before each practice, every session was agony. One of the assistant coaches started to ride me about coasting, not hustling. In a fit of irrational anger and frustration, I quit, turned in the uniform. Many weeks later the blisters healed, but I was too proud to ask for another chance. I was *not* a quitter . . . but I quit! How I regretted that one impulsive decision to give in to pain and cash in my chips.

My house in Tucson was located three blocks from the University of Arizona campus. Male students often walked by my house going to and from classes wearing their ROTC uniforms. The idea of having to wear a uniform on campus was a real turnoff for me. I knew that my next venture after high school was to attend the University of Arizona. So, in an effort to avoid having to take mandatory ROTC, I joined the Arizona Army National Guard, 158th Infantry Brigade, located in Tucson. Basic training was at Fort Ord, California, and then it was on to Fort Gordon, Georgia, for training as a manual teletype operator. On returning to Tucson after that training was completed successfully, I was placed in the Guard Unit's Communications Platoon.

Next, it was on to college at the University of Arizona. Textbooks in hand, I walked the sunbaked campus each day, searching for a friendly face among the hordes of students going to and from classes. Over 20,000 of us were registered;

all ages, races, nationalities, and levels of commitment were represented. I was one of the uncommitted, taking a full course load but not sure why, not certain I even wanted to be there but plugging away at the course work anyway in the event something fired my interest enough to major in that subject.

I was bored. In a desperate attempt to shore up my dreary social life, I joined one of the most prominent social fraternities on the Arizona campus, Phi Gamma Delta. I became a "house man." We house men lived, ate, slept, and breathed fraternity. We were like brothers, feeling a closeness many family members never experience. To be able to afford my school tuition and fraternity house dues, I worked as a "scully" in the fraternity kitchen, serving food, clearing tables, and washing pots and pans. School holidays were spent working at my stepfather's business in downtown Tucson. I was also a lifeguard at the downtown Sands Hotel during summer vacations.

My carefree college days came to a disastrous end late one night in May 1964. The evening began harmlessly enough. Several fraternity brothers and I went to a local pub to celebrate the conclusion of semester final exams. Several pitchers of beer later, it was closing time. We were all soused, thoroughly wiped out. I climbed into the back seat of Paul's Volkswagen. Chris got in the passenger seat, and we waited while someone coaxed Paul down from the roof of the pub where he was pouring beer down on the heads of departing customers. That should have been a red flag that Paul was in no shape to drive, but I was too befuddled to care.

Paul drove us home, weaving recklessly, taking corners on two wheels, running over curbs. He blew out a right front tire about six blocks from the fraternity house. We bumped to a halt behind another parked VW. Paul or Chris (it matters not who, in retrospect) suggested we switch tires—take a good tire from the other car and replace it with our flat tire.

I wanted no part of this drunken caper, especially since I was planning a law enforcement career after college. While they worked clumsily under an alcohol fog, dropping hubcaps, cursing, and laughing merrily, I left and walked home to the fraternity house and collapsed into my bunk on the sleeping porch. About 4:00 a.m., a bright flashlight shined in my eyes and a stern-faced cop whispered loudly, "You're under arrest for Grand Theft!" My two "brothers" had wilted when the cops demanded to know who the third thief was. The

Volkswagen theft owner had initially reported three culprits were stealing their tire. My life then ricocheted off in another direction.

Rather than hire a lawyer and have my family find out about it, I chose to plead guilty to a lesser charge of tampering with a motor vehicle, a misdemeanor, and accept a fine along with my cohorts. That was a mistake. Page two of the local Sunday paper had an article on the incident: "University Students Arrested for Grand Theft." There was my name in print—local boy turns bad.

I dreaded facing my mother, but it had to be done, thanks to the press. The year before, her husband (my stepfather) had died of a heart attack. He meant little to me; we rarely spoke, and then only when it was unavoidable. But his untimely death staggered my mother. He was the aggressive, take charge, decisive, type-A businessman. His loss left a vacuum in her life. She was slowly rebounding, and then this had to happen. She heard my side of the story but remained stoic, only berating me for not obtaining a lawyer. She never mentioned it again. I loved her for that.

Other "friends" and family were not so kind. I became a nonperson. People I had known for years avoided me. I was summoned to the dean of students soon after the tire caper and was told the university was suspending me for one semester. "We are cracking down on student troublemakers who give the university bad publicity." I then died a thousand deaths carrying my class withdrawal slip up the stairs to my law enforcement curriculum advisor. He was a stern, righteous, retired Detroit police captain, and he had read about me in the local newspaper. Not a word did he utter, nor would he look at me, as he scribbled disgustedly on my drop sheet. He reacted characteristically, as I had known he would, as if I were a despicable, unclean leper.

A long period of depression set in. I grieved over my lost self-esteem. My plans for a law enforcement career were over. I spent the remainder of that summer and fall employed at a local hospital as a surgery orderly, counting the days until I could be readmitted to the university. Graduation from college a year later was anticlimactic. I found no great clamoring for public administration graduates, especially for ex-law enforcement majors with arrest records. The best job I could get in Tucson was as a credit manager trainee at Sears—a decent enough job—but not stimulating. I felt unfulfilled, sedentary, stifled. I wanted a challenge.

My six-year total service obligation in the Army National Guard was completed in 1966. Nearing the end of my active reserve commitment, I'd been offered a promotion to sergeant if I reenlisted, but I turned it down, seeing no future for me continuing with the National Guard, so that was not an option.

One evening in the summer of 1966, after another boring day at work reviewing credit histories, I sat down in front of the television to watch the evening news. A serious-looking Marine captain was being interviewed about a battle his unit had just fought. His self-confident demeanor and squared-away appearance started me thinking that I'd like to be on his team, so to speak.

I contacted the Marine Corps recruiting office in Los Angeles to explore the possibility of me becoming an Officer of Marines. The Marines needed officer material, and I hoped they wouldn't turn down a willing, qualified, college graduate just because he got out of line once while under the influence of alcohol. Five potential Officer Candidate School (OCS) recruits and I met at the Sands Hotel in Tucson with the Marine Officer Selection representative. Three of us, including me, had misdemeanor arrest records (all alcohol related) and needed a special waiver to be accepted. My waiver was granted. No one would expect Marines to be choir boys—we were no exception.

Pending the results of my physical exam, the next step would be to report to Quantico the following October to commence Officer Candidate School. One problem—I wore glasses to correct my mild farsightedness. Believing (erroneously) that this would prevent me from being accepted into OCS, I went to the medical school library at the University of Arizona and checked out several ophthalmology textbooks showing various eyesight exam charts. I memorized three different eye charts. When it came time for my eye exam at the clinic, I instantly recognized that the medical office eye chart was one I'd memorized. My medical records subsequently indicated a vision score of 20/20 in both eyes.

As my overall health was excellent, I embarked on a conditioning program to prepare myself for the demanding physical challenge ahead at OCS. I jogged 2 miles to the city park and back daily, then did as many pull-ups and push-ups as I could manage in the garage. The workout routine was the same as I'd followed preparing for the start of football season in high school; only, had I known what hell was in store for me at Quantico in a few short months, I'd have worked out three times as hard.

The Change of Command

My reverie was abruptly terminated. The unmistakable, rhythmic squeal of many tank shock absorbers protesting their 52-ton burdens was detected approaching C-2 from the north. A dust cloud rising outside the minefield gate heralded the approach of three M-48A3 USMC Patton medium tanks. They lurched to a halt in the vicinity of the diesel fuel truck, keeping a healthy distance from one another, while the first tank crew refueled from the diesel truck.

I didn't have to find the captain. He also heard the tanks arrive. In a flash, the captain jumped in, started up the jeep, and accelerated over to the nearest tank. Tom Barry was just removing his headgear when he spotted us. He emerged from the tank commander's cupola and sprang to the ground, grinning from ear to ear as he approached. Slight in stature, he almost bounced with enthusiasm when he walked. "Jimbo, how the hell are ya!" he said warmly, ignoring the captain.

Noticing the dirty bandage on his left cheek, I quipped, "Cut yourself shaving, Tom?"

"Ho, ho! All we need around here is another comedian. You know, I nearly bought the farm the morning this happened. I was standing on the front slope plate of my beast there, when mortar shells started dropping all around me. I flopped down into a prone position under the gun tube and froze; a piece of shrapnel hit me in the face. There I am, too petrified to move, blood pouring out of the hole in my cheek, praying to God for all I was worth."

"Was that your first or second Heart?" asked the captain earnestly, an anxious expression on his face.

"Second," said Tom. "The first was only a scratch." He turned away from the captain and continued, as if annoyed at the captain's question: "Watch your ass up there on Con Thien, Jim. The gooks love to mortar tanks. They got our positions zeroed in." He whispered the last, as if this was confidential information he didn't want overheard.

Tom spun around and called for his crewmen to get everyone together by his tank. Refueling halted while a dozen crewmen from the three tanks gathered in a group next to Tom. "Listen up, the captain here has a few well-chosen words to say to you."

Ignoring the dig, the captain said, "Gents, this is Lieutenant Coan, your new platoon leader." I cringed inwardly as he said "new." But then he mentioned my one month of experience at battalion headquarters before coming to Alpha Company. I thanked him silently for not presenting me to these men as a total novice in Vietnam. My gaze shifted from face to face, studying those grimy, combat-wizened Marines, veterans of many continuous months of operations in this area. Something akin to intuition warned me that the next few minutes in front of these men would either win their confidence or cast some doubt in their minds as to my competence.

When he finished his little speech, I nodded knowingly at him and requested the senior sergeant to join me in a huddle—better that only one man should know the extent of the new platoon leader's inexperience. The captain introduced me to a skinny, dark-tanned Marine of Mexican American ancestry, Sergeant Guivara. He appeared tired, maybe bored; I couldn't tell for certain. He was cordial, anyway, as he pointed out my tank, A-12, and told me the names of my other crewmen, which went in one ear and out the other in the stress of the moment. He explained the refueling procedure, then excused himself as it was his turn to refuel his tank.

Tom strode over to me just then, a subdued, serious look in his dark eyes. "Okay, Jim," he sighed. "It's your baby now. I want to wish you all the luck in the world." The depth of his sincerity brought me up short for an instant. This wasn't the same cocky, macho, irreverent Marine I had known two weeks earlier back at Phu Bai.

"Thanks, Tom, I'll need it all, it looks like . . . by the way," I asked, almost as an afterthought, "what's up with you and the CO?"

"You'll have to find that out for yourself," Tom replied quietly as he walked away. I knew better than to pursue the matter further. Tom wasn't the game-playing type. Something was going on, but he didn't want to share it with me. I could accept that, but my antennae were going to be aroused until I learned what was behind Tom's barely concealed animosity.

All of this talk was making me more apprehensive, if that was possible, so I said my final goodbyes to Lieutenant Barry and the captain. Obviously, Tom had no reservations about returning to Dong Ha. The hot showers and mess hall food would be a blessing compared to what he had lived with for the last nine days at Con Thien. He was scaly with accumulated dirt, as were the rest of the men. I made a mental note to check into that once we got up to Con Thien.

While the other tank crews were finishing their refueling, I had a good look at A-12 (alpha one-two), "my" tank. Even at rest, it was a thing of awesome beauty; its smooth, sun-warmed, forest green steel surface conveyed power, almost invincible strength. Pity the poor foot soldier faced with an armored assault coming at him; that would be a terrifying experience, with or without antitank weapons.

Those 52-ton "iron monsters" carried a crew of four: tank commander, gunner, loader, and driver. The M-48A3 medium tank held 375 gallons of diesel fuel and traveled at speeds of up to 40 mph (downhill) with a 300-mile range. What differentiated the M-48A3 from the A1 and A2 models was the diesel engine (as opposed to an explosion-prone gasoline engine), infrared capability, and special 360-degree vision ring around the base of the tank commander's cupola. Mounted in the turret was a 90mm tank cannon that could fire a 32-pound, high-explosive projectile 4,400 meters distant on a direct-fire basis, or up to 19,560 yards in indirect fire. A coaxially mounted .30-caliber machine gun was placed immediately to the left of the 90mm main gun breech in the turret. The loader was responsible for keeping both the machine gun and main gun loaded and functioning during a firefight—a tough job, but a crucial one. Also in the turret were the gunner and tank commander, sixty-two rounds of assorted 90mm ammunition, 6,000 rounds of .30-caliber ammo, and 500 rounds of .50-caliber ammo for the tank commander's cupola-mounted .50-caliber machine gun. The driver sat in his own compartment up front, physically isolated from the others.

I climbed around and over A-12, noting track tension and wear on the track blocks. The sprocket teeth and road wheel rubber were worn, but not badly. Attached to the rear of the turret was a storage area called the "gypsy rack"; personal gear was stowed there. I added my bundle to the already stuffed gypsy rack, making certain that my gear was safely secured in the event we hit some rough terrain.

"All set, Lieutenant. Should we crank 'em up?" The question came from the tank commander who had just finished refueling A-13.

"Right, Corporal. Let's move out." I scrambled up the side of A-12's turret and dropped through the hatch in the tank commander's cupola, flipped on the master control switch, and pulled a hard-shell communications helmet snugly down on my head until both ears were comfortable.

"Driver, this is the TC," I spoke confidently into the intercom. "Crank 'er up!"

"Aye, aye, sir!"

The throaty growl of our 750-horsepower, 12-cylinder, turbo-supercharged diesel engine and the sweet smell of engine exhaust fumes from the tank in front of me made the morning's anxiety vanish. I was ready now, ready to tackle whatever lay ahead.

As the tanks idled for a few moments to allow their engines to warm up, I checked the interior of A-12. The deck was covered with dried mud streaks. My .50-caliber machine gun was showing some rust spots. It was apparent even to my novice eyes that this vehicle badly needed crew maintenance. I knew things must be hectic at Con Thien, but this was unacceptable. Siege conditions might make equipment maintenance difficult, perhaps even hazardous, but there was no excuse for the poor condition of this tank's interior. I held my tongue, though, until I could check out the living conditions on Con Thien for myself; also, being a rookie platoon leader, I wanted to hear what my platoon sergeant had to say about what I could or could not expect out of these men in a combat situation.

Con Thien

Until the spring of 1967, Con Thien was occupied by only a few South Vietnamese and US Army Special Forces personnel operating out of an abandoned, French-constructed fort. US Marines moved onto The Hill in the spring and were given full responsibility for its defense.

Late one black, moonless night in early May, soon after the Marines had taken up defensive positions around the perimeter, two battalions of NVA Regulars assaulted Con Thien and came perilously close to overrunning its defenders. The first wave of enemy sappers was past the wire obstacles and tossing satchel charges of C-4 and TNT into bunkers and fighting holes before the unsuspecting infantrymen from Company D, First Battalion, Fourth Marines, realized they were under full-scale attack. Only the courage of individual Marines completely isolated in the confused cacophony of exploding mortars and satchel charges averted a catastrophe.[3] The one major penetration of the defensive perimeter was pinched off almost immediately by officers and NCOs who rallied their men to counterattack at the crucial area and close the gap in their lines, regaining fire superiority in the process. Then, it remained only for those well-disciplined infantrymen from 1/4 to wait in their foxholes until dawn.

When daybreak finally came, the Marines still held Con Thien, but blackened, smoldering hulks of what used to be amtracs, bulldozers, and trucks littered the perimeter, attesting to the ferocity of the struggle. A few remaining enemy soldiers were lying hidden in the elephant grass within the perimeter, trapped when the initial penetration was sealed off. As the sun rose higher and higher, these last remaining survivors of the unsuccessful night assault were picked off one at a time by grim-faced Marines waiting patiently for them to rush out of the tall grass in last-ditch, one-man "banzai" charges.[4] The enemy lost 197 confirmed dead; Marine losses were put at 49 killed and 100 wounded.[5]

The Marines labored all summer in the broiling sun to improve Con Thien's defenses. Sporadic shelling by enemy gunners firing from heavily camouflaged positions within the DMZ did not prevent the fortification of this, the finest natural outpost along the entire length of the DMZ.

On September 3, 1967, free elections were held for the first time throughout South Vietnam. I remembered from reading daily after-action reports at Battalion Headquarters in Phu Bai that, prior to the elections, Con Thien rarely received more than a few rounds of incoming mortar or artillery fire during any single 24-hour period. Then, on Election Day, a fierce enemy bombardment rained down upon the hill's defenders. That marked the beginning of North Vietnam's campaign to besiege Con Thien and force an American withdrawal. From that day forth, a steady barrage of enemy shells pounded the hillsides of Con Thien.

The next day, September 4, a platoon from Company I, Third Battalion, Fourth Marines, tangled with an NVA company about 4 miles south of Con Thien. Before long, the rest of India Company, as well as Mike Company (supported by tanks), were engaged in that fight. The enemy lost thirty-seven soldiers killed.[6]

On September 7, Company I of the Third Battalion, Twenty-Sixth Marines, encountered a large enemy force only 3 miles south of Con Thien. Company K came to the rescue with tanks. In the ensuing five-hour battle, fifty-one NVA soldiers were lost.[7]

O

My arrival on Con Thien that tenth day of September would find the struggle for control of the firebase developing in earnest. With an overhand throwing motion of my right arm, I gave the signal to the other tanks to move out. My tank clanked slowly into position about 15 meters behind the lead vehicle. Gradually, our three-tank caravan began to pick up speed, and we headed north on the hard-packed dirt road leading to Con Thien, where the other two tanks in my platoon were located.

The chances of an ambush this late in the morning were quite slim, but we observed proper road-march discipline anyway. The lead tank kept its main gun straight ahead, mine was pointed to starboard, and the trailing vehicle covered the port side of the road. My own tank gunner kept his eyes glued to the periscope in front of him as he traversed the turret back and forth, never losing sight of the lushly vegetated tree line paralleling the road.

We rumbled along at 25 mph in our 52-ton armored chariots, with the wind in our faces and the rhythmic roar of mighty engines pulsating through our bodies. *Con Thien . . . no longer just another Vietnamese name; it would soon be my home for weeks to come.* Our heavy section of three tanks continued to negotiate the main supply route as it gradually climbed toward the crest of a broad plateau. At last, my tank reached the top of this high ground and there, rising sharply before us, was the three-pronged hill mass called Con Thien. A haphazard pattern of sandbagged bunkers, hootches, and outdoor privies littered its otherwise bare, reddish-brown slopes. The surrounding deep green grasslands and ancient, abandoned rice paddies created a striking contrast with the exposed red clay hillsides. Dense thickets of shrubs and trees ran to the south and southeast.

A surge of anxiety gripped my insides as I viewed my new home for the first time. We cruised rapidly up to the minefield gate, then slowed to a walk as we proceeded along the narrow dirt avenue through the minefield. Halfway through, the entire six-gun battery of 105mm howitzers on Con Thien opened fire; I jumped reflexively at the sudden, jarring sound and almost ducked down in the turret.

I noted that the 105s were dug into a hollow at the base of the center hill. This defiladed position was ideal for a high angle of fire weapon such as the howitzer; also, it afforded some protection for the exposed gunners. Seeing that we had some fire support on position with us was a real morale booster. Their instant reaction capability during enemy shelling would be a blessing to The Hill's defenders.

We had approached Con Thien from the south. The northern slopes of Con Thien faced the densely vegetated DMZ 2 miles away, where an estimated 20,000 NVA soldiers waited in hiding for the signal to mass for an assault on Con Thien. By approaching and leaving through the south gate, much of The Hill's activity was masked from enemy eyes.

Once through the 75-yard-deep minefield that encircled Con Thien like a medieval moat, our three tanks split up, and each tank went to its assigned position around the perimeter.

My tank pulled alongside a sandbagged bunker on the southwest corner of the perimeter, just behind the infantry lines. The bunker was rectangular in shape, about 5 feet tall, and large enough to hold five or six men comfortably. I had to probe cautiously with my left foot inside the darkened bunker doorway to ascertain the distance down to the dirt floor. When I was safely inside, I sat back on an unoccupied cot shoved in a corner.

More so than at any previous time in my life, I felt completely, unutterably alone. There I was in command of a platoon and all of these men were distant strangers. What was I supposed to do now?

Lance Corporal Bert Trevail, the driver on A-12, must have sensed my mood. "Have a beer, Lieutenant!" he offered, as he stabbed his bayonet into the top of a can of beer that he had been saving for some "special" occasion. I gratefully wolfed part of the warm beer down and passed the can back to Trevail, who finished the rest off in three swallows. Trevail was a strongly built man, six foot two or three. He had close-cropped reddish hair, a brushy moustache, and bright, twinkling blue eyes that rarely stopped smiling.

"Never thought warm beer could taste so good," I lied, still tasting the bitterness on my tongue.

"We only go first class here, don't we, lads?" replied Trevail. This brought forth some cynical comments from the other two crewmen, and some laughter, which helped break the ice even more.

Corporal Sanders, a wiry, gregarious, black Marine about twenty-one years old, was seated on a cot across from me, alternately spooning and slurping from a can of C-ration peaches. "Now, take my man Johnson over there." He gestured sweepingly with his plastic spoon in the direction where the third crewman, a slender, shaggy-haired youth in filthy utility trousers rested lethargically on an air mattress. "He don't care 'bout nothin' 'cept gettin' his young self home to the world where he belongs . . . right, Johnson?"

"Uh-humm," Johnson grunted, obviously more interested in dozing than talking.

"Where do you come from, Trevail?" I was curious about his clipped, almost British manner of speaking.

"Canada, sir. I served in the Canadian Army, then went to college there for a few years, but quit to join the US Marines so I could come to Vietnam."

"It beats all, don't it, Lieutenant?" Sanders chimed in. "The pacifists back home are runnin' off to Canada to avoid getting drafted and Trevail here comes to America to volunteer. Now, ain't that a switch."

Trevail shifted uncomfortably, then spoke in a serious tone: "You're losing seven men from this platoon real soon, sir. That's the word we got. They're all due for rotation back to the States. Corporal Johnson is leaving with them."

I had taken over a platoon dominated by "short-timers" who obviously cared only about staying alive for a few more days; then, they would be home free. They had come to Vietnam together as members of a twenty-man tank platoon shipped over from Okinawa in August 1966. One year later, seven men were left out of the original twenty. The others had either been killed or wounded too severely to return to combat. I was the new, untried lieutenant to them, but when their green replacements arrived in a few days, I would be the veteran who greeted the "newbies."

"Lieutenant, let me show you around this place while there's no incoming," said Trevail.

"All right, but we'd better make it quick because I have to report to the Battalion CO right away."

"No problem, sir, just follow me."

Grabbing my steel pot off the tank, I buttoned my flak jacket and prepared for an introductory tour. "What about incoming? Aren't we taking a chance?" I spoke calmly, trying to hide my concern for our safety.

"Not really, sir. They usually don't start shooting again until around noon. That gives us a good half hour."

"Oh, that's nice of them," I replied, wondering if he was kidding me or not.

Trevail led the way and I followed like his shadow, not wanting to be caught in the wrong place should the enemy's timetable for shelling be moved up a half hour. He indicated that infantry from Third Battalion, Fourth Marines, were dug in all around the defensive perimeter. He pointed out Con Thien's three small hills known as Observation Posts (OPs) 1, 2, and 3. OP-1 faced west; OP-2 was atop the center hill, facing directly north toward the DMZ; OP-3 overlooked Leatherneck Square to the southeast and the 200-yard-wide cleared "trace" leading eastward to the Gio Linh firebase 6 miles away. Our artillery forward observers manned bunkers atop each hill.

The protected valleys and flat spaces behind and below the OPs were used for storing ammunition and for helicopter landing zones (LZs). There were two helicopter LZs: one for resupply near OP-3, and one for medevacs between OP-1 and OP-2 next to the Battalion Aid Station (BAS). The remaining terrain was occupied by supporting artillery, mortars, tanks, amtracs, engineers, Ontos, and such. Better than a thousand Marines garrisoned The Hill that day, dug into an area covering two large city blocks.

Linking the Chain of Command

"Say, Trevail," I asked, "where's Gunnery Sergeant Hopkins around here?"

"He's on the other side of OP-2. It was his turn to be on the north lines last night, but he wanted to stay there during the day, today, and try to knock out some gook bastards that shot at him last night with a fifty-seven-millimeter recoilless rifle. Those gooks are rather poor shots; besides, that HE round they're using is too small to seriously hurt our tanks."

"Well, after reporting in to the CO, I've got to find the gunny. Can I make it okay on foot?"

"It's too risky, sir. We usually take the tank over there, rather than walk, because anything moving in the open is a fair target once you're on the north side of OP-2."

"All right," I said. "Meet me back at the bunker in thirty minutes and we'll take the tank over. Right now, I'm going calling on the colonel."

I located the command post (CP) bunker built up against the steep reverse slope of OP-1. The bunker was massive, by far the most prominent structure on Con Thien. It seemed almost impossible for an enemy artillery shell to land on the CP bunker because of its ideal location. I climbed up some dusty, wooden stairs to the narrow bunker entrance, asking Marines along the way where the CO was. Everyone pointed inside, so I followed my nose, looking for silver lieutenant colonel's insignia on someone's collar. Not having any luck, I approached a crimson-faced staff sergeant who was just inside the bunker doorway, busily scribbling something on a clipboard.

"Sergeant, I'm Lieutenant Coan, the new tank platoon commander replacing Lieutenant Barry. Can you tell me where the colonel is?"

"Yessir, he's right over there, but he's real busy now, 'cause we're getting set to move the hell outta here. Another battalion is relieving us today, thank heaven."

"Is that right?" I was surprised to hear that 3/4 was leaving Con Thien, because none of the tankers, including my CO, even mentioned it to me. "Well, good luck!" I replied, walking over to where a slender, graying lieutenant colonel was speaking with some other officers.

Just as I reached the colonel's side, he pivoted toward me and glanced at the gold second lieutenant bars on my collars and my shined boots. He greeted me as if he had been expecting me.

"You must be Tom Barry's replacement," he said warmly, yet briskly, as if he only had a few seconds of his valuable time to spare. "Tom gave me your name. I was looking for you to be here about now. I'm Colonel Bendell. The man you want to talk to is over there, though, because my battalion is leaving Con Thien today."

"Yes, sir. That's what I understand." Before I could say more, Lieutenant Colonel Bendell motioned for me to follow him. We stopped before two senior officers. The nearest man, a tall, large-boned, husky officer with dark, piercing eyes, was introduced to me first. He was Major Cook, the commanding officer of Third Battalion, Ninth Marines.

"Welcome aboard, Lieutenant," he said gruffly, as he shook my hand. "This is Major Gardner, by the way. He's our XO. You'll be seeing more of him than me, I assure you." He grinned knowingly, and I returned the grin, not exactly sure what he meant by that, but I suspected the worst.

"Major Gardner, glad to meet you, sir." Smaller in stature than Major Cook, he gripped my hand firmly, staring intently into my eyes as if attempting to size me up. I stared back, until my instincts told me that the formalities were ended, and any further delay in my departure might bring about a hint in that direction. "Well, I'll be checking back in later to see what's happening, sir. Now, I have to locate my platoon sergeant."

"All right, Lieutenant, and don't forget our briefing here tomorrow at 1600."

"Aye, aye, sir," I responded, and spun on my heel, relieved to have the required military formalities done with. On my way out of the CP bunker, I noted the firm, wooden deck and 12-inch by 12-inch upright beams spaced every 6 feet along the center of the bunker. Maps and plotting boards were located on almost every wall. This bunker was the most important place on The Hill— Con Thien's nerve center—so sturdily reinforced that I doubted if anything but a lucky direct hit by the largest-caliber enemy weapon could damage it.

While walking back to my bunker, it seemed unreal to me that we could be shelled by the enemy at any moment. I was alert, but not alarmed at the prospect. I patted the fiberglass plates on my flak jacket, wondering if the jacket really was much protection. And the helmet? It wasn't good for too much except heating your shaving water, I concluded.

Routine tasks were being performed all over the hill as if we had nothing to worry about. C-rations were distributed, "water buffaloes" were drained, and cases of shells for the mortars and artillery were broken open and the ammunition passed into gun pits. Some 81mm mortar crews fired their weapons furiously, dropping one mortar round after another down long, black tubes, then ducking down away from the muzzle blast. Two amphibious tractors (amtracs) loaded with mortar ammo chugged up a steep hill beside me as I passed by the Battalion Aid Station. *I could duck in here if any incoming landed nearby,* I thought absently, walking by hurriedly.

Then, 80 yards behind me on the crest of OP-1, enemy mortars landed. WHOOMP! KA-WHUMP! WHOMP! Clouds of greasy smoke and dust boiled skyward.

"Incoming!" Shouts rang out all over the hill. I sprinted the last 30 yards to our bunker, my heart in my throat, and almost dove through the doorway.

"What's the matter, Lieutenant," chided Trevail. "Those rounds weren't even close to . . ." BAMM! A rocket or artillery round slammed into the earth right next to our bunker, cutting Trevail off in midsentence. We all flinched involuntarily and held our breath, staring up at the bunker roof, fearing that the single projectile would soon be followed by more. Sand particles trickled down gently from overhead. No one dared to move for several seconds, lest their movement might somehow trigger another blast.

Our bunker was constructed of wooden ammo boxes filled with sand-bags and braced by steel engineer stakes. I noticed this, wondering if it could withstand a direct hit. The answer had to be negative. The roof was made of 4-inch by 6-inch beams laid side by side and covered with three or four layers of sandbags, not much more than protection from the elements. A direct hit by anything larger than an 82mm mortar would disintegrate it. Everyone in the bunker was thinking the same thing; it was written plainly on all faces.

A few more incredibly tense minutes elapsed without any incoming. No one in the bunker appeared even to breathe. "Let's get out of here and go see the gunny," I said, hoping that purposeful activity would combat the choking fear that threatened to evolve into panic if more shells impacted close by.

After listening by the doorway for a few seconds to detect any enemy guns fir-ing from the DMZ, I shouted, "Let's go!" We sprinted one by one to the tank and scrambled through the nearest open hatch, which happened to be the loader's.

"Crank it over, Trevail, and move us out of here!"

We roared away from the bunker, spewing smoke and dust behind us. The narrow dirt road we followed led up a knoll to the base of OP-2, then turned to the right and circled around to the exposed north side of OP-2, just inside the perimeter wire. Marines in this area walked bent over in a shuffling crouch, ready to hit the deck in an instant. I thought better of riding with the upper half of my body sticking out of the cupola, so I dropped quickly down inside the tur-ret and looked through my bullet-proof vision ring . . . just in case.

The DMZ was a few miles to the north. The thickly vegetated, rolling ter-rain was pockmarked by thousands upon thousands of bomb craters, the result of months of merciless pounding by our B-52s. Primary targets were NVA troop concentrations, gun emplacements, and infiltration routes through the DMZ into South Vietnam. The Ben Hai River, which ran almost the entire length of the DMZ, meandered lazily off in the distance like a giant serpent flowing into the South China Sea.

We reached the side of Gunny Hopkins's tank, A-15, and came to a halt. His hatches were all buttoned up. The main gun tube was traversing slowly back and forth as though searching out a target. The loader's hatch opened a few inches and a crewman inside motioned urgently for us to move away. I realized my mistake instantly. We made choice targets sitting so close together.

Sanders said, "Lieutenant, there's a good spot over there where we can lie low." He indicated a depression about 30 yards behind us.

"All right, Trevail, take us straight back. . . . That's good, now a hard turn to port. Okay! Wait for me, I'll be right back." I jumped to the ground and ran over to the gunny's tank, climbing onto the rear deck behind the turret gypsy rack. As I banged on the loader's hatch with my helmet, the hatch opened a crack and I shouted, "Let me in! It's Lieutenant Coan!"

WHEEOOW—BANG! A recoilless rifle round zipped overhead like an angry hornet and exploded on the hill behind us. *They're shooting at me!* I ducked down behind the gypsy rack feeling very naked and very scared. I had to get inside that tank; another near miss might riddle me with shrapnel. WHEEOOW—BOOM! *That one was close!* I tasted fear in my mouth like stale bile. I pounded furiously on the hatch, ready to court-martial someone if that hatch wasn't opened in two seconds. "Goddammit, Gunny! Open up before they blow me away!" The hatch opened immediately and I piled in head first, dropping right on top of a crewman named Apodaca. I panted heavily, lying on my back in the bottom of the turret, looking sheepishly up at the half-amused, half-irritated lance corporal.

"Gunny, I'm sorry about crashing your party like this, but they almost had me out there. . . . Guess we'll be working together from now on. . . . What a way to get started!"

"Hell, Lieutenant, we'da let you in sooner, but you disappeared after that first shot. We couldn't find you. Anyway, I'm mighty glad to have you with us. It's damned hard tryin' to locate those gook bastards out there with that peashooter makin' life miserable for us folks." Gunnery Sergeant Hopkins was sitting shirtless in the tank commander's seat, peering through the range finder. He traversed the turret with his tank commander's override handle as he spoke. He was about my size (185 pounds) and had some gray hair creeping in at the temples. "Damn those gooks! They're shootin' from behind a hill out there, and we cain't see 'em 'cause the recoilless rifle back blast is bein' funneled into a cave."

I detected a southern accent—West Virginia was his home. He had served eighteen years in the Marine Corps, was a Korean War veteran, and this was his second tour in Vietnam. The gunny had spent his first tour around Da Nang where the US Marines first landed in 1965.

His turret was snowy white inside, as it should be, and his crewmen were relatively clean, the complete opposite of my tank. Obviously, he and I thought alike about maintaining the appearance of men and equipment in this type of combat situation, where the crewmen had many hours of idle time on their hands.

The gunny's eighteen years of experience in tanks would be invaluable because I had so many things to learn. The main problem facing both of us was our newness to the platoon; he had only just reported in three days earlier.

"Gunny, we've got some filthy guys in this outfit. Is there some reason they can't or won't maintain their personal hygiene? Is water scarce up here or something?"

"No, Lieutenant. They's plenty of fresh water in them five-gallon cans in the bunkers. Somebody, namely you and me, needs to keep on the tank commanders about that. There ain't no need to be that dirty here, and they's no excuse for the piss-poor shape of those turrets, either. The guns and ammo need to be cleaned every day. Don't worry, short timers or no short timers, those turret decks *will* be clean enough to eat off." He paused to gauge my reaction, staring intently at me with his gray eyes, waiting for a sign of approval or disapproval of what he stood for.

"That sounds mighty fine to me, Gunny." I was openly relieved. There would be no conflict between us on this matter; in fact, he appeared more eager than I was to get these tanks and their crewmen cleaned up. We exchanged brief smiles; he winked and gave me a thumbs-up sign. We were a team.

I carried a small notebook in my trouser pocket and copied the gunny's list of names, ranks, and serial numbers of all the men in First Platoon in the event we had casualties to report back to Alpha Company in Dong Ha.

The five tanks in the platoon were spaced around Con Thien's perimeter.

My tank would be A-12 until the short-timers left. The other tank commanders were Sergeant Guivara on A-11; Corporal Aranda on A-13; Sergeant Weicak on A-14; and Gunny Hopkins on A-15. We agreed to talk further about each crew when his tank returned to our bunker the next morning. I needed to know who the seven short-timers were so we could talk about where to assign the replacements.

"Oh, one more thing, Gunny. What about 3/9 replacing 3/4 today. Do we need to watch out for anything unusual tonight?"

He paused thoughtfully. . . . "Not a bad idea. It'd be a good time for them gooks to try something. I'll pass the word for everyone to be especially alert tonight."

It was time to leave. I felt very satisfied climbing out of his tank. The gunny and I would make a good team. That strange feeling of vulnerable nakedness returned as I jumped off the rear of A-15 and sprinted for my tank. . . . *God, don't shoot now*, I prayed silently, knowing that I was being observed by the enemy. In one mighty bound, I leaped onto the side of A-12 and yanked open my tank commander's cupola hatch. In another second, I hoisted myself halfway through the hatch and was congratulating myself on a successful and speedy trip, when my flak jacket got hung up on the .50-caliber machine gun trigger assembly protruding into the cupola. I was stuck! My entire upper torso was exposed to the enemy—*a great target!* At any second, I expected to be blown to bits. I struggled and yanked furiously. Finally, I disengaged my snagged flak jacket and dropped into the turret, shouting, "Let's get the hell away from here!" Trevail ignited the engine without a second's hesitation and we were on our way back to our "sanctuary" on the perimeter's south side.

Later that afternoon, my crew and I worked on cleaning up the machine guns in our tank. After they were all oiled and the ammunition was checked for corrosion and dirt, I passed the rest of the day making a partial inventory of A-12's equipment, which was, at best, a hit-or-miss operation, because it wasn't healthy to spend a lot of time walking around outside the tank, either on it or alongside it. We weren't missing anything crucial, but much of the tank's equipment inside the turret was in deplorable shape. The communication helmets were battered, microphones cracked, binoculars broken, and the flashlights needed batteries. The first aid kit was practically empty, and, worst of all, my radio set was barely operable. The gunny and I faced a real challenge with these tanks because they had been knocked around considerably in the year since their departure from Okinawa.

That evening, after a welcomed meal of C-rations, my crew and I relaxed inside the bunker. We talked or read by candlelight until about 2200. That was a pleasurable respite from the day's earlier excitement because, once the sun set, night brought a measure of stillness to Con Thien. The enemy's guns ceased to torment us, and our own weapons were muzzled, except for occasional H&I (harassment and interdiction) fire directed toward suspected enemy locations. We were expected to stand watch on the lines at night in our tank from 2200 to 0600. The eight-hour watch was divided into two hours per crewman, but it was still an unpleasant chore, one that I had to perform with everyone else.

How do the duties and responsibilities of an infantry platoon leader and a tank platoon leader differ? The latter is first of all a tank commander: he has to supervise the maintenance and operation of his own tank and be responsible for the welfare of his other three crewmen; also, he must command his own tank in battle. Second, he is responsible for the deployment and combat readiness of his other four tanks. His five-tank platoon is divided into a heavy section of three tanks and a light section of two. He commands the heavy section. Because the tank platoon leader is also a tank crewman, he must stand night watches like the others or risk forfeiting the respect of his men. A slacking tank officer who pulled rank and refused to share this duty would either be canned or have an "accident" eventually.

My two-hour watch lasted until midnight. The minutes crawled by as I willed my heavy eyelids not to close. Standing on the lowered tank commander's seat, I was able to rest my elbows on top of the cupola and peer out into the blackness with an unobstructed view, but this permitted the mosquitoes a grand opportunity for attack. The only solution was insect repellent, squeezed out of a plastic bottle onto my fingers and then smeared over all exposed skin. The stuff was greasy and pungent smelling, but it worked. The mosquitoes whined furiously near my ears, but they stopped biting. Periodically, a friendly mortar illumination round would pop open just outside the perimeter and light up the immediate vicinity for a brief minute as it drifted silently to earth beneath a gently swaying parachute.

Infantrymen from 3/9 were huddled in the trench line to my left front. This was also their first night on the lines at Con Thien. Nearby, a machine gun crew smoked and talked quietly, oblivious of the targets their glowing cigarette butts made in the darkness. It was so peaceful, so tranquil; the Con Thien night had a deceptive charm all its own.

My watch ended and I went into the bunker to awaken Corporal Johnson for the next watch. He moved as if by instinct after thirteen months of this routine. I fell, exhausted, onto the empty cot staked out earlier in the day as my own. Covering my head with a lightweight poncho liner to ward off the mosquitoes, I soon entered dreamland, but not until I had said a silent prayer asking for help in facing the challenging days to come.

2.
MEETING THE CHALLENGE

Theirs not to make reply,
Theirs not to reason why,
Theirs but to do or die.

—Alfred, Lord Tennyson (1809–1892), "The Charge of the Light Brigade"

With 3/9 solidly entrenched on The Hill, life on Con Thien grew increasingly perilous. The siege was beginning to take effect. US Marines were locked in a struggle with the NVA 324B Division over control of Con Thien. The victory would go to whichever side possessed the firepower to overwhelm its opponent's guns and the willpower to endure the mental pressures of a prolonged bombardment.

The Second Day

The bunker was cold and damp when I awoke. A peculiar sweet-sour odor, like mildew, hung heavily in the stale bunker air. I crept to the narrow doorway and peered out. Con Thien was beginning to stir with the scattered activity of sleep-drugged men as they staggered up to urinals or sandbagged outdoor privies. I needed something to combat the early morning chill in the air, so I made some C-ration instant coffee, heating water in an empty fruit can with the aid of a chemical heat tab. No one else was making wake-up noises yet, so I walked outside, enjoying the warmth of the coffee-filled can in my hands.

A squad of Marines from 3/9 was trudging toward the minefield gate. They appeared to be returning from a night ambush position somewhere outside the perimeter wire. Their weapons glistened and their uniforms were soaking wet from the early morning dew. Marine infantry—best assault troops in the world. They looked positively lethal. Bandoliers of M-16 ammunition hung from their shoulders and necks; some men had machine gun ammo belts crisscrossed on their chests. I noted that each man wore a buttoned-up flak jacket and steel helmet. *Good discipline. No "individuals" allowed here.* They obviously hadn't detected any NVA outside the perimeter because they ambled along quite nonchalantly, not in any hurry to get back home.

My gaze shifted toward the 105mm howitzers from Battery "D" 2/12 located 40 yards away. In complete contrast to the infantrymen, the artillery gun pits were swarming with hectic activity. Marines looked through sights on their guns at aiming stakes, some stood by with earphones on, while others were breaking open wooden cases of 105mm ammunition. *Our guys should start shooting momentarily.*

My reverie was rudely interrupted by enemy shells screeching in from the north, crashing all around OP-2. That first salvo was enough for me. I jumped back in through the bunker doorway, sloshing coffee on one of my sleeping crewmen in the process.

"Goddammit to hell! Oh, sorry, sir," said a disgruntled Corporal Johnson. I apologized to Johnson, but he resented being awakened more than he resented the coffee on his trouser leg.

More incoming shells arrived. Then, our artillery opened up with a resounding barrage. They sent round after round back toward the enemy gunners who had greeted us so rudely a few minutes earlier. The duel was short-lived, as we received no return incoming.

My rumbling stomach told me it was time for breakfast. Eating C-rations was not exactly an epicurean experience; in fact, some men detested "C-rats," but the food was wholesome and nourishing. A case of "Cs" had twelve different meals. I could eat all twelve meals cold and still enjoy most of them; although I could do without ham and lima beans (also called "ham and mothers"). We had a stockpile of heat tabs (smokeless chemical briquettes) and were usually able to eat our rations heated.

Cooking C-rations in the field required some schooling. First, a small, empty can was used as the "oven." Several holes were punched in the side of the can to allow for proper oxygen circulation. Then, a heat tab was lit on fire and dropped into the well-ventilated oven. A handy field expedient the old salts preferred was to take a pinch of C-4 explosive and drop that in the can. It burned quite hot and did the heating job in only seconds.

The main meal—franks and beans, tuna casserole, diced ham and eggs, among others—was opened by a miniaturized can opener device (called a P-38) and the can placed on the oven for three or four minutes until heated. Most meals also contained canned fruit, crackers or biscuits, and cheese, peanut butter, or jelly; also included were matches, toilet paper, cigarettes, gum, instant coffee, powdered cream, and sugar.

After breakfast, relaxing with another cup of C-ration coffee, I reflected on the comradeship and warm conversation we shared at times like this, making any hardships endurable. The nagging worry that one was in a dangerous situation was pushed into the subconscious, and men laughed and talked comfortably. Only when one was cringing from a near miss did he feel the fear rise up in his throat; his palms began to sweat, and his stomach churned into knots that threatened to make him vomit.

Gunnery Sergeant Hopkins and his crewmen bounced through the bunker entrance and greeted us cheerily. The gunny was elated to be alive. He had narrowly escaped getting "blown away" earlier that morning in the first salvo of enemy artillery that had landed so unexpectedly around the base of OP-2. Caught outside of his tank relieving his bladder, only the close proximity of a trench line saved him. Winston Churchill once said: "Nothing in life is so exhilarating as to be shot at without result." The gunny would certainly vouch for that. He filled up a steel helmet with water from a five-gallon can and washed the scaly grime from his hands. He made eye contact with me and winked, but in such a way that no one else would notice.

"I believe I'll do the same, Gunny," I said, pouring some water into my own helmet after removing the helmet liner.

"Come on, lads, you won't melt. It's high time you all splashed a little soap and water on yourselves, too," chided the gunny, gently but pointedly, amid some muffled protests in the background.

"Aww, Gunny, why you gotta mess with us," said one of the men.

"Mess with you? Boy, *look* at you! You're a damned disgrace, not only to the United States Marine Corps, but to your family name as well!" Gunny Hopkins's neck grew redder; his voice took on the hard edge of a drill instructor chewing out a reluctant recruit. "Now, hop to it!"

Silence. All eyes were on Gunnery Sergeant Hopkins. It was a classic military showdown, short-timers versus seasoned "old salt." I feared that a nasty scene was brewing. No way could these men lie there any longer and keep their stripes, and everyone knew it. Then, amid some mumbling about being "too short to sweat the small stuff," everyone joined in and started washing up. Just a few pointed, well-chosen barbs from the platoon sergeant had done the trick.

My personal philosophy regarding disciplinary matters, hygiene, equipment maintenance, and such, was that the platoon sergeant and I (the platoon leader) would set standards. If he either wouldn't or couldn't enforce them, after agreeing upon them, then I would. Afterward, I would request another platoon sergeant. Future problems with my own tank crew, however, would be handled by me as their tank commander. But this first time, it was enlightening for me, a rookie, to see a real pro in action. Colonel Chaplin was right about this senior sergeant's value to me, a novice lieutenant trying to establish himself.

The agony of a cold shave passed, momentarily; then, I felt totally refreshed, ready to do lieutenant's work all day. First, I rechecked the list of names and serial numbers copied from Gunny Hopkins the previous day. Next, Hopkins explained our daily routine of providing two tanks for the morning mine sweep of the MSR as far south as C-2; calling on the radio back to Alpha Company Headquarters at Dong Ha every day; and attending the afternoon CO's briefing for all attached unit leaders (my platoon was now attached to 3/9). The gunny also told me how incoming mortars and artillery arrived at certain times of the day in barrages. But one couldn't set his watch by them; they weren't that punctual.

The first shelling of the morning was over, an opportune time to make additional liaison with the newly arrived staff of 3/9. I donned a flak jacket and helmet, cocked an ear to the north for a few seconds (just in case), and struck off for the battalion CP. Passing by the Battalion Aid Station, I saw a dead Marine lying outside on a stretcher. He was covered by a blanket; only his boots with the toes pointing skyward were uncovered. I wondered absently what his face looked like, then repressed the thought. The pungent smell of death reached me as I approached closer, trying not to look, but unable to resist. Carmine stains on the earth nearby meant that other corpses had rested there recently. That was a sobering and depressing sight. The artillery barrage that morning must have been responsible.

My pace quickened. Areas of dense elephant grass were located on either side of the wire-bordered path leading from the medevac LZ to the CO's bunker. Triangular signs labeled "MINES" were spaced regularly along the wire fence. The story I heard was that those mines were emplaced without any definite pattern by the ARVN when Con Thien was first used by them as an observation post early in the war.

When the Marines moved onto The Hill in the early months of 1967, they expanded the original perimeter and fenced off all the old booby-trapped areas. Clearing those abandoned, unmarked minefields was considered too hazardous; besides, the limited number of Marine engineers in the area were more urgently needed to prepare Con Thien's new perimeter minefield. Inside the CO's bunker, I met briefly with Major Gardner. He was concerned about my tank crewmen strolling around Con Thien without helmets. I assured him this would be corrected immediately. He also wanted to make certain that my tank platoon would be participating in SITREPS on the lines at night.

SITREPS meant Situation Reports, a procedure the infantry used to receive reports periodically at night on the status of each position or unit stationed on the lines. All of my tanks had PRC-25 radios, so we'd have no problems monitoring the grunt frequency at night and participating in SITREPS; besides, it helped one stay alert during his two-hour watch.

After only one day on The Hill, I was beginning to get adjusted to my new home. Many varied sights and sounds were ever present: guns booming, tanks and amtracs rumbling, jet planes carrying out air strikes nearby, friendly artillery shells whooshing softly overhead toward the DMZ, and helicopters lifting in and out with their cargos of men and material; it was all strangely captivating. Occasionally, the distressing sound of incoming enemy ordnance shattered the spell and reminded me of that Greek legend of the "Sword of Damocles," where a king suspended a sword tied with a hair and hung it directly over Damocles's head to impress on him the perils of a ruler's life.

Later that afternoon, my crew and the gunny's crew sat around in the darkened bunker, passing time with tales of home, girlfriends, cars, food, and assorted combat exploits. I overheard Lieutenant Barry's name mentioned and focused on that conversation.

"Yep, Mr. Barry took some crazy chances. I never seen nothin' like it . . .

ridin' on the front slope plate of the tank, sprayin' a tree line with his rifle. I don't think the captain approved of his tactics; that must be why he relieved him."

"He was *real* unhappy 'bout the captain relieving him, too. He dug this stuff, man," said Sanders. Even Tom Barry's own crewmen thought he was being removed from command by the captain. Tom must have thought the same. No wonder he seemed to hold the captain in something less than the highest esteem.

"I really doubt that the captain had anything to do with Mr. Barry's departure," I chimed in. A few heads spun toward me, perhaps surprised at my comment, or perhaps surprised that I was eavesdropping. "That's right," I continued, "Lieutenant Barry was doing a good job from what I understand, other than getting himself wounded twice in two weeks."

It was Trevail this time. "No disrespect intended, but no one gets relieved from command in the bloody Marine Corps just because he got two Purple Hearts. There has to be more reason than that."

I started to share what Colonel Chaplin had told me back at Phu Bai about Tom Barry's situation, when WHAMMM!! We were stunned by a blast from a very close near miss. Sand poured down from the ceiling for a few seconds and dust particles floated in the air. I had flinched, as had everyone else. *"Damn! What the hell was that?"* Everyone else must have been thinking that also because I heard no response. I stared hard at the gunny. Gunny Hopkins's facial expression was that of fear personified. He looked exactly like I felt.

When it was 1600, the CO's afternoon briefing beckoned. To walk over would be suicide because a heavier shelling than usual was pounding Con Thien. "Let's take the tank over to the CP," I told my crew. No one protested. They were glad to get out of that flimsy bunker.

Pausing by the doorway, I listened for the telltale "boom" off in the distance that indicated the firing of enemy guns. No booming sounds could be detected. I counted to three and bolted for A-12. The rest of the crew was right behind me. Trevail fired up the tank engine and we raced toward the CP.

Geysers of greasy, black smoke and dirt again erupted along the battered crest of OP-2. Some poor bastards, probably our forward observers (FOs), occupied a bunker up there. We pulled to a stop within 30 meters of the CP bunker entrance. That was as close as we could come in the tank. A densely grassed area ringed off by barbed wire marked the end of the road. A narrow path through the grass was bordered by triangular warning signs reading "MINES."

"Shut it off, Trevail." I wanted to be able to hear any more incoming ordnance, and that noisy diesel tank engine would prevent that. With my ears straining to detect any distant sounds that would indicate enemy guns firing, I jogged up along the minefield path, praying that no incoming arrived for a few more seconds. One flight of wooden stairs to negotiate and I made it up to the bunker porch—*safe!* From there, I waved to my tank crew and indicated through hand gestures that I would meet them back at our bunker when the CO's briefing ended. They understood and roared off immediately.

Much activity was evident in the CP. The volume of incoming had increased in the last few hours, and the recently arrived staff of 3/9 were apparently attempting to work out better procedures for plotting reported enemy gun locations. Coordination of air and artillery support with helicopter resupply and infantry operations, and the numerous other details to be arranged with all the attached units on Con Thien, were substantial undertakings.

Throughout the briefing, sporadic, muffled thuds from exploding enemy shells around the perimeter reached our ears. We sat there stoically, feigning unconcern. The only comment on the shelling was made by the CO of 3/9, Major Cook, who said, "I shouldn't have to tell you men how important it is to wear flak jackets and steel pots at all times out in the open; yet, I see bareheaded Marines all over this perimeter. I want the word passed on this right away."

Most of the attached unit leaders, myself included, stared straight ahead with poker faces. He had not singled anyone out, but I knew my tankers were among the worst violators.

The steel pot was the second-most important piece of headgear to a tank crewman. His hard-shell commo helmet was essential; the steel pot was only considered an accessory to be stored in the bottom of the tank's gypsy rack. Obtaining compliance with this unpopular order would be difficult, especially among my short-timers, but I had to do it, not only for the safety of my men, but also to keep 3/9's staff from reprimanding me and Gunny Hopkins.

Genuine concern was expressed during the briefing over an encounter the previous evening between the Third Battalion, Twenty-Sixth Marines, and what appeared to be an entire NVA regiment 3 miles southwest of Con Thien.

Some of the enemy assault units wore US Marine helmets and flak jackets, but the ruse failed. The enemy broke contact before midnight, having lost 140 confirmed and an estimated 315 KIAs.[1] The number of Marine casualties was not mentioned, but we all knew without being told that much American blood had been shed in that struggle to protect Con Thien's left flank and rear. Two Marine tanks were also knocked out in that battle.[2]

We were not alone at Con Thien. I began to realize this at the briefing. In the previous week, two significant battles had been fought to the south and southwest of our position by infantry units whose ultimate mission was to prevent the encirclement of Con Thien by the NVA.[3]

Just before the briefing ended, Major Gardner described the tactical deployment of 3/9. Two full companies were being held in reserve at "Yankee Station," a nub of high ground densely overgrown with shrubs and trees about 400 meters south of Con Thien's outer perimeter wire. Each evening, prior to dusk, two of my tanks would be sent out there as part of a reaction force in the event that the NVA successfully overran a portion of Con Thien's perimeter. Those two reserve companies, supported by my light section of tanks, would then attempt to seal off the incursion and rout the remaining NVA. It seemed to be a solid plan on paper, but I wondered if these infantry officers fully understood the difficulties inherent in moving tanks and infantry together in a night counterattack. I hoped that it never became necessary to make them understand.

I left the briefing with a premonition that something was wrong and ran the entire distance back to our bunker. Something had happened, but not what I feared. An ugly, blackened hole about 3 feet wide was located between our bunker and the machine gun position 10 yards away—another near miss.

"Looks like they almost nailed you guys," I said, entering the bunker. No one smiled or even looked up. "Say, what happened? Did someone get hurt, Gunny?"

"Well, none of us, but one of the boys next door got blown away by a rocket while you was in the meeting. It sure can mess a guy up."

The other men gradually came out of their shock and reiterated the story of what had happened in my absence. A 122mm rocket, weighing 125 pounds, had screamed into the earth near our bunker and caught two infantrymen sitting outside the machine gun position next to us. One man was killed instantly; the other was critically wounded. Trevail had dashed outside, loaded both casualties onto A-12, and drove them to the Battalion Aid Station. Trevail's fast action probably saved the life of one man. Nothing could be done for the other casualty; large chunks of jagged shrapnel had ripped right through the back of his flak jacket.

The grim reaper had arrived close to home. I knew those men, vaguely, as one would come to know his next-door neighbors in any big city. I'd spoken briefly with them earlier in the day when they came over to borrow a shovel. Now, they were gone—one dead, the other in critical condition.

I stared at the charred crater made by the NVA rocket. The tail assembly of twisted aluminum lay nearby as mute evidence of the blast that had claimed a young Marine's life. Two surviving members of the perimeter strongpoint stared out at me from inside their bunker with a hollow gaze. Their eyes beseeched me for an answer. I could not give them one and turned away.

Our bunker was quiet that evening as we heated C-rations. Everyone was deep in thought. *Could it happen to me?* We were all probably thinking the same thing. Our bunker began to bounce and vibrate rhythmically to the sound of a series of continuous explosions some distance from Con Thien. Someone shouted, "That's an Arc Light! Those B-52s are blowin' the hell out of 'em!"

US Air Force B-52 bombers were conducting another raid in defense of Con Thien. The target was probably NVA troop and artillery concentrations. B-52s are huge, swept-wing, eight-jet bombers that flew so high one could barely detect them in a cloudless sky. Their approach was silent. The first hint of their deadly presence was the screeching howl of hundreds of bombs plummeting earthward. Each plane carried a 27-ton payload of 108 mixed 500- and 750-pound bombs, with an occasional 1,000-pounder added in. A four-plane bombing run could lay waste to an entire grid square (an area 1 kilometer square).[4]

Morale of the men began to pick up markedly after the bombing. Laughter once again warmed the confines of our musty bunker. The horrors of sudden death had been pushed gradually back into the recesses of our subconscious as we made plans to spend another night on Con Thien. My watch did not begin until midnight. I lay back on a cot, gazing at the dull orange glow cast on our bunker ceiling by a solitary, flickering candle, and pondered the events of the previous year that had led to me becoming a tank platoon leader in the Marine Corps.

O

October 1966, I was one of two dozen anxious, yet controlled, young men, sitting pensively in our seats, gazing out the bus windows at Quantico's red brick barracks, hoping for some indication of what lay in store for us that day. Even though parked in the sun on an asphalt parking lot, the autumn weather felt cool. We were 30 miles south of Washington, DC, near the Potomac River, not far from several famous Civil War battlefields in northern Virginia. The surrounding hills provided a breathtaking backdrop of colorful autumn foliage.

An olive-drab military bus slowly approached our civilian bus from across the lot. I looked around at the others waiting on the bus with me. Nervous chitchat ceased abruptly. The tension mounted as a tall, gaunt gunnery sergeant bounded up the stairs of our bus.

"Are all of you men candidates?"

We nodded, wide-eyed in unison, expecting the worst. "Follow me, then." He was almost cordial. *What a letdown! When were they going to start yelling at us like they did in all the Marine Corps movies?* We filed silently aboard the gunny's bus, travel bags gripped tightly in sweaty hands, ready to jump out of our skins at the slightest startle.

Our bus lurched to a halt a few minutes later outside a large, gray, prefab building. Butterflies gripped my stomach as I glimpsed a few of the NCO cadre for the first time. They were standing outside in twos and threes, some smiling, some sneering. Then we heard: "Get off that bus, people, and LINE UP!" The bus emptied in five seconds.

As we stood braced at attention, the NCO cadre strolled arrogantly along the outskirts of our formation, faces full of contempt, surveying the civilian slime, the college-boy maggots. "Look at those sideburns on Elvis, there. Hey, sweetheart! You sure got purty hair." Squinting into the blazing sun, my right cheek twitched once, then again. *Oh, God! Don't give me away! Please stop!* I silently pleaded. Perspiration trickled down my ribs from my armpits.

At the order to march, we headed toward our barracks, more or less in step. "Stop pushing, dammit!" A long-haired New Yorker, two ranks to my front, had protested to a mean-looking black sergeant. I couldn't believe my ears. He had to be a fool, ignorant, or both, to do that.

"You shut yo' #&*%!@# mouth in fo-mation, CANDIDATE, or you gonna have a boot up yo' ass!" That relieved the tension. This was the Marine Corps! Welcome to OCS!

Officer Candidate School at Quantico was ten weeks of tough, demanding challenge; physically tougher than any of us could have imagined back home when we started getting our beer-bloated bodies back in shape after college. Those few among us who came to OCS directly from boot camp at Parris Island or San Diego Marine Recruit Depot confirmed our suspicions: OCS was tougher physically than the boot camp they had endured.

Marine Corps OCS was a weeding-out process, weeding out the physically unfit, the mentally slow, those who failed to function under stress, and those lacking leadership qualities. We came to OCS in all sizes, shapes, and levels of fitness, and our backgrounds were as diverse as any collection of college graduates' backgrounds could be. My platoon had a former defensive back from the University of Southern California Trojans football team, a professorial English teacher from a small eastern college, an Aggie country boy from New Mexico, two former enlisted Marines right out of boot camp from Parris Island, and a reformed "flower child" from San Francisco. We had two crucial things in common, however: we wanted to become Marine Corps officers, and we were willing to endure any hardships to get there.

The hair went first. Sheared off practically to the bare scalp, we instantly lost our individuality. We drew an initial issue of uniforms, boots, underwear, and such; took our physical exams; and then it started.

Every morning before breakfast that first week of OCS, we formed up sleepily outside the Quonset hut barracks and went for a run in the dark across uneven, rocky fields, stepping in holes and falling over each other in domino fashion if the leading man tripped and went down. If you had anything wrong with your knees, if you lied to the doctor during your physical exam about old sports injuries, they were bound to act up again. Several candidates washed out after that first week due to "previously undetected medical problems," so there was a method to all that madness. After one week, the morning "fun runs" ceased.

Daily, without fail, we put on our yellow USMC T-shirts after the noon meal and ran to the exercise field. First it was calisthenics, then we jogged to the pull-up bar, shouted out each pull-up until we hung there exhausted, then did *"one more for the Corps!"* Eighteen pull-ups the desired goal, many of us achieved it. Next, we did grass drills (nonstop calisthenics) for thirty minutes, then we ran through the obstacle course, 100 yards of assorted log barriers and walls to go over and under, finished by a 20-foot rope climb. We waited by the obstacle course, panting, chests heaving, until everyone was through it, then we went for a run. Always the runs—miles and miles—up hills, down hills. We ran to class, from class, to chow, and back to the barracks.

Each week, the company went on a forced march. Helmet, rifle, canteens, and light marching pack were required. Led by our company commander, the major, we charged single file up the infamous Hill Trail, weighted down by all that gear, leg muscles straining, lungs bursting, stumbling over unburied roots and rocks; the pace, almost a run, never slackened. Yet we had to keep the proper interval behind the man in front. "Forty inches front to back!" bellowed the cadre. "Keep your proper interval, candidate!" Occasionally, another candidate would be passed out or semiconscious beside the trail, vomiting, eyes rolling back, face contorted, mirroring my own agony as I passed him, struggling to keep going. "Forty inches front to back!" Up and up we climbed, no end to the hellish ordeal in sight. "Keep your forty inches, candidate, or you get a leadership chit!" Oh, the dreaded leadership chit (three, and you washed out of OCS). I couldn't quit. I quit once before in high school . . . never again. After 3, 4, or 5 miles, who knows how many, the cursed trail ended and we could walk a bit.

Somehow, the captain leading our platoon and the NCOs badgering us from the rear never looked as bushed as we did. The added equipment we carried made the difference, but I was too cowed to recognize that; I really believed they were in better shape.

Unlike enlisted Marine boot camp, we were on our own. One never stopped for another who fell out of formation. We had to be able to take care of ourselves first. "How can you lead fifty men if you can't take care of *yourself*?" was constantly pounded into us. Plus, we didn't have time to spare helping the slower ones. If a man couldn't get organized, couldn't make his pack up right, or couldn't drill his squad properly, he fell by the wayside; no one could learn it for him. And we were graded individually on everything we did.

Every other week we were given a sheet of paper and told to rate all of our OCS squad mates from first to last in answer to this question: "Whom would you want to have leading you into combat?" Those who averaged last place in the "peer reviews" were sent the following day to Parris Island, where they would attend boot camp and then become enlisted Marines.

We were at a place called Camp Upshur (soon referred to as Camp "Rupture"). We dealt with pain; I had it constantly: a sprained elbow, pulled groin muscle, and bruised heel. But going to sick bay was not an option to pursue in Marine Corps OCS unless you wanted a drill instructor on your case for days afterward. "Pain is weakness leaving the body" was the philosophy we had to mentally internalize.

Everything was "candidate" this (or *canadate* if said fast) and "candidate" that. "Get your piece squared away, there, candidate!" . . . "Are you in love with me, candidate!? Then, keep your #@x#@ eyes straight ahead." We were, for the most part, highly motivated college graduates, but if we got too impressed with ourselves, there was always the equalizer: "It didn't take an act of congress to make me a gentleman, CANDIDATES!" The good sergeant was referring, of course, to the officer's commission conferred by the president of the United States through the secretary of the navy.

Then there was Staff Sergeant Ledford, a wiry, carrot-topped, bantam-weight Marine from Tennessee—hardly the recruiting poster image of a Marine—but he was steady and tough, and, he wore a Silver Star medal for heroism in combat in Vietnam.

"You all march like a buncha turkeys bobbin' fer bugs!" he said to us after one exasperating day on the drill field. And his shrill voice hounded us all the way up the tortuous Hill Trail: "Get up the *heel*! Get up that *hee-ul*! You better *pray* I don't pass you up, *candidate*!" In the chow line at every meal, "Take all you want, but *eat* all you take!" That was our watchword, and Ledford could always be counted on to remind us.

The bottom line on everything we did was the ability to function effectively under stress, to keep a clear head in the midst of confusion, to persevere in the face of seemingly impossible situations. "Do the best you can with what you've got." That's not particularly profound advice, but it was one of the slogans pounded into us that typifies US Marine Corps tradition.

We returned to the barracks late one evening after chow, having completed a three-day "war." We were all exhausted, dirty, but warmly excited at the idea of a nice shower and a good night's sleep between clean sheets. Instead of the anticipated command to fall out of formation into the barracks, however, we were told: "Lights out in thirty minutes. You *will* be prepared for a full field gear inspection at 0700 tomorrow. Dismissed!"

At first, we were stunned. Lights out meant no one was supposed to be out of his rack! How on earth could we prepare a "junk on the bunk" display in the *dark*! But, we persevered anyway—most of us, that is. Three candidates decided it was ridiculous to attempt it in the dark and chose to go to sleep, telling themselves they'd get up early and then complete that "impossible" task. The rest of us snuck into the lighted head (naval term for bathroom) in relays to spit shine combat boots, clean rifles, scrub our smoke-blackened mess kits, and clean our filthy web gear. We arranged the 782-gear display on our bunks by the light from cigarette lighters and flashlights and then slept on the deck. As you would expect, no one passed inspection, and Captain Harrison made a big show of his displeasure because no one passed, but we hadn't quit. We followed orders; we did the best we could under the circumstances. Perhaps it was coincidence, perhaps not, but those three who chose to sleep that night, rather than attempt the impossible, never saw graduation day from OCS.

Twenty-nine of our original fifty-man platoon completed OCS and were commissioned as second lieutenants in the US Marine Corps. At last, we were "butter bars." We were junior officers, true, but we didn't know anything about being officers. The Basic School at Quantico was our next assignment. There, we would spend four and a half months (normally six months before the Vietnam War required a drastic increase in the output of new officers) learning the skills of our new profession. The Basic School graduate was intended to be a qualified infantry platoon leader, a leader of Marines. He also had to know ceremonial functions as well as combat techniques.

We shared two-man rooms at the Basic School bachelor officers' quarters (BOQ); kept an M-14 rifle chained under our beds when not being used for drills, tactics, or marksmanship qualification; and awoke each morning to a recording of reveille broadcast over a distant loudspeaker. We had less emphasis on physical training but more mental challenge laid on us than in OCS. We attended classes on tactics, self-defense, first aid, personnel administration, military law, Marine Corps history, map and compass orientation, and weapons (both infantry weapons and supporting arms). We were tested, graded, evaluated, and critiqued at every turn.

Sometimes, as my gaze wandered over the classroom, taking in the serious, intelligent, alert faces of my young cohorts with their burr-headed crew cuts, I wondered how many of us might be dead in a few short months. But it was only fleeting, morbid curiosity, not a grave concern to be dwelled on. Vietnam was too far removed and foreign to evoke any stirrings of alarm or fear, either for myself or my classmates. Besides, I knew I wasn't going to get zapped.

Training at the Basic School was thorough. I lacked a feeling of urgency, however, knowing that it was only practice, that it was simulated, but I learned my lessons anyway, motivated more by a desire to be a competent officer than by worry over going to Vietnam. We had textbook principles to memorize: five-paragraph orders, enfilade fire, channeling the enemy assault forces, flank security during marches, and L-shaped ambushes.

While undergoing hand-to-hand combat training, we learned that there were two kinds of bayonet fighters: "the quick and the dead!" And we all shouted in unison, "The spirit of the bayonet is to *kill!*" Then there were the unwritten maxims we internalized: Marines never retreat; Marines never leave their dead behind on the battlefield; Marines never surrender as long as they have the means to resist. One did not ask, "What if?" We had no time for intellectual debates on these matters. We were told what was expected of us as Officers of Marines, and we could either measure up to those standards or face the consequences of failure.

On graduation from the Basic School, many of my buddies received orders sending them immediately to the western Pacific (probably Vietnam, but possibly Okinawa) as infantry officers. I was one of two dozen officers selected for additional training at the Tracked Vehicle Officer's School, Camp Pendleton, California.

Camp Pendleton, with its nearly treeless, grass- and shrub-covered hills, was situated on the Pacific Coast, north of San Diego. A huge tank park was located practically on the beach. Many an early morning, we headed up the beach single file in our M-48A3 tanks, our faces feeling the sting from flying grains of sand kicked up by the preceding tanks, and the faintly sweet smell of diesel engine exhaust lingering in our nostrils.

We took turns during the day being driver, loader, gunner, or tank commander, as we familiarized ourselves with each crewman's functions. Tanks were complicated. We had to be able to set the timing on a .50-caliber machine gun, operate communications equipment, operate the range finder and ballistic computer, and maintain and repair track, road wheels, torsion bars, idler arms, sprocket, and the rest of the suspension equipment, and we had to know how to deploy our tanks in combat.

Tank school was only six weeks, not nearly long enough to master all facets of the "iron monsters," but it was commonly understood that our real training in tanks would be "on the job" in Vietnam.

We had a few precious days of leave granted after tank school, then, the first week of August, our class was on our way to Vietnam. We had no parades and no patriotic speeches to see us off. It was almost as if we were placed on a gigantic conveyor belt stretching across the ocean, to be used as replacement parts for America's burgeoning war machine—all so damned impersonal.

Our military passenger jet landed in Okinawa, loaded with replacements for Vietnam. I spent three boring, sweat-drenched days awaiting orders. The humidity was abominable. Few things in the military are more worthless than a green second lieutenant sitting around, awaiting his first real duty assignment. I practically ran to the personnel office when told that my orders came in.

Third Tank Battalion, Third Marine Division, Phu Bai, Republic of South Vietnam; that was my destination. Half of the eighteen tank officers from my class were reporting to First Marine Division Headquarters in Da Nang. I was in the other group going up north, where much of the combat action had occurred that summer near the Demilitarized Zone dividing South and North Vietnam.

We flew by military passenger jet to Da Nang from Okinawa and spent the night on cots in a flimsy wooden shack right next to a runway. Sleep was impossible. Jet fighters screamed up and down runways all night at five- to ten-minute intervals. By morning, I would have volunteered for anything to get away from there. I didn't have to, though. We were put aboard a C-130 Hercules transport plane and flown up north to Phu Bai before noon.

Third Tank Battalion was actually located a few miles from Phu Bai's airport in a dust bowl called Gia Le. We saw our first Vietnamese civilians that day, clad in black silk pajamas and white conical hats; they looked through us blankly as we passed them in our truck going toward Gia Le. No waves, no smiles, no hint of recognition shone on their faces. Some uncomfortable insight was gained at that moment. We were only being tolerated by the Vietnamese. Little real gratitude or indebtedness was likely felt in the hearts of the common people.

Instead of receiving one of the coveted platoon leader billets in Third Tank Battalion, several other recent arrivals and I had to cool our heels and accept a staff assignment at Battalion until a platoon leader slot opened up.

I was made the Assistant S-3—Operations and Training—in charge of conducting evening briefings for the Third Tank Battalion commander and his staff. My boss was Major Bruce McLaren, the S-3. Our daily activities were routinely dull. The August heat and dust at Gia Le combined to create a stifling, energy-draining setting. The end of each day was celebrated as one less to endure there. Observing Vietnamese peasants was the major diversion, and that novelty faded after a few days.

As the S-3 Alpha, I reviewed the incoming dispatches from Third Marine Division to glean information pertinent to Third Tank Battalion. Then, I would piece together a summary of the previous day's action reports and present it to Colonel Chaplin and his staff after our evening meal.

The battalion's three companies, A, B, and C, were heavily committed to providing direct support for Marine infantry units spread out just below the entire length of the DMZ from Khe Sanh to Gio Linh. In between were places like Camp Carroll, Cam Lo, Dong Ha, the Rockpile, and Con Thien, which were Marine bases or outposts strategically located to maintain a watch on the Ben Hai River. North Vietnamese Army units were constantly attempting to infiltrate southward past these outposts, and US Marine, Army, Navy, and Air Force firepower blasted them wherever they were detected, around the clock.

In late August, I was instructed to accompany the colonel on one of his periodic tours of the outposts where Third Tank Battalion had units stationed. He liked to bring mail and cold beer for the men, which made his brief visits understandably welcome. In two days, we traveled by jeep from Dong Ha (where we shared a tent at Alpha Company's area) to Gio Linh, Con Thien, and Camp Carroll. Luckily, nothing memorable happened at those outposts. We were able to ride in, visit, and depart without getting shelled or sniped at—no easy feat, either, I learned later.

At the end of our second day, I was resting on my cot in our tent at Camp Carroll, when Colonel Chaplin shuffled in, sighed deeply, and sat down heavily on his nearby cot. "We had a bad one down south of us today," he said wearily, his normally ruddy face pale with concern and fatigue. "Listen to this message com-center received an hour ago." He pulled a scrap of folded paper from his utility shirt pocket, waved it open, and read aloud: "One tiger made a bird; we have Kilo Indian boys." He shook his head slowly as he explained, "That means a tank hit a mine and all four crewmen were killed."

"Some mine, Colonel. That's incredible," I said.

Just then a runner came to the tent with more news of the incident: "Sir, Charlie Company says that tank ran over a 500-pound bomb; it was command detonated. Three tanks from Gunny Keith's platoon were going down a road and the gooks set off the bomb under the second tank. It blew the turret completely off. Three of the four crewmen just disappeared."

"Good God!" we both said, almost in unison. I didn't know if this was an extraordinary event or not, due to my limited experience "in country," but I gathered from the reactions of the others that it didn't happen very often; not like that, anyway.

The next morning, we flew out of Dong Ha on a hot, noisy C-130 Hercules and returned to battalion headquarters at Gia Le. I had a new appreciation for the Marines out in the field after my recent, brief tour. Sudden, violent death was quite remote from us, the staff drones back in the rear, plodding along with our mundane, routine, day-to-day existence. Consequently, we were ignorant of the realities of coping with a combat situation. Unless one had been under fire before, it was impossible for him to identify with the experiences of the combat veterans. Each day, we blandly reviewed the after-action reports submitted to Division by various Marine Corps units, recorded some of them, and saved the spicier accounts for the colonel's evening briefing. The fear, exhaustion, terror, and emotion experienced by the individuals who participated in those battles and skirmishes could never be communicated to us, the staff, so out of reach back in the rear. We dealt with statistics: cold, impersonal information to be analyzed, processed, and forgotten.

I was always taken aback when seeing the wild eyes and tight lips of our tank crews just returning from a combat zone, as they wheeled into the Third Tank Battalion area amid choking clouds of dust churned up by clanking treads. They obviously knew something, or else had experienced something, that separated them from the uninitiated. Now, I'd gone forth to learn the mysterious secret they shared . . . to become one of them.

O

A rustling noise in the shadowy corner near my cot meant that our friends, the rats, were back foraging for food scraps. Con Thien was rat infested. They slept by day, and at night they scurried around inside the various living areas, quarreling over bits of food. If they had kept quiet and not bothered us, their presence would have been tolerated, but they constantly uttered little screeching sounds that made one's scalp crawl, and they had the disconcerting habit of jumping up on sleeping Marines in search of a meal. More than one man had awakened with a rat sitting on his chest. One Marine sleeping barefoot had his toe chewed on by a rat. He was subsequently placed on a medevac chopper and sent back to Delta Med at Dong Ha where he underwent a series of painful rabies shots. Every night spent in a bunker was spent with the rats.

Gunny Hopkins had his section of tanks out at Yankee Station with the reaction force, so my crew stood watch in our tank by our bunker. SITREPS proved to be a blessing, for they helped keep a man alert while on watch. Every half hour the stillness would be broken by a call on our radio: "Alpha one-two, request SITREP, over."

We answered, "Alpha one-two all secure, over."

"Roger one-two, out," came the bored reply of the grunt radio operator.

At 0200, I woke my relief for the next watch and climbed onto my cot for a most welcomed night's rest—the rats be damned.

The Company Gunny's Visit

Our bunker was beginning to worry me. Not only was it little protection from a direct hit by artillery or rockets, but it did not keep out rain. A drizzle during the night revealed what a sieve our bunker roof could be. Rain dripped in on us from a dozen places.

A brief but concentrated shelling attack ended about 0830. Several near misses around our bunker finally convinced me that the time was at hand for us to reinforce our flimsy bunker roof and waterproof it with some canvas tarps we had scrounged from near the LZ. As soon as we were certain the morning shelling had ceased, we dashed outside and began the much-needed repairs, working feverishly in order to finish before another barrage of shells rained down on Con Thien.

Trevail, Sanders, and I filled dozens of empty, wooden, 105mm ammunition crates with dirt and rocks, and Johnson laid them side by side across the already sandbagged bunker roof. Our newly acquired canvas tarps were laid out over the ammo crates. We then added two more layers of sandbags. The sweat on my brow soon merged into rivulets of perspiration on my face and body in the humid morning sunshine.

While we labored so industriously, an air strike was being delivered about 1,000 meters west of our position. An O-1 single-engine, light observation plane (Bird Dog) circled slowly in the area for almost a minute, then it banked into a steep dive and fired a white smoke rocket at a clump of trees. As the Bird Dog pulled out of its dive and flew a safe distance away, two F-4B Phantom II jets with MARINES in block letters on the fuselage streaked single file over the smoke-marked target area. No bombs were dropped on that first run. They banked sharply and swung around for another pass. It was almost like watching trained falcons zooming in on their prey for the kill. On the second run, the lead plane raced in much lower and released two fin-stabilized 250-pound "Snake-eye" bombs over the target. KARUMMP—WHUMP! Twin geysers of reddish-brown earth and smoke erupted skyward. The second jet screamed in behind the other and released more Snake-eyes. The bombing runs continued until all ordnance was exhausted, then the Phantoms climbed up out of sight. Seeing those Marine Corps jets in action was a real morale builder.

We completed our bunker repair job by emplacing two 12-inch by 12-inch beams upright in the center of the bunker to shore up the sagging roof. I was mildly curious about the source of those beams. "Say, where'd you find these babies, Trevail?"

"Well, Sir . . . let's just say they weren't requisitioned through normal supply channels." His mischievous grin and twinkling eyes told me everything I needed to know. Trevail had a unique gift for acquiring items we lacked, by barter, con job, or otherwise. His enterprising spirit and resourcefulness never ceased to delight us. I asked no more about the beams.

Three days had passed since my last bath, and the odor of accumulated perspiration followed me around like a second shadow. It was time to wash up and change into my spare set of clothes. I filled my steel pot with cold water and hastily soaped and rinsed my head, armpits, crotch, and feet in that order, and replaced my odorous, sweat-soaked T-shirt, socks, and utilities with clean ones— truly amazing how wonderful a bath and clean clothing could make a man feel.

Gunny Hopkins returned with his crew from the morning mine sweep just as I finished cleaning up. The gunny's jaw was set, and he appeared quite upset. He was reluctant to talk at first, but I eventually coaxed the story from him. While moving his tank slowly along behind a mine sweep team of Marine engineers sweeping the dirt road from Con Thien to C-2, he was jolted by a sudden blast several yards from the road, almost to the tree line. When the smoke cleared, what remained of an infantryman lay in a twisted heap, his legs blown off; he was dead before the corpsman reached him. The man was part of a squad providing flank security to protect the mine sweep team from an ambush when he apparently triggered a booby trap.

The wretched irony of the incident quickly altered my optimistic, adventurous mood. I was becoming filled with distaste for Con Thien, Vietnam, and the whole ugly war. I exited the bunker and climbed into A-12 to pull myself together. Safe inside the steel womb of my tank, I sat back in the commander's seat, letting my thoughts wander. . . . *I could get blown away, too; any of us could. It could happen in a flash—here one moment and gone the next.* The reality of it was sobering. I made a determined effort to repress those thoughts. Dwelling on such things was not healthy.

Noon was fast approaching. Occasional eruptions of smoke from OP-1 and OP-2 indicated that enemy mortar shells were again landing up there. From our location, it was impossible to tell if they were inflicting any casualties, however.

We rarely heard about casualties unless they occurred in our immediate vicinity. Our bunker was situated on the southwest portion of the perimeter behind a rise of ground that shielded the medevac LZ and Battalion Aid Station (BAS) from view. After each heavy bombardment, a steady stream of casualties, both walking wounded and stretcher borne, flowed into the aid station. The more seriously wounded were evacuated from the LZ by USMC UH-34D helicopters within minutes after being hit. The dead lay outside the BAS in body bags or on blood-soaked stretchers, covered with muddy blankets, awaiting their turn. They could wait. It was a godsend for us to be spared a view of the BAS LZ.

In the midst of a depressing afternoon, the Alpha Company gunnery sergeant and his driver stopped outside of our bunker in a heavily loaded jeep.

"Hey, you old hillbilly. . . . How ya' doin' up here?" said the company gunny warmly, as he greeted Gunny Hopkins exiting our bunker.

"Well, if it ain't the rear-area commandos, come to see how the fightin' Marines live."

"Stow it, Gunny. I can always take the beer home and say that the road up here was blocked."

"Oh, Lord, just kidding, just kidding. Come on in and set a spell."

Several cases of cold beer and a large nylon mail bag stuffed to the brim were gleefully carried inside the bunker by our crewmen.

"Let's make sure this beer hadn't gone stale. What do ya' say, old cob?"

"Outstanding idea! You'll make sergeant major yet, Hopkins."

While the two gunnery sergeants sampled the beer "to make sure it was still fresh," they sorted out the mail for each crew. That seemed like an opportune moment for me to take advantage of a lull in the shelling and contact Alpha Company in Dong Ha on the powerful jeep radio. I had to submit a spot report on three 90mm high explosive (HE) rounds expended by Sergeant Guivara's tank earlier in the day. He was shooting at a suspected NVA forward observer's position 1,300 meters west of the perimeter.

"Local Train Alpha, Local Train Alpha. This is Local Train Alpha One, over." I released the handset push-to-talk button and awaited a reply. The steady hum of the radio filled my ears.

"This is Alpha," came the operator's voice. "Go ahead, over."

"Roger, spot report follows . . . from Alpha One to Alpha Six . . . Mike Oscar Mike Mike November Tango (brevity code letters standing for the date-time-group, 12/1130 hours) . . . from Hernando's Hideaway (code name for Con

Thien); A-11 fired November Pebbles (high explosive 90mm rounds) at a Fox-trot Oscar (forward observer [FO]) in a tree line with negative results, over."

Just as I said "over," a screeching blast jarred the handset from my grasp, momentarily stunning me. Someone nearby screamed, "*INCOMING!*" My ears rang. I fought to clear the cobwebs from my brain. *MOVE LEGS! GET ME OUTTA HERE!* I staggered the few short yards to our bunker and fell through the doorway. Short of breath, my heart palpitating wildly, I huddled in a corner of the bunker as more artillery shells slammed into the earth nearby.

That first round had landed close to the jeep! It must have been no more than 20 yards away. A minor miracle had just occurred, because I was unscathed.

Either it was coincidence, or an NVA FO called that "arty" down on me sitting exposed in the open using the jeep radio. It had to be more than coincidence because we were starting to receive incoming on our side of the perimeter whenever any type of vehicle stopped outside of our bunker. Perhaps we were zeroed in. Lieutenant Barry warned me about that. At any rate, I was determined never to be caught sitting in the open like that again.

The company gunny decided that Con Thien was not such a nice place to visit, and, soon after the shelling ceased, he and his driver started up their shrapnel-ventilated jeep and sped through the south gate, never looking back.

That close call earlier had shaken me up, and rather rudely at that. While hoofing it over to the CP later for the afternoon briefing, I imagined enemy eyes were on me all the way. I tried to reassure myself. *Shake it off, old man; you're getting paranoid. They missed you, thank God, now forget it!* But that peculiar, naked feeling stayed with me.

Once inside the CP bunker, I collapsed into a chair, confident of being temporarily out of danger. Much of the briefing was routine; very little information was passed that directly concerned my platoon. A B-52 strike shook the earth beneath our feet violently near the briefing's conclusion.

While exiting from the CP bunker, I observed an ominous, dark gray curtain of smoke hanging in the northwestern sky about 3,000 yards distant, caused by the B-52 strike a few minutes earlier. Several smiling Marines were standing on the CP bunker porch watching the show. I joined them, curious to see how an

Arc Light bombing mission appeared in daylight.

A moment later, the familiar sound of hundreds of 500- and 750-pound bombs roaring earthward reached our ears. Then, CRUMP! CRUMP! KA-RUMP! BOOM! The earth beneath us trembled violently even though the bombs were striking miles away. More pillars of black smoke boiled upward and thickened the already impenetrable shroud blotting out the northwestern horizon. *How could anyone survive such a pounding?* I wondered. The concussion alone could kill a man dozens of yards from point of impact.[5]

Several spectators on the porch cheered lustily; others gaped in awe with me at the destruction unleashed by our bombers. Suddenly, ssss-BAM! A single 61mm mortar round landed 40 yards behind us. Our impromptu cheering section rapidly dispersed, somewhat chagrined by our adversary's show of defiance. We were being taunted. That single mortar round was a pointed reminder that the enemy was still out there, prepared to withstand our most devastating weapons.

Night Attack: September 12/13

My crew was preparing to spend the night on the northern perimeter. We rotated this duty since it was less pleasant on that side of the perimeter at night—no bunkers to sleep in.

After a C-ration supper of franks and beans, I climbed aboard A-12 to await the rest of the crew. Trevail ignited the diesel engine and allowed it to warm up for a few minutes. We had a healthy engine; one could tell because of the smooth, purring sound she made while idling.

Dusk was on us as we traversed the narrow road around the perimeter to the same spot where I had been sniped at by a 57mm recoilless rifle that first day. The chances of receiving enemy shelling were reduced sharply once the sun set; therefore, we were much more relaxed than the last time we visited "Dodge City," as this portion of the perimeter was so aptly christened.

One infantryman was standing by as we backed into our firing slot and cut the engine.

"Say, Marine, where is our infantry support?" I asked.

"I'm it," he answered nonchalantly, shrugging his shoulders.

"Are you serious?"

"Afraid so. There's another guy 'bout fifteen yards away, but you can't see him from here 'cause he's behind a mound of dirt."

"Oh, that's just great," I muttered, not sure whether to laugh or complain to someone about the situation.

The lone Marine began rigging several Claymore antipersonnel mines in front of us. Each mine was connected by an electric wire to a firing mechanism located at his foxhole. In the event of attack, the command-detonated mines would spray deadly shrapnel in the direction of the enemy. The man apparently knew what he was doing, so I decided to wait until the next day to ask Major Gardner about our thinly manned northern perimeter.

My crew and I passed the time chatting quietly in the turret until 2100. Sanders was feeling drowsy and wanted to sleep, but his watch was from 2200 to midnight. I told him I'd stand his watch if he would agree to stand my watch from 0200 to 0400. The sleep-hungry tanker readily accepted the trade.

SITREPS weren't done on this side of the perimeter; in fact, we didn't even have radio communication with the infantry company manning the northern perimeter. We could only communicate with the 3/9 Battalion CP. That was another matter to be taken care of in the morning. Until then, we would just hope that nothing serious happened during the night.

My watch passed routinely. One occurrence did prove interesting: a TPQ strike (ground-controlled radar bombing) was run directly to the north of us by a solitary jet aircraft. The jet was locked on to a radar beam that operated in conjunction with a computer to provide corrections in air speed, altitude, and heading to the aircraft, thereby directing it over the target. A rapid series of blinding flashes was followed a split-second later by two simultaneously erupting mushrooms of smoke and flame resembling miniature atomic blasts. Bull's-eye! The TPQ had scored a direct hit, resulting in two secondary explosions.

At midnight, I woke up Trevail; then, I spread a blanket out on the steel rear deck of the tank to sleep on. Another blanket was folded neatly into a compact square to serve as a pillow. The camouflaged poncho liner was used as a combination blanket and mosquito barrier. When my humble bed was ready, I wrapped myself up carefully in the poncho liner to allow room for breathing yet protect my head, neck, and hands from nocturnal swarms of ravenous mosquitoes. Within minutes, I was submerged in the depths of slumber.

About 0300, something startled me. I awoke briefly, but on sitting up and looking around, I could not see that anything was amiss. I lay back down and was drifting off to sleep again when a peculiar POP! POP! PA-POP! POP! sound made me open my eyes. Green, glowing tracer bullets were snapping over my head, just clearing the top of the turret. An NVA machine gun northwest of Con Thien was spraying the slopes of OP-2 behind us. *We're under attack!* I started to jump through the loader's hatch but hesitated and ducked back down behind the gypsy rack. Those bullets were popping by me too close! I had to get inside that tank because, if it was an assault, my tank's firepower would be desperately needed; it would also be a prime target of enemy sappers.

One, two, three, go! I lunged for the hatch and squirmed through, stepping on a prostrate Johnson in the process. "Okay, let's get with it! We're being hit, dammit!"

I peered out through the tank commander's 360-degree cupola vision ring. Everything was pitch black except for green tracers whizzing around and over my tank. Mortars and artillery began exploding in the minefield and along the wire to our front with blinding flashes. I couldn't tell if it was a rolling barrage by the enemy or our guns firing. My chest heaved with excitement as adrenalin coursed through my body.

I grabbed the tank commander's override handle and traversed the turret left to the northwest where the heavy machine gun fire was originating, estimated the range at about 800 meters, and gave my fire command: "Gunner, one round HE . . . NVA machine gun . . . eight hundred . . . Fire!"

"Up!" shouted Sanders, the loader, as he flipped the safety switch off.

"On the way," said Johnson, the gunner, followed a split-second later by WHAMM!! Our tank recoiled sharply. The 90mm projectile exploded out into the blackness, its red phosphorous tracer element glowing brightly as the round streaked toward the target. The expended brass cartridge clanked loudly on the steel turret deck. Sanders slammed another round of high explosive into the main gun breech and shouted, "Up!" The gun was reloaded, ready to fire.

The first HE round exploded with a dazzling white flash just beyond the target. "Depress the tube, Johnson," I said. "We're a bit too high." The gun tube hummed as it was depressed electrically a few degrees. Acrid fumes from the first round permeated the close turret atmosphere. "Stand by . . . Fire!"

"On the way," said Johnson . . . WHAMM!! Again, a glowing red projectile streaked out into the night. This flash was right on target. No more green tracers sprayed the hill behind us.

"We got the bastard! Now, use the coax and hose down the area to our left front!" I shouted. Shadowy figures silhouetted by exploding mortars and incoming artillery flashes could be seen sprinting toward the outer wire 100 yards away. Our chattering .30-caliber machine gun spewed streams of bullets into the midst of the oncoming enemy. We still had no flares illuminating the battlefield. I cursed vehemently at our faulty communications with the infantry.

Without any warning, a US Army truck-mounted quad-fifty to our left opened fire, its four .50-caliber anti-aircraft machine guns spitting streams of glowing red tracers. Since the quad-fifty was mounted in the open bed of a truck, it had to be wheeled into action from behind its protective berm. A veritable fountain of tracer bullets was sprayed into the attacking enemy's flanks by the Army quad-fifty and my .30-caliber machine gun.

"Fire more HE at 'em!" Six more of our 90mm shells split the night air with their high-velocity KRACK!

Shouts went up and down the line to cease fire. No more enemy movement was noticeable outside the wire to our front. The focus of the main assault seemed to have shifted to our left, northwest of OP-2 and more toward OP-1. Some sporadic firing was still continuing over there, but it was all one-sided; our weapons were making all the noise.

I was almost choking from propellant fumes polluting the atmosphere inside the turret. Raising the tank commander's hatch, I stuck my head out cautiously into the deliciously fresh night air and inhaled deeply. One flare illuminated the quiet battlefield. Many twisted human forms lay sprawled outside the perimeter wire to our left front.

My hands were shaking from the excitement of the last half hour. "We stopped 'em!" I kept repeating.

"We blew them suckers away!" Sanders voiced unrestrained glee at the havoc we brought to bear on the NVA sappers. "We wasted those gook bastards."

They weren't human beings; they were "suckers," "gooks," or even "slopes." We felt no more concern or empathy than if we had just flushed a covey of quail and blasted them. But the NVA were our enemy—trained killers out to dispatch us from this earth. We got to them first, and it was thrilling, exhilarating—a primitive urge unleashed—defeat of your enemy in mortal combat.

When the rising sun had cast enough light to see clearly, I peered out through my vision ring at the battlefield. Great gaps had been blown in the concertina wire and numerous craters pockmarked the minefield to our left front. It appeared as if the NVA had first tried to breach the minefield by blowing up as many mines as possible with a concentrated shelling attack.

To my complete amazement, not a single enemy body was left lying out there. I knew we had hit several of the enemy sappers, otherwise, they would have penetrated our lines. *Had my eyes been deceiving me earlier?* I had seen men sprinting toward the wire, stopped short by a murderous wall of machine gun fire. Their comrades must have evacuated all their dead and wounded under cover of the predawn darkness.

Several empty 90mm brass casings had collected on the turret deck during the attack. Sanders was tossing them out one at a time through the loader's hatch when a shout to the rear made me stand up in the cupola and look around. There stood Major Cook and Major Gardner, in the midst of making a tour of the perimeter to assess the extent of damage.

Major Cook asked, "Did you tankers hit anything, Lieutenant?"

"Yes, sir . . . well . . . I know we did, sir, but there aren't any bodies left out there now."

"That's all right. You tankers did your job well. We were hit by what we estimate was an NVA reinforced company, and they never made it to the wire. Good show!"

As the two senior officers moved off on their inspection tour to the next position, I knew thereafter we were going to be considered an integral part of Con Thien's defenses, not merely clumsy iron monsters that tore up telephone wires and churned roads into rivers of mud when it rained.

My own confidence had improved immensely. I no longer doubted my crew's ability, or the defensive capabilities of the Marines on Con Thien. The NVA might overrun us, but they would have to be willing to pay a very dear price to achieve such a Pyrrhic victory.

One Lucky Day

As soon as we had eaten a C-ration breakfast back at our bunker, my crew and I went to work cleaning and oiling our weapons and replenishing the expended ammunition.

Gunnery Sergeant Hopkins had left earlier with his tank to provide security for a team of engineers whose risky mission it was to repair the damaged minefield, replace mines and restring concertina wire. Engineers were frequently mortared while working in Con Thien's minefield—a terrifying experience—nowhere to hide. Gunny Hopkins went along to provide direct fire support in the event the engineers drew enemy fire again.

Marine engineers at Con Thien had an uncomfortably high casualty rate. At the CO's briefing the previous afternoon, I had met the engineer lieutenant. He possessed that resigned look of a brave man who is all too aware of the steep odds against his safe return home.

As I was struggling to put my freshly oiled .50-caliber machine gun back into position in the cupola, the unmistakable report of tank cannon fire reached our ears, coming from the northwest where Gunny Hopkins was located. Fearing that he might be in trouble, I turned on our tank radio and tried to contact him. He didn't answer.

"Listen up," I said to the crew. "We're going out there and see what's happening. The gunny might need some help. Keep the hatches closed in case we get shelled on the way out."

We made our way through the minefield gate and cautiously followed in the gunny's tracks around the outside of the perimeter wire. The sunbaked hard terrain was ideal for tanks.

As we approached within a hundred yards of the other tank, it fired a second round at a target to the northwest. A great cloud of white smoke spewed forth from the main gun barrel, temporarily obscuring the tank. I halted our vehicle and again tried to raise the gunny on the radio, without success.

Just as I was going to move my tank closer, Gunny Hopkins popped up through his tank commander's hatch and gestured urgently for me to leave the area. He pointed to his commo helmet and gave a "thumbs down" sign, meaning that his radio set was malfunctioning. Through his improvised sign language, I was able to interpret that his lone tank was tolerable to the NVA FOs, but two tanks were fair game and would attract enemy fire like magnets.

Within seconds after we reversed direction and moved back the way we had come, artillery shells screamed down around us. "Step on it, Trevail! Maybe we can outrun them," I shouted into the intercom.

KRUMP! KRUMP! KA-WHOOMP! Rounds exploded on all sides of our tank as we rumbled resolutely forward, bouncing and swaying crazily over the uneven ground outside the perimeter. Not until we were almost to the gate did the shelling cease.

I had made a stupid move by venturing out there like that and could only pray no one got hurt because of it. Gloom saturated my spirit. My help was not needed, and I only jeopardized the engineers further by my unwanted presence. *When would I learn not to bunch up my tanks!*

A half hour later, as I sat in the bunker dejectedly stirring a cup of hot cocoa, Gunny Hopkins's tank pulled up to a halt outside. *Oh, brother,* I thought. *Here's where an officer gets chewed out by his platoon sergeant.*

The gunny bounded through the doorway, a broad, beaming grin on his face. "Say, Lieutenant, you were mighty unpopular out there this morning."

Thinking that he was referring to the animosity the engineers must have felt toward me, I replied dully, "Any of those guys get hurt because of me, Gunny?"

A flicker of insight made his eyes narrow quizzically. "Oh, you thought you messed up by comin' out there? Hell, Mr. Coan, thanks to us, nobody got hurt. We attracted so much attention that the gooks never even bothered them engineers working in the minefield."

I was taken aback for a second, then, tears of relief squeezed into my eyes, but I fought them back, somehow. "Thank God! I just knew I'd screwed up. Boy, Gunny, you don't know how low I felt coming back in."

"No problem, 'Skipper.' Them engineers probably figured we sent you out as a decoy on purpose. Now, why don't we catch some shut-eye while we got the chance. I'm all wore out." He wasn't the only one. We were all weary—bone tired and dragging. We had experienced a night with little rest followed by a hectic morning. One by one we drifted off to sleep, oblivious of the soggy morning heat and sudden, jarring blasts of artillery fire from the nearby 105mm gun battery.

Shortly after noon, I was awakened from my nap by the clanking sound of a tank outside the bunker. It was Sergeant Weicak. He had brought his tank over from his position on the northeast side of Con Thien and parked it alongside our bunker.

"What's up, Weicak," I said, my tongue slurred from sleep. I noticed his cheek was swathed in bandages. "Did you get hit?"

"Yes, sir. I was talking with two grunts about an hour ago, and a mortar round dropped right next to us. One guy was killed, and the other got messed up really bad. I only got a piece in my face."

His normally tan complexion was quite pale, and his lips trembled as he spoke. It must have shaken him profoundly, but he wouldn't admit it. I was checking my notebook for his serial number so I could radio a spot report back to Alpha Company, notifying them of the casualty in my platoon, when a barrage of mortar shells exploded all around us with their characteristic smacking thuds. No one flinched; our bunker was safe from mortars, but I was concerned. This was the second time a tank had halted outside the bunker and we'd been bracketed by mortar fire.

An NVA forward observer likely had our position pinpointed. Any time a lucrative target presented itself, such as two tanks parked outside our bunker, we could expect to be shelled. The next time it might be artillery, not mortars, and then we would be certain casualties if an artillery shell hit the bunker. I passed the word to all of my tank commanders, through Gunny Hopkins, that only one tank at a time was allowed near our bunker. Any others must stay a healthy distance away. Life was perilous enough on Con Thien without taking unnecessary risks.

The noon bombardment by NVA mortars and artillery was not particularly heavy—I slept through most of it—but the shelling continued intermittently throughout the afternoon; that was highly unusual. Previously, we had been able to count on a two- or three-hour lull between bombardments.

The daily CO's briefing time–1600–was nearing. I had to run the gauntlet, again, from my bunker to the CP. My sweating palms and stomach butterflies told me how much I dreaded performing that duty. I was vulnerable to enemy shelling the entire distance. Strangely, I cancelled out the urge to drive over in my tank. The idea somehow seemed cowardly. I would rather risk death on foot than risk having my comrades-in-arms question my courage. How insane it all was, yet, at the appointed hour, there I was, striding doggedly toward the CP, praying fervently all the while for just a few more minutes without incoming. At last, my suspense-laden journey was completed. All the bottled-up fear was exhaled in one mighty breath as I reached the CP bunker's womb-like sanctuary. Others already present on the bunker porch acknowledged my arrival with nods of recognition and knowing smiles. They had experienced the same terrors as I; they understood.

At the briefing, I sat between the engineer platoon leader and the sergeant in charge of the amtrac section. The faint, thudding sound of incoming mortars and artillery was a nagging reminder of the hazardous return trip awaiting me once the briefing was terminated. Major Gardner informed us officially that the early morning attack on Con Thien was made by a reinforced company of NVA Regulars. He gave us a thumbs-up, reporting proudly that we had all done a good job. No enemy body count was given, but, sadly, we had lost four Marines killed and fifteen wounded.

Much too soon for me, the briefing ended. I had to go out *there* again—no holding back because everyone was watching. One by one, we climbed down the stairway that provided access to the bunker porch. As soon as one man reached the bottom of the stairs, another started down. Inevitably, my turn came; I climbed grimly down the stairs, never looking back, my ears straining to detect the telltale whoosh of an incoming mortar or screaming artillery shell. *You never hear the one that has your name on it,* I remembered. That familiar, nakedly exposed feeling returned once again.

Along the narrow minefield path, past the BAS bunker, and around the artillery battery, I moved with a determined purpose: to reach my bunker before the next enemy shells arrived. *Only a few more seconds . . . 20 yards . . . three more steps . . . safe!* Not a moment too soon, I jumped inside the bunker. WHAM! WHAM! KA-WHAM! A salvo of artillery rounds exploded viciously in the nearby minefield.

I was alone; the bunker had been deserted. *They must be riding the bombardment out inside the tank,* I surmised. My sweat-soaked clothes were uncomfortable, and I craved a drink of water, but the ultimate priority was staying alive. I waited by the doorway until it was relatively quiet outside, then sprinted over to my tank and climbed aboard. *Safe again*, I sighed, and closed the tank commander's hatch over my head.

"Mr. Coan," said Sanders. "You look beat."

"No lie. It's getting hairy out there. Charlie must be pissed off about something."

I watched through my vision blocks as round after round of enemy mortar fire raked over the crests of OP-1 and OP-2, spewing forth geysers of black smoke that enshrouded the two hilltops. Our own 81mm mortars, 4.2-inch mortars, and 105mm howitzers were returning countermortar and counterbattery fire furiously from their positions located at the base of OP-2. The volume of noise was deafening.

One 81mm mortar crew caught my eye. A Marine was dropping rounds down his mortar tube as rapidly as possible with one hand and holding his helmet on his head with the other. An enemy shell exploded nearby, obliterating the Marine in a cloud of black smoke. When the smoke and dust cleared moments later, there was that mortar crewman, crouched lower, but still dropping rounds down his red-hot mortar tube as fast as ever.

The artillerymen earned my deepest respect for their unfaltering courage during these artillery duels. Other Marines referred to them as "cannon cockers," but that term was not meant to be taken as derogatory. Each gun in the battery was situated in a scooped-out depression and encircled by a sandbag-lined parapet to protect the gun crew from flying shrapnel, but nothing except their maker could help them if an enemy shell exploded within the parapet confines. This brutal fact did not prevent them from carrying out fire missions in the midst of enemy artillery attacks, completely ignoring the crashing shells exploding nearby.

I watched as the nearest gun crew ran from the safety of their bunkers to their 105mm gun, seemingly oblivious of the shelling ravaging Con Thien. One Marine sighted in the gun while another with earphones crouched alongside. A third man cradled a shell in his arms and stood by the breech, anxiously awaiting the signal to load. NVA shells screamed out of the sky, exploding with ear-splitting blasts as they ripped into the earth. One incoming round hit atop the gun parapet, spraying jagged pieces of burning hot metal through the air.

One man went down holding his bloody face in his hands. Another Marine ran from his bunker to his fallen comrade's side, carried him out of danger, then assumed the wounded man's role on the gun crew. Round after round flew out of their smoking howitzer toward the enemy. Another salvo of exploding shells bracketed them, yet no one flinched; they continued their fire mission without letup. The entire hill mass was alive with blasting guns and bursting shells. I wanted to do something, to shoot back at our tormentors, but we were not laid in with the artillery for indirect fire support.

As quickly as it had begun, the enemy shelling ceased. No more rounds were incoming; they were all outgoing. Marine gunners had triumphed through sheer courage and expertise. They had refused to retreat to the safety of their bunkers and sit out the attack; instead, they faced squarely into the withering storm of whining shrapnel and detonating projectiles until the duel was over. Was this heroism, or merely their duty? Undeniably, a very fine line separates a heroic act from mere performance of duty under fire.

Marine A-4 Skyhawk jets dropped napalm and Snake-eye bombs in the area to the north where the NVA guns were emplaced. The fluttering whoosh of friendly 155mm and 175mm artillery shells passing overhead meant that our big guns at C-2, Cam Lo, and Camp Carroll had joined in as well.

Late evening darkness soon descended on us. Con Thien was peaceful once again. I climbed wearily down from the tank and joined my crewmen in a subdued meal of rations. Would they attack again tonight? What would happen tomorrow? These questions seemed uppermost in everyone's thoughts.

Candles flickered in the close, musty air of our bunker and cast dancing shadows on the sandbagged walls. I lay on my cot, daring to contemplate the simple pleasures of home: hot running water; flush toilets; clean, crisp sheets; and long walks in the park, blissfully relaxed and unconcerned. With visions of happier, carefree days floating before my eyes, I tuned out the ugliness of Con Thien and drifted off to sleep.

3.
THEN THE RAINS CAME

'Tis the only comfort of the miserable to have partners in their woes.
—Miguel de Cervantes, *Don Quixote*

With each passing day, the fighting for Con Thien grew more intense. The North Vietnamese were taking a pounding from our artillery, planes, and naval gunfire, yet they continued to increase their pressure on Con Thien through stepped-up rocket, mortar, and artillery attacks.

"Give 'em ten for one!" That was the watchword of the Marines on Con Thien. Our gunners had a goal of returning ten rounds at the enemy for every one fired at Con Thien. In order for us to maintain this 10:1 ratio, both of our ammunition resupply channels had to be kept open. The main supply route (MSR) from Dong Ha to Con Thien provided access for truck convoys; CH-53 resupply helicopters brought in ammunition periodically during the day in cargo nets hung beneath them. As long as these resupply arteries remained viable, enemy attempts to besiege Con Thien would be thwarted.

The Short-Timers Depart

We had spent a miserable night. At 2200, we were placed on high alert because some NVA infiltrators were detected outside the minefield. An AK-47 automatic rifle opened up with a staccato burst of gunfire just before midnight, followed a short while later by a Bangalore torpedo explosion in the outer perimeter wire. We knew it was merely harassment—an attempt to make us trigger happy. No one fell for the ruse.

My crewmen and I passed the night in our tank, sleeping fitfully, waking up every two hours whenever someone new assumed his watch. The morning sun was high over the horizon before we stirred awake enough to contemplate starting a new day—my fifth on The Hill.

The date was September 14, target date for my short-timers to be pulled out of Con Thien. Hopefully, their new replacements freshly arrived "in country" would be at C-2 around noon. I spent a busy morning making certain, among other things, that everyone due to rotate was notified of the departure time. The tank crew assignments had to be juggled so that all seven short-timers were on the two tanks going to C-2; I would be on one of the tanks.

The short-timers were nervous, almost paranoid. Every incoming round was meant for them. Each moment was filled with worry—no one wants to be killed, especially not on his way home.

"Well, Corporal Johnson," I said jovially. "You're almost on the road back home. How does it feel to be this short?"

"Sir, this is the worst day of all. . . . I'm worried. . . . I just pray that I'll make it through one more day; that's all, just one more day, and then they'll never see my ass over here again. I'll be back in the world."

"You'll make it, Corporal," I said. "My whole purpose in life right now is to get you short-timers out of here in one piece. Stay inside the tank and don't do anything stupid like walking around the perimeter to say goodbye to everyone."

"Oh, don't worry about that, Lieutenant. For the rest of the morning, I'm not even peeking out to see who's winning the war."

And so it went: each man living in his own private hell, counting the minutes until he could bid adieu to Con Thien.

It was almost noon when I finally received clearance from the CP to leave. The chances of an ambush along the way were slim; nevertheless, I saw that all the short-timers rode inside their tanks with the hatches closed securely. They were taking no chances. A-13 was attacked during a routine mine sweep the week before I came to First Platoon. A solitary RPG-2 antitank rocket was launched from the high grass beside the road, and it struck A-13 in the gun shield, missing the driver, Lance Corporal Bores, by inches. One man in the loader's seat was wounded severely when the projectile's shaped charge penetrated through the homogeneous steel and burst inside the turret, spraying white-hot shrapnel in his direction. A squad of Marines scoured the area immediately afterward, but not a sign of the phantom attackers was found. It was a hit-and-run attack for harassment purposes only.

With no infantry support to impede us, we traversed the 4 miles from Con Thien to C-2 in a dozen tense minutes. The welcome confines of C-2 soon appeared. We slowed to a walk while passing through the minefield. I spotted a diesel fuel truck and the captain's jeep parked in a cleared area adjacent to the road, approximately 30 meters from the minefield gate.

Our two mud-spattered tanks separated: mine going to the fuel truck; the other traveling 50 meters farther down the road. It was a habit learned at Con Thien. Bunched up tanks invited trouble.

My short-timer crewmen, so withdrawn and apprehensive earlier, were now joking and grinning. They were the picture of unrestrained happiness. The new men stood apart shyly in their fresh jungle utility uniforms. Bulging olive-drab waterproof bags stuffed with extra clothing and blankets were slung over their shoulders. The contrast between the fresh replacements and the thirteen-month veterans was striking. Each of the seven surviving veterans of one terrible year in Vietnam possessed almost nothing except the faded, torn set of utilities on his back; a grease-stained flak jacket; muddy boots; a dented, muddy helmet; and a .45-caliber pistol. But they were ecstatic. They had made it. They had survived Con Thien and all of its horrors. They were returning to Dong Ha for hot showers, clean clothing, mess hall meals, and a flight home.

The captain approached me urgently as I jumped to the ground from the tank's front slope plate. "Lieutenant Coan, did you bring all the short-timers with you?"

"Yes sir," I answered, slightly miffed that he would even ask such a question.

"Good job, Lieutenant. I was afraid you might have difficulties in getting them all out at once. What's it like up there on the hill?"

"It's no picnic," I replied, wondering why he had not come up to Con Thien to see for himself—at least once. "It's like being fish in a barrel, only we fish shoot back every time they shoot at us."

The captain had a look in his eyes that I interpreted as respect. A mere five days earlier, he regarded me as a nervous, untried rookie; now, I was almost a veteran.

As soon as the refueling was completed, my new crewmen climbed aboard our tanks for their first visit to Con Thien. I counseled them thusly: "When we stop the tanks outside of my bunker, don't hesitate. Move inside as quickly as possible. Charlie is particularly fond of shooting at our tanks when they congregate in that area."

Fear was evident in some of the new men. Their wide, glassy eyes stared vacantly at nothing. *Let them be scared*, I thought, *then they won't be wandering around sightseeing and get hurt.* We all knew moments of fear at Con Thien. It was not cowardly to be afraid, as long as you could perform your duties, follow orders, and fight the enemy when called on. One learned to accept it and live with it; or, one could not cope with living on a red clay bull's-eye like Con Thien.

The captain gave me a thumbs-up sign and shouted something at me. I waved goodbye, and we headed back up the road, disappearing in a dingy screen of diesel smoke.

Just as I predicted, the two tanks had barely stopped alongside my bunker at Con Thien when a mortar barrage peppered the area. The new men had listened well to what I said earlier; none were caught outside.

Our replacements were the epitome of attentiveness as Gunny Hopkins and I talked to them. The gunny recorded their serial numbers, and I told them what they could expect to be doing, plus how to avoid becoming a casualty. They trusted me. I was their leader. No longer was I the new officer trying to lead salty short-timers.

Three crewmen from A-11 rotated home, leaving behind their driver, Lance Corporal DuBose. I moved over to A-11 and assigned two of the replacements to go on it with me: Sergeant Howard, a wiry, squinty-eyed "old man" of thirty, who had served one four-year hitch in the Corps back in the 1950s, returned to civilian life for a while, then reenlisted when the Vietnam War heated up; and, Corporal Irizarry, a shy lad of Puerto Rican descent, perhaps twenty. Sergeant Carter, a drawling, lanky southerner—Alabamian to be precise—was assigned as tank commander of A-12, my former tank.

Howard had been through amtracs training, but was not too familiar with tanks; therefore, the gunny and I concluded that he should obtain some more on-the-job experience before being given a tank to command. He was in his element, though. He yearned to be there. He left a steady civilian job with a construction company because, in his words, he never truly realized how much the Corps meant to him until he gave it up after his first hitch. He had to go through the hell of boot camp all over again, but he dearly wanted to be an active-duty Marine and, like Trevail, he possessed the air of a contented man, thoroughly enjoying his current station in life.

75

The other replacements were scattered throughout the platoon so they could be absorbed with the least amount of disruption. I gathered my gear from A-12 and carried it over to A-11. Lance Corporal DuBose was sitting in the driver's compartment; barely disguised gloom enveloped him. "Say, DuBose. You look like your dog ran away and you lost your best friend at the same time."

DuBose never changed his morose expression. "Sir . . . I hated to see those guys go. We were tight . . . saw a lotta shit together . . . some really hairy stuff."

I understood then. DuBose, a serious, huskily built youth from Louisiana, was grieving over the loss of his buddies from A-11 who had just gone home. He was the only one left of the original crew.

"You know," I spoke gently, attempting to say something to help snap him out of his depression. "The name of the game here is that short-timers leave, and the rookies replace them. Most of the rookies survive to become short-timers. Before too long, you'll be short, going back to the world."

"Right, I'll be goin' back one way or the other—holdin' my sea bag, or a body bag holdin' me."

"DuBose, you'll be going back home the way you started out—walking on two feet. I intend to see to that."

He gazed into my eyes briefly, as if wanting to trust in my promise to him. But we both knew the score. Either of us could be blown to bits in an instant. I left him to his thoughts and stowed my gear in the nearly empty gypsy rack attached to the rear of A-11's turret.

We had not taken much incoming in the morning; therefore, I decided it would be a good day to make the rounds of my tank positions, check to see how the new men were becoming situated, and deliver some mail the captain had brought to us earlier at C-2. I buttoned the narrow helmet strap snugly under my chin and snapped my flak jacket closed. Hanging out of the turret, I could not fix on any sounds that might mean trouble, such as booming gun reports coming from the north. I slung the mail bag over my shoulder and made my way around the perimeter on foot from one tank position to the next. Each time I left the security of a bunker, I scurried along like a gopher looking for a hole, staying close to trenches and moving in spurts from one sanctuary to another. It was risky moving around the perimeter; one never knew when an enemy shell might crash down on him without warning—the Sword of Damocles syndrome.

All movement in the open was hazardous, but everyone had his duties to perform and errands to run; I was no exception. Our crouched, shuffling quick-step was labeled the "Con Thien shuffle," a natural posture assumed while walking around under constant threat of sudden death. All senses were finely tuned in this grim comedy of survival: the eyes searched for trenches or depressions to dive into; ears strained to detect the distant *thump! thump!* of NVA artillery pieces opening up, or the whoosh of falling mortars before they struck. A fraction of a second's warning might mean the difference between life and death.

The time was rapidly approaching 1600 when I left Sergeant Weicak's bunker located east of OP-2, almost in "Dodge City." To save some time, as I was almost late for the afternoon briefing, I chose to follow the most direct route to the CP. That meant being exposed in the open more than I liked, but the shelling had been light throughout the day. I gambled that no shells would fall in the next five minutes.

With lengthy strides almost resembling a trot, I ate up the distance to the CP. Past the mortar pits, keeping both ears and eyes alert, I hoofed it along the road behind the BAS. Then, three distinct booming sounds reached my ears from the north. I had five seconds to act . . . *where was a bunker!! . . . nowhere to hide! I'm trapped in the open!*

I dove into a deep rut gouged in the road where one of my tanks had once been stuck in some mud. My fingers clawed the hard clay as several shells screeched earthward. WHAM! WHAM! KA-WHAM! Shrapnel whizzed over my head. Dirt clogs splattered down on my helmet and back. Someone nearby yelled, "Corpsman! Corpsman!"

More shells plummeted into the ground close by with crushing blasts. My spine crawled as I drew on all reserves of will power to defeat the urge to leap up and run away. I knew better.

Our 105s suddenly opened fire, sending a salvo of shells whistling northward. Again and again they fired. Several more terrifying moments passed, during which I scarcely breathed, before I felt like risking a run for it.

Completely out of breath, I staggered into the CP bunker and sagged against the nearest wall. The briefing was already in progress.

"You're late, Lieutenant," whispered a crinkle-faced gunnery sergeant good-naturedly.

"Late, yes, but not dead," I panted. "It's a minor miracle I'm still alive after just getting bracketed out there in no-man's land."

Much of the briefing's content did not register on me. I was slightly delirious and could not concentrate on what was being said until the meeting had almost ended. Perhaps it was a mild case of shock. After returning to my bunker, I crumpled onto a cot and lay there. To put it mildly, I'd had a strenuous day.

Hesitate, and You're Dead!

This was my night to go outside the perimeter along with another tank, A-13, and sit in battalion reserve at Yankee Station. I was pleased at the thought of leaving The Hill for one evening because it would be a rare opportunity to unwind; also, we would not have radio SITREPS to answer while on watch.

We waited until barely enough light remained in the cloud-smudged evening sky to see our way safely through the minefield gate. Then, after the two steel behemoths, A-11 and A-13, idled their purring diesel engines for several minutes, I told DuBose to drive over to the gate where Sergeant Osborne in A-13 would meet us. Osborne, one of the recently arrived replacements, took over as tank commander for Corporal Aranda, one of the short-timers. My tank led the way through the minefield and we followed the dirt road out to Yankee Station, about 500 meters south of Con Thien.

Lima and Kilo Companies were dug in so well at Yankee Station that we were inside their perimeter almost before we realized it. This puny, insignificant nub of high ground was ideal for staging a reaction force because its natural vegetation screened all friendly activity from the enemy. Numerous tall trees, intermingled with dense foliage, provided excellent camouflage for the reaction force.

An infantryman ground-guided us to our positions for the night. We came to a halt in the middle of an ancient rice paddy, immediately behind the defensive lines. The ground was spongy. I was concerned that we might sink during the night and become mired down by morning, but the other tank could tow us loose, I rationalized, so we remained in place.

We sat atop the tank, relaxed and carefree for the first time in several days. Periodically, one or more friendly mortar rounds burst outside the defensive perimeter in a shower of glowing white phosphorus resembling a Fourth of July aerial fireworks display. These mortar rounds were being registered around the perimeter to mark the location of our night defensive fires in the event of an all-out enemy assault.

I excused myself, broke out a blanket—my bed for the night—and arranged it on the rear deck of the tank. That was my favorite sleeping spot. It was relatively level, and being directly over the engine, the steel remained warm long after the engine was stilled. Wrapping a poncho liner around my head and upper torso to ward off the mosquitoes, I sank into a deep slumber akin to unconsciousness.

Sometime during the night, I was awakened by a gentle rainfall. I snatched up my dampened bedding, climbed into the already cramped quarters of the turret, and secured the hatches overhead. The rain continued steadily without letup throughout the night.

Daylight approached reluctantly the morning of the fifteenth, managing only to change the soaking-wet blackness of night into a sodden, gray dawn. Great splashing buckets of rain cascaded down on us, bringing misery to friend and foe alike.

I was deeply troubled over our location in the rice paddy. Water had collected in puddles around the tank. I was certain that if we remained there much longer, we would be too bogged down to move. Every tanker dreads that possibility, and I was no different. Without bothering to prepare breakfast, I had DuBose crank over the diesel engine; it coughed to life and idled smoothly. The other tank commander, Sergeant Osborne, heard my vehicle start up, and his tank engine also sprang to life, sending forth billowing gray clouds of diesel exhaust.

"DuBose, let's try it straight back the way we came in," I said over the intercom. "Take it slow and easy because we don't want the treads to slip in this muck."

"Okay, sir." Gingerly, he applied pressure on the accelerator, and we began to move backward slowly.

"That's right . . . straight back . . . don't turn it!"

As we edged our way out of the paddy onto firmer ground, I breathed an audible sigh of relief. We had extricated ourselves from a potentially serious predicament. Our treads had sunk nearly a foot into the rain-softened rice paddy overnight. One more hour, and even another tank with towing cables might not have been able to dislodge us.

Our next goal was to locate the mine sweep team of engineers and their infantry escort. Like angry, prehistoric beasts, our 52-ton iron monsters crashed out of the dense undergrowth onto the road. I questioned a few sleepy, miserably wet Marines huddled under ponchos nearby, but they had no idea where the mine sweep team could be found.

Up and down the road we traveled, asking everyone we met where the tanks were supposed to meet up with the engineers. Some ignored us, others shrugged their shoulders. Then, the combination of an empty stomach plus soaking-wet clothes, made worse with every passing second I spent exposed to the downpour, changed me into a cursing madman.

"Where the hell is the goddamned mine sweep detail?" I bellowed at a group of Marines lounging under a tarp alongside the road. They stared back dumbly and made no reply. "Listen, goddammit! You had better answer up or I'll hang your asses!" I instantly regretted saying those words. If they defied me, I was going to have to follow through on my threat, and that was a problem none of us needed that miserable morning. Fortunately, one man snapped alert and gestured in the direction from whence we had come, telling us to turn right at the big tree and go about 50 yards down the road.

Corporal Irizarry, one of the replacements acting as my loader, had an expression of alarm on his face as I dropped down into the turret, slamming the tank commander's hatch closed. That was the first time he had been with me in the tank, and I was fuming out loud in a fit of temper. He must have thought he had a hot head for a platoon leader.

We intercepted the mine sweep team plus infantry security right where we'd been told to go. Raindrops splashed in my face as we assumed our position about 25 yards behind the engineers. Sergeant Howard, another new man, sat in the gunner's seat. My tank covered the port side of the MSR, and Osborne's tank had responsibility to starboard.

The engineers commenced swinging their mine detectors from left to right and back again, moving ahead at normal walking speed. Our tanks lurched forward in low gear. We would maintain a proper interval of 25 yards behind the engineers throughout the mine sweep. I felt compassion for the hapless grunts as they slogged through liquid mud and rivulets of water beside the road. Every man's clothing was sopping wet in spite of ponchos and rain jackets. The intensity of the downpour increased by the minute. We were ripe for an ambush. The incessant rainfall had markedly limited visibility, and each Marine was lost in his own wretchedness. Only the self-discipline instilled in boot camp long ago forced these men to peer off into the tree line for signs of an ambush as they trudged forward.

The crushed-rock road supported our tanks nicely. If forced to leave the road, it almost certainly meant becoming mired down in the soggy rice paddy country. I hoped fervidly that no ambush was forthcoming.

While rounding the bend leading from Yankee Station to the Rocky Ford a mile distant, we came up on the rear elements of a large unit of Marines moving southward in two columns strung out on either side of the road. It occurred to me again that 3/9 was not alone on Con Thien. Those Marines had probably been operating to our south for days.[1] Their vacant eyes stared out from muddy, unshaven faces as they plodded numbly onward. They were beyond feeling. I was reminded of a procession of cows coming in single file from pasture looking neither right nor left, nor caring to.

The pelting rain had diminished to a faint mist by the time we neared the Rocky Ford, halfway to C-2. Rocky Ford bore that name even though it was no longer necessary to ford the creek where it intersected the MSR, Route 561. Marine engineers had installed a culvert that permitted the creek water to flow unimpeded beneath the graded road, but runoff from the early morning cloudburst had created a lake on one side of the built-up road, which was now acting as a dam. The dual, corrugated steel conduits under the road were not large enough to accommodate such a tremendous volume of rapidly accumulating rainwater. Two huge fountains sprayed forth under pressure from the lake side of the culvert. The roadbed appeared sound despite the water backed up on one side. We ventured cautiously over the culvert, flanked by infantrymen from the previously mentioned Marine battalion, and continued on with the mine sweep to C-2.

I had made arrangements with Alpha Company the previous day to have a diesel fuel truck awaiting us when we arrived at C-2. It was there, parked in the usual location, just inside the minefield gate next to the dirt road. Whatever reservations I harbored concerning the efficiency of our rear echelon support were quashed then and there. We were getting excellent logistical support.

When the refueling operation was completed, the infantry squad and the engineer team loaded aboard our two tanks, and we moved swiftly back up the road to Con Thien. As we cleared the crest of a small hill and started on the downgrade toward the Rocky Ford culvert, we observed a platoon of five tanks bucking and rolling in rough, sparsely vegetated terrain about halfway between us and Rocky Ford. They were moving rapidly on line, approaching Route 561 from the west.

"Stop, driver! Whose tanks are those?" I asked, totally surprised and alarmed to see another group of tanks marching so purposefully toward our road, less than a thousand meters from us. For a brief instant, I feared they might be North Vietnamese Army tanks charging the infantry battalion strung out on both sides of the road before us.

DuBose was the first to respond. "That's Alpha Company's Fifth Platoon."

"How can you tell from here? You got x-ray vision or something?"

"No, sir. Just binoculars." He raised up in his driver's seat and grinned mischievously. He'd broken free of the previous day's doldrums. That was a good sign.

"Okay, driver, move it out." As we lurched forward, I wondered how that other platoon of tanks was able to negotiate such rain-saturated terrain and not get bogged down as we almost had back at Yankee Station earlier.

My gaze shifted to the culvert we had to cross again. I noted that perhaps 10 percent of the road on the side backing up the floodwaters had crumbled away. Two columns of infantry were still crossing the culvert without hesitation despite gushing torrents of muddy water spewing out of the culvert pipes. The backed-up runoff was level with the road and threatening to overflow the dam-like obstacle at any moment.

"Hold it up, DuBose!" I shouted over the intercom. "That roadbed looks weak; it might not support us. Let me get a closer look." I climbed hurriedly down from A-11 and jogged up to the crossing. It looked extremely hazardous. The road's capacity for withstanding the rapidly multiplying volume of water surging against it was growing more tenuous with each passing minute. We had to get across or risk being cut off from Con Thien and the rest of the platoon, if and when the culvert gave way.

I walked back to my other tank and inquired of the driver, "Piggy" Bores, who had a year's experience driving tanks over every type of terrain possible in Vietnam. "What do you think, Piggy . . . can we make it across?"

He replied without the slightest hesitation: "Let's go on over, Lieutenant. It's not gonna hold up much longer."

"That's what I'm thinking." I jogged around to the front of my vehicle, the lead tank. "Get ready, DuBose, we're gettin' set to give it a go!" I scrambled up the front slope plate and jumped into the tank commander's cupola. As I reached behind me to retrieve my com-helmet, I looked directly into the intense, searching stares of a half dozen worried infantrymen riding aboard my tank. That Marine Corps adage from OCS echoed in my mind: *Hesitate and you're dead!* . . . I hesitated. My mind was in a turmoil of indecision. I could not make myself tell DuBose to move out. We had to get across the culvert immediately . . . *but all those men—God help us all if* . . . KA-WOOSHH! The culvert was no more, it washed away in a mighty, raging torrent of pent-up water pressure.

In shocked silence, we gaped at the mighty surge of water as it flipped those two enormous steel conduits end over end in an avalanche of cascading water like paper straws. "Holy Jesus!" I muttered. Then, the sickening realization came to me that some men walking over the culvert had been swept away and might be drowning.

Men began to shout. Two Marines instantly shed their equipment and flak jackets and jumped into the muddy, churning, swift-moving water to rescue two men who somehow had grabbed on to tree branches near the bank. They pulled them out of the water, then sprinted along the bank looking for others less fortunate.

I jumped to the ground, threw off my helmet, flak jacket, and pistol, and ran over to the scene of the tragedy, but there was nothing more I could do there. One man was missing and presumed drowned. Not a trace of him could be found. Heavy jungle undergrowth prevented searchers from going more than 50 yards from the road without machetes to hack their way through.

What had been a lazy, meandering creek a week earlier was now a raging river, 10 feet deep and 100 feet wide. NCOs and officers physically restrained several men from stripping down and diving into that deathtrap. Others stood helplessly along the riverbank, sobbing and cursing with rage.

The word was passed from man to man that their navy corpsman, "Doc," had met his fate that morning. He was a noncombatant whose duty was tending to the hurts and wounds of his grunts, often at the risk of his own life. Weighted down with all of his equipment, he never had a chance. Vietnam had claimed the life of another American boy.

Shock, outrage, and disgust were mirrored in every man's face. What a horrible way to die! He'd survived bullets, artillery, booby traps, and disease only to drown like a trapped rat. The senseless tragedy sickened me. I was forced to turn away. A search party equipped with machetes, ropes, and stretchers struck off to attempt a retrieval of the drowned man. Other Marines rigged ropes to allow those stranded few to cross the washout who were not chosen by fate to be on the culvert at the instant it gave way.

The only thing we could do was turn our tanks around and return to C-2. Attempting to cross that raging torrent was out of the question, and it would continue to be impassable for several days.

With one hard downpour, Mother Nature accomplished what the NVA could not. Con Thien was cut off and isolated. No more resupply runs could be made on the MSR until the washout was repaired.

Rain started to fall again as I trudged wearily back to my two tanks. "Piggy" Bores looked at me with glazed eyes; his face was ghostly pale. "We-we c-c-could have . . ."

"That's right, Bores, we could have, but we didn't. Forget about it. The most important thing to do now is get situated somewhere out of the rain and contact Dong Ha on the radio." Bores nodded dumbly in agreement. I understood exactly what was bothering him; we had come so awfully close to being swept away with the others. If I had not hesitated, many of us would have been killed. That old Marine Corps maxim, "Hesitate, and you're dead," did not hold true that day.

Rained In: September 15–17

The infantry and engineers riding on my two tanks were as soaked to the skin as miserable mutts in a thunderstorm by the time we returned to C-2. I halted my tanks in front of the most imposing bunker, surmising that some high-ranking officers, either infantry or artillery, would be located within.

"Sergeant, come on in with me and let's make arrangements to contact your people back at Yankee Station," I said to the senior enlisted man on the mine sweep detail. The rangy, hollow-eyed southerner was not the least bit reluctant to follow me into the bunker after being out in the rain all morning.

I spoke to a major standing at the shoulder of a communications operator and reiterated the story of how the culvert collapsed, preventing us from rejoining our outfits on Yankee Station and Con Thien. The major had problems of his own, as several bunkers on C-2 were flooded out due to poor drainage, but he allowed the sergeant to use his radio to make contact with the mine-sweep sergeant's parent unit.

A gruff-looking, leathery-faced master sergeant handed me a cup of steaming hot coffee. "Here ya' go, Lieutenant. This'll cut that chill a bit." I thanked him for his hospitality and leaned back against a rough-hewn timber upright supporting the bunker overhead. The memory of that terrible rush of muddy water sweeping those steel conduits end over end was still fresh. I could not erase that vision from before my eyes.

"Sir," said the mine-sweep sergeant, obviously elated about something. "They're sendin' trucks out here from Dong Ha to pick up me and my men and take us back to the rear. How about that!"

"Good deal. Go on out and pass the news to your men."

Pandemonium broke loose outside as the drenched, shivering infantry-men riding atop my tanks learned of their impending trip back to Dong Ha. Much whooping, cheering, and back slapping ensued. In Dong Ha, the men would get hot showers and clean clothes, the first such creature comforts for them in many weeks. It also meant another precious day or two removed from danger in their battle with fate to stay alive. The grins lighting their faces despite the downpour told the whole story.

When the infantry and engineers dismounted, I told Sergeant Osborne to follow my tank down the road. We had driven almost to the south gate of the enclave before I located a suitable area in defilade with good drainage, firm ground, and easy accessibility to the road. Two other tanks sat in defensive positions along the perimeter wire about 100 yards away. I learned that they were from the Second Platoon of Alpha Company and introduced myself to them so they'd know who we were.

We halted our two iron monsters parallel to each other, about 5 yards apart, and traversed the main gun tube on each tank until it pointed directly at the turret of the other. This formed a perfect center beam to support a 15-foot by 25-foot canvas tarp that Bores kept aboard A-13 for just such an occasion. By tying the four tarp corners to the inboard tank fenders, we created a dry, slant-roofed shelter roomy enough to walk around in without stooping. Howard and Irizarry used entrenching tools to dig shallow paths around and through the sheltered area to channel the runoff, thus permitting the mud floor of our "tent" to dry out. The few cots we carried in the gypsy racks were set up, and we were in business, prepared to wait out the rainstorm.

The downpour had slowed by noon to a fog-like drizzle, but the heavy, gray, impenetrable skies promised no change in the weather for some time to come. I climbed into A-11 and attempted to make radio contact with Alpha Company in Dong Ha. My CO did not appear to be upset over our predicament. His instructions were to remain where we were until the rain lifted. If we needed rations or water, I was to contact the other tank platoon commander stationed at C-2.

We had nothing to do but sit and wait . . . and wait . . . and wait some more. After the prolonged strain on my nervous system from the previous week at Con Thien, I was perfectly content to lounge around on a cot and gaze up at our tarp absentmindedly. Some men occupied their time by engaging in a card game called Tonk; others were lulled asleep by the constant pit-a-pat sound of raindrops striking our canvas tarp.

With the arrival of dusk, we made ready to spend the night as comfortably as possible under the circumstances. Since we were not anywhere near the C-2 lines, and we were not responsible to anyone except ourselves, I dispensed with night watches, provided that someone volunteered to sleep inside the turret of each tank. Irizarry and Burnett volunteered without a moment's hesitation.

Our second day marooned at C-2 was no different from the first: it alternately poured and drizzled; ominous, dark clouds drifted low overhead; and gusts of wind threatened to snatch our precious tarp from us. After our morning meal of C-rations was consumed, we set about oiling all exposed metal surfaces on the main gun breech and on our machine guns. We also wiped down any ammunition exposed to the elements.

About mid-afternoon, one of the crewmen from the Second Platoon tank nearest us came over to say hello. He and his crew were curious about why we had set up camp there at C-2. When I explained that we were marooned on this side of the washout when the culvert collapsed the day before, he informed us that several amphibious vehicles called "Otters," loaded with supplies for Con Thien, had tried to negotiate the flooded washout that morning and one of them had capsized. That was surprising news to us because Otters were Marine Corps tracked amphibious vehicles designed to swim through bodies of water carrying personnel and supplies.[2]

The remainder of the day was unstructured; one could think, talk, read, write letters, or play cards—whatever passed the long, boring hours sheltered from that incessant downpour. I chose to think, reliving those numerous close calls the past week on Con Thien. My luck would not hold up forever. I concluded that from that day forth, my primary goal in Vietnam was to be a survivor, not a hero—especially a dead hero. Vietnam was not worth losing my life over. But I had my pride; I was an Officer of Marines. I would do my job, do whatever was required, but focus on keeping myself and my Marines alive. I was determined to be careful, prudent, and smart, not do anything foolish that lowered my odds for survival. *But what about fate?* I asked myself. If that bullet or piece of shrapnel has your name on it, it's curtains. I concluded that the old cliché about your number being up was valid—too many men were killed by accident in Nam to discount that theory—but taking unnecessary risks such as sightseeing, thrill-seeking, or "John Wayning it" only tempted fate. I was going to be a survivor, unless fate deemed otherwise. And, if my ultimate fate was to become a casualty, so be it. Worrying about it wouldn't keep it from happening.

Like most of us serving in Vietnam, I found the will to plod through each day because of a deep need for respect, respect for one another and respect for myself. The Vietnamese weren't exactly erecting monuments in our honor, and the American people back home—most could care less. We only had one another and ourselves to face, and we fought and died out of fear we would lose the respect of our peers and ourselves if we allowed the instinct for self-preservation to gain the upper hand and convince us to run away and hide from it all. As Marines, nearly two hundred years of honor and tradition permeated our every waking moment. Ever present, yet unseen, it was there with us, almost a part of us, almost a burden to bear. Too many good men had preceded us over the generations, men who had fought to the death because they were loyal US Marines. No, we could not give any less than our best in this stalemate at Con Thien. No matter how indifferently our allies or our business-as-usual fellow Americans back home treated us, and no matter how we felt about the congressional limitations that prevented us from going after those NVA guns in the DMZ with an air/ground assault, we were US Marines. We would persevere.

Tim O'Brien said it best in his novel on the Vietnam War: "They were tough. . . . They carried their reputations. They carried the soldier's greatest fear, which was the fear of blushing. Men killed, and died, because they were embarrassed not to. It was what had brought them to the war in the first place, nothing positive, no dreams of honor and glory, just to avoid embarrassment. . . . They were too frightened to be cowards."[3]

Late in the afternoon, another tank pulled up alongside of us and halted. It was the Alpha Company "dozer" tank, so-named because it had a hydraulically operated blade attached to the front of the tank that allowed it to function as a bulldozer. A diminutive, raspy-voiced black Marine was the tank commander. "Who are you guys?" I shouted over the diesel engine noise.

"Corporal Brown—Lance Corporal Charlie Brown, to be precise—and who might you be, sir?"

"I'm Lieutenant Coan, First Platoon, Alpha. Come on in outta the rain. This makeshift abode isn't real fancy, but it's home." My offer didn't have to be repeated; Brown and his crew wasted no time getting under our canvas tarp. His additional crew made twelve of us seeking shelter from the elements. "We got cut off from Con Thien when the Rocky Ford washed out. How about you?"

"We got orphaned when the Cam Lo River flooded, and we also got some engine problems—we're barely able to roll. The CO said to tie up with you dudes, so we'll be riding out this damned storm together, I guess. . . . You got any cards?" The glint in his eye when he made such an innocent-sounding request should have been a clue. We were fat, dumb sheep in for a shearing, only we didn't know it.

After several hours of poker and blackjack, my crewmen retired for a final smoke before turning in for the night, their wallets considerably lighter than before Charlie Brown and his crew arrived. Charlie sat back contentedly in his personal folding aluminum and canvas lawn chair, sipping C-ration cocoa, alternately humming and smiling to himself. "Sure enjoyed playing cards with your men."

"Yeah, I bet you did, Brown."

"On the serious side, though, I been in this green machine almost as long as these dudes been on this earth. I been promoted and busted back down again more times than I can remember. I was Staff Sergeant Brown at one time even. I've served in just about every tank outfit in the Corps. Everybody knows Charlie Brown, and everybody knows Charlie Brown don't forget a favor. Next time we meet, hopefully under better conditions, the drinks are on me."

The remainder of that evening, Charlie Brown, Howard, and a few corporals who had been around the block once or twice swapped an unending parade of sea stories: "I remember the time back in [Da Nang, Subic Bay, Naha, Gitmo, Yokosuka, or wherever Marines had liberty in foreign ports] and we picked up on these two broads who . . ." I dozed off after a while, warm and reasonably dry, wrapped in my poncho liner, the pit-pat of raindrops on our overhead tarp lulling me to sleep for the night.

Dawn broke on the third day at C-2 without the usual gusty winds that had plagued us previously. A light rain continued to fall in intermittent showers. The date was September 17, the start of my second week as a tank platoon leader. The novelty of freedom from anxiety had worn off. I wanted desperately for the rain to stop so I could have the platoon united once again, even if it had to be on Con Thien.

About 1100, we received a surprise visit from my company commander and the Third Tank Battalion executive officer (XO). I walked cautiously toward their jeep and saluted, not certain why they had come. *Was I to be commended or court-martialed?* The XO had been dispatched from Third Tank Battalion Headquarters to observe firsthand what was happening in Alpha Company. I was only one of many stops the captain would be making with the XO that day because better than half the tanks in Alpha Company were bogged down or stranded. The entire Fifth Platoon, which we had observed two days earlier just before the culvert collapsed, had become hopelessly mired in mud about 150 meters from the MSR, not far from Yankee Station. All five tanks had to be abandoned with their guns and equipment left intact. Also, three tanks from the Third Platoon at Gio Linh were bogged down in mud and forced to spend a long, apprehensive night outside their perimeter wire illuminated by mortar flares to inhibit NVA infiltrators from approaching the helpless giants and knocking them out with antitank rockets.

I began to understand, then, why the XO had a nervous tic in the corner of his right eye, and why my captain's face appeared so drawn and pale. The brass at Third Division must have been directing some pointed queries at my superiors.

Just prior to departing, the XO asked me about the road conditions from C-2 to the washout. I replied briefly: "Sir, I doubt that the road has been swept since the washout occurred. It's probably been mined."

A momentary expression of annoyance passed over his face, and then he said almost sarcastically: "I'll take a look, anyway. Thank you, Lieutenant." They drove toward the north gate at a rapid speed. Two minutes later, however, the jeep returned and exited rapidly through the south gate, headed back to Dong Ha. Neither the captain nor the XO glanced my way as they scurried past. I guessed that either they were denied permission to travel unescorted to the washout by sentries at the north gate, or else they thought better of going down that unswept road once they got to the gate.

The prolonged spell of sitting in one confined area invariably made several men "itchy." They asked permission to hitch a ride into Cam Lo, 2 miles south of C-2. I sent them on their way because they needed a break from the daily routine. Much to everyone's satisfaction, they soon returned with beer, candles, and cigarettes, which they were able to purchase for several hundred Piasters from some Vietnamese civilians at a roadside stand. The black market was well stocked with American-made products in those days.

Lance Corporal Brown headed his dozer tank back to Dong Ha in the afternoon. His engine problems had cleared up, and he felt optimistic about his chances of successfully fording the swollen Cam Lo River. He had been such a stimulus to everyone's morale that I wished he could remain with us.

By late afternoon, I was craving a nap. The only logical, quiet place around was inside of A-11. I made a bed out of a smooth plank, 3 feet or so in length and 1 foot wide, by padding it with a doubled-over blanket and laying the plank across ammo storage boxes on A-11's turret deck. It was not exactly the Hilton, but it was dry. On arising sometime later, I could hardly believe what my eyes were seeing—enough stacked cases of shrimp, rice, pears, pineapple, and who knows what all else, to make a shoulder-high wall along one end of our hootch. "Where in the heck did this stuff come from?" I asked incredulously.

"The cook over at the main mess tent just gave it to us," answered a highly pleased and exhilarated Sergeant Howard. "As soon as we told him we was from Con Thien, he gave us all the rations he could spare."

"And he said nothing is too good for you poor bastards up at Con Thien, didn't he," chimed in a wide-eyed, breathlessly excited "Piggy" Bores.

"Yeah, right, that's what happened," chorused the others.

My suspicions were, though never proven, that the food was carted off from the rear of the main mess tent at C-2 when some cook's back was turned. At any rate, we enjoyed a rare feast that evening.

The Washout Fiasco

The rain had finally stopped! After three days and nights of almost constant downpour, we gazed out at patches of blue in the morning sky. The date was September 18.[4]

That prolonged spell of dampness had a corrosive effect on metal surfaces; similarly, the endless monotony of the previous three days had engulfed everyone in a state of lethargy that threatened to corrode our very spirits. A thorough cleaning of our tank weapons and ammunition was needed to combat both types of deterioration. I set my two crews to the task of dismantling and oiling their machine guns and examining each bullet in the ammo boxes for rust.

In spite of our damp, muddy clothing and boots, morale spiraled upward as the morning's purposeful preventative maintenance progressed. The rain's cessation meant we would soon rejoin our comrades on Con Thien, and this knowledge injected an additional measure of enthusiasm into our labors.

Just before noon, my captain arrived unexpectedly back at our position in his mud-coated jeep, accompanied by the Alpha Company gunnery sergeant and a lieutenant I was not acquainted with. A gigantic tank retriever followed behind the captain's vehicle. His order to "break camp and mount up right now" surprised me. My men were also momentarily taken aback, but they snapped to, hastily reassembled their weapons, and tried to dismantle as rapidly as possible their three-day collection of rain-defeating implements such as ponchos, plastic sheets, and Bores's canvas tarp. However, we weren't swift enough to satisfy our impatient CO, and he grumped about as though we should have been prepared to go the moment he arrived, even though we no more expected to have him there than General Westmoreland himself.

In spite of the confusion and chaos aggravated by the fussing of my two sergeants and myself, we broke camp and reloaded the tanks in a matter of minutes. Much of the contraband we hoarded had to be left behind, but a crate of Washington apples and a dozen bottles of hot sauce did go with us.

We were going to attempt to ford the Washout (no longer called Rocky Ford) if the water level had receded sufficiently. We had no infantry support with us, and the MSR from C-2 to Con Thien had not been swept for mines in three days. The CO drove his jeep rapidly along the unswept road, apparently unconcerned about the possibility of mines. I led my two tanks completely off the MSR; the tank retriever followed in our tracks.

The lieutenant riding with the captain was the unfortunate Fifth Platoon commander who was forced to abandon his entire platoon of tanks near Yankee Station at the height of the deluge two days earlier. Two of his tanks remained bogged down in the mud, and he was along to see if they could be dislodged with assistance from the mighty tank retriever. His other three vehicles were at Con Thien, having been towed safely out of the enemy's reach by Gunny Hopkins and my other tanks.

We approached the Washout cautiously; the ambush potential was extremely high. Each tank covered a side of the road, while the CO's party reconnoitered the now placid creek area for a fording site. It was eerily quiet. Not a single bird call could be detected in the thick jungle tree line on either side of the road. The washed-out road was now a jagged gorge, 25 yards wide and 10 feet deep.

The company gunny hurried over to my tank and said: "There's a good spot about 75 yards to the west of this road. The banks aren't too steep, and the creek bottom is real sturdy. . . . Follow me." We lurched along in the gunny's steps toward the fording site.

The captain and the lieutenant were standing expectantly on the far bank as DuBose edged our tank down an incline into the water. I elevated the main gun tube to prevent jamming it into the ground, then DuBose stomped on the accelerator and we plowed across the creek, our momentum carrying us up and onto the opposite bank. A soft mud underfooting caused by the recent flood threatened to suck us down if we slowed for an instant. I yelled at DuBose, "Go! Go! Don't stop until we hit the road!" Huge chunks of mud flew off the tracks as we steered for the safety of the firm roadway 75 yards distant. With one mighty surge, we clawed our way up the steep, rocky roadbed and triumphantly slammed forward onto the road surface. We had made it. "Hold it up, DuBose. That was nice driving." Rivulets of sweat trickled down my cheeks, and a clammy feeling permeated my back and armpits. The humidity was fierce.

Next to ford the creek was the retriever. It followed in my tracks, but did not remain on the road. The driver headed his retriever off into some grassy terrain adjacent to the MSR. I also thought it would be best to get away from the unswept road. "Driver, move up a few yards and pull off where that retriever is going. We should be safer over—BLAMM!!" Our tank lurched violently and ground to a halt; particles of mud and debris rained down around us. We had detonated an antitank mine.

I silently cursed the captain for ordering us out of C-2 without taking some basic precautions, such as having a mine sweep team at the Washout to meet us. Since the tragedy at the Washout, there had been no mine sweeps conducted on that portion of the MSR, Route 561. The NVA must have sown the stretch of road from there to Con Thien with numerous mines.

No one was hurt by the explosion, and we were not in much of a predicament because we had a tank retriever with us and plenty of daylight left. We immediately set to the task of fixing the pretzel-shaped tank tread and unbinding two sets of damaged road wheels and road wheel arms.

KA-BOOM! My other tank hit a mine in the water at the fording site. Bores managed to pull up on the opposite bank, but we were in serious trouble nonetheless. Both tanks were knocked out! I could not understand how my tank and the retriever could have crossed at the identical location and not hit that mine.

Without any offer of assistance from the captain, or any instructions, he and his party moved on ahead with the retriever to attempt to pull both of Fifth Platoon's tanks out of the mud. We were left behind to repair our damaged tanks. I protested that we might need help (both crews and I were relatively inexperienced at performing field repairs), but my protestations were drowned out by the mighty roar of the departing retriever's diesel engine. We were abandoned with no infantry support along and no prearranged radio communications established. I was filled with misgivings. The retriever soon vanished into the trees about a half mile up the road. *God help us all if the gooks decide to spring an ambush now,* I thought to myself.

I experienced an odd sensation that made my scalp begin to crawl; I felt like we were being watched. Fifty yards of open grass lay between us and the hostile jungle on both sides of the road. We were sitting ducks for a sniper. I could not tell which made me more apprehensive: the thought of a sniper zeroing in on my head, or an antipersonnel mine on the ground in the vicinity of the exploded antitank mine.

As a precautionary measure, I warned my crewmen not to leave the road, because there might be booby traps buried in the soft shoulder.

Beeowww! A sniper round whined over the top of Osborne's tank. Everyone hugged the ground. Beeowwoo! Another bullet whizzed overhead. Osborne gestured wildly from his tank cupola toward the jungle to his front.

"Blast him with your fifty caliber!" I shouted. He fired two long bursts in the direction of the sniper and waited. No response was forthcoming. "Let's keep working," I said to no one in particular, "but keep low; we might hear from the little bastard again."

The hours ticked by. I tried to reach the tank retriever down the road by radio, but their set was either not tuned to the Alpha Company frequency or it was shut off. We needed the retriever to hold the track away from the sprocket so it could be untangled.

I was becoming more anxious by the moment. While turning dials on our radio as a last futile gesture to obtain help, I stumbled across a conversation between two Marines who were using the call sign "Carrot-top." I knew that Carrot-top was the code name for Second Battalion, Ninth Marines, and that they were operating in the vicinity of Yankee Station. An idea came to me. *Maybe we should let 2/9 know of our predicament at the Washout. Then, if anything happened, we could get help.* I soon reached the CO of 2/9, after violating almost every radio communication rule in existence; however, my sloppy radio procedure was necessary to explain who I was and what two mine-damaged Marine tanks were doing at the Washout.

That battalion commander was angry. The more he lectured me, the angrier he became. "Why didn't you damned idiots let us know what in the hell you were up to!" I wanted to explain to him that I was only a second lieutenant with eight days of combat experience, following my captain's orders, but I held my tongue, "yessirred" and "rogered" him, and he soon cooled down. Before he signed off, he promised to look into the matter. I had some rather mixed emotions over my chat with Carrot-top Actual—relief at knowing we were not alone anymore, and disgruntlement over receiving what I felt was an undeserved ass-chewing.

Looming, dark gray clouds obliterated the blazing afternoon sun; rain began to fall again. A steady drizzle soaked everyone, but we continued to labor over our damaged tank tracks.

I glanced up the road and saw, to my complete surprise, a squad of Marines walking single file in our direction. They had been sent to provide us with security by the irascible CO of 2/9. In charge of the detachment was a husky, black sergeant. His men were obviously intent on catching a few hours of much-needed shut-eye once they were displaced in a loose perimeter around the two tanks. I was appalled by the men's condition. Open, festering sores covered some men's hands and faces, likely from infected mosquito bites. They were filthy beyond belief, and their eyes had that vacant, thousand-yard stare common to infantrymen who have seen too much combat. One man stated that he had averaged less than one meal of C-rations a day for the last week, and he hadn't eaten yet that day. His gaunt features and dark-circled eyes told me everything. I broke open our crate of apples and made certain that each man was given all he could carry; then, we divided our extra case of C-rations with those half-starved Marines. I also gave them all the heat tabs we could spare. God knows they needed them worse than we did.

Although the sudden downpour endured less than a half hour, the water level in the creek had risen noticeably. Our chances of recrossing it were growing slimmer with each passing minute. My crew was making some progress, and the track on Osborne's A-13 was almost buckled together again. All we could do in that situation was to keep working away and hope that the captain brought his retriever back while we had sufficient daylight to complete the short-tracking of my tanks.

Shortly after 1800, with less than an hour remaining until sunset, I could see the huge retriever belching forth greasy-black clouds of diesel exhaust as it and a mud-caked tank drove toward us. My pulse began to race in anticipation of finally extricating ourselves from our dilemma.

Disappointment was printed plainly on the captain's face as he pulled abreast of us and shouted: "Why aren't the tanks fixed yet?" I explained that we could have completed the job sooner with the aid of his retriever, but it was like talking at a wall—I couldn't get through.

The gunny and the captain brushed me aside and attempted to force the twisted track off the sprocket by yanking on it with a cable hooked onto the retriever, but their hurried, uncoordinated actions only made the situation worse; they undid in minutes what it had taken us over an hour to accomplish. My tank was then totally immobilized.

We were in a sticky situation. Darkness was rapidly approaching, the creek had risen, and one tank was incapable of repair before nightfall. Privates looked to their sergeants; sergeants looked to their lieutenants; and the lieutenants, in turn, asked of their captain that age-old military question: "What now, sir?" The captain jumped aboard his tank retriever and desperately attempted to contact someone on the radio back at Dong Ha, advising them of our plight.

The company gunnery sergeant climbed into the abandoned Fifth Platoon tank and cranked over the engine. Then, without checking the creek's water level, the gunny stepped on his accelerator and aimed for the fording site. With a mighty splash, his tank entered the markedly swollen creek. Water sloshed into the driver's compartment. The tank made it halfway up the opposite bank, then stalled. In complete disbelief, I watched the dead-engined tank roll back into the creek and settle stern first into the muddy water. White clouds of steam billowed up from the submerged engine as the gunny tried to restart it. It sputtered once, then died again with a clearly audible death rattle. Our only avenue of escape for the retriever and my two tanks was blocked.

Dusk was upon us. Our infantry support had orders to report back to their company before dark. In order to remain with our tanks overnight, the captain thought we should have at least a company of infantry support around us in the event of an attack. Our tanks were immobile and would not be of much help if the NVA decided to attack us, but finding a spare infantry company on such short notice was probably impossible. We were up a creek without a paddle . . . literally.

The captain ordered me to prepare to abandon my tanks. I was shocked.

Surely there was a better solution, but the decision was made and I had to comply. I was told to take my crewmen and go on foot with the infantry, spend the night with them, and attempt to return to Con Thien the following morning. As soon as practical, I was to return to Dong Ha so my seven crewmen and I could be reoutfitted for a return to Con Thien with two other tanks. The captain and his party, plus the retriever crewmen, would remain with the three abandoned tanks and the tank retriever until they received further instructions from Third Division Headquarters.

My two tanks were abandoned according to standard operating procedure (SOP) regulations: firing pin removed, engine starter-relay switches taken out, and radio sets disconnected. All machine guns were taken out and placed on the retriever, the only vehicle out of four that was still mobile.

I felt sorry for the captain. He would have to bear the burden of responsibility for the entire mess. I wanted to say something consoling, but the right words escaped me in those last moments. I said nothing. With a brave grin and a wave of my arm, I bid farewell to those remaining behind. They would have to deal with the three tanks and the retriever at the Washout.[5] My little band of seven "desperados" fell in behind the infantry security squad, and we moved off with them to join up with their company.

We were a ragtag bunch of Marines. Some of my men wore rain boots instead of jungle combat boots; others had cut off their utility trousers at the knees (to fight heat rash caused by broiling temperatures inside the sun-cooked tank turrets), and Howard and I were the only ones wearing helmets—the rest wore camouflaged slouch hats or utility covers. We all had flak jackets, fortunately. In addition to the .45-caliber pistols we were required to carry, some men had M-16 rifles; others brought along the .45-caliber submachine guns (called "grease guns" by tankers) from our abandoned tanks. And Sergeant Howard had cigarettes. When I passed the word earlier to prepare to abandon our tanks, the men were told to travel lightly and take with them only the *most* important things they possessed in the whole world, including weapons and flak jackets. Howard retrieved several cartons of Camel cigarettes from his tank and stuffed them in his shirt pockets and trouser pockets. They were his highest priority belongings.

We followed clumsily after the boondocks-toughened grunts until it became impossible to see. The blackest of Vietnam nights was upon us. We linked up single file with each man grasping the belt on the back of the man in front, and, as if we were a procession of blind men, we stumbled and fell over every log and boulder in our path, cursing silently all the while.

The entire infantry company from which this squad originated was similarly hooked up and awaiting our arrival. As soon as we stumbled into their midst, off we went again, hanging on tenaciously and praying we did not become separated. Sergeant Howard brought up the rear of our little band of grounded tankers. He sent head counts up to me every few minutes.

I was not exactly cheered to learn from the man in front of me that we were going to spend the night in an area that had been rocketed two nights earlier. His outfit had suffered numerous casualties in that vicious attack.

The fate of our comrades left behind at the Washout was far from our minds. We had our own problems. God only knew what lay in store for us that night. At long last, we passed through 2/9's lines and reached our destination. I had not the faintest idea where we were. The word was passed on that I wanted to speak with the infantry company commander, and I was immediately ushered over to where a captain was slumped wearily on the ground against a tree stump. "Well, Lieutenant," he said cheerily, "I understand you have decided to join the infantry for a while."

"Hopefully not, sir. As soon as possible, I have to get my men back up to Con Thien."

"That's no problem. You can wait until morning, can't you? Besides, we can use your extra weapons tonight to fill in some gaps in our lines."

I felt like informing him that the just completed night march had permanently dampened any enthusiasm I might have once held for joining the infantry, but his tone of voice meant that he was telling me, not asking me, to remain through the night with his Marines. Rather than have him embarrass me by ordering me to stay, I offered my services thusly: "Show me where to set in my men, and we'll be glad to help out, sir."

"Good show! Sergeant, inform the lieutenant here where he can have his men fill in on the lines."

Raindrops began to filter through the leaves above us as we followed that sergeant to our nighttime positions—two-man foxholes covered by ponchos. Marines near us were relishing their first C-ration meal of the day, whispering softly, and preparing as best they could for another rain-soaked night. No fires were allowed to ward off the dampness; strict light discipline was in effect.

My belly grumbled its displeasure at not having had any food since morning; it would have to do without, because 2/9 had no food to spare.

Sergeant Howard and I gravitated toward the same fighting hole. He was a good man to have along in tense situations—courageous, cheerful, cool-headed, and a damned fine Marine. His outstanding attitude and military bearing had propelled him right back into the NCO ranks within only a few years. If we ever made it back to Con Thien, I promised myself that Howard would be given command of a tank at the earliest opportunity.

Before "bedding down" for the night, I made a tour of my men's positions to see that all was well. It was so dark I could not even see the ground beneath me. I'd only walked a dozen steps away when I fell into a hole, knocking the breath out of myself and losing my helmet. I crawled the rest of the distance to my men's fighting holes. When assured that they were set in for the night, I crawled back to rejoin Howard, minus the helmet I gave up as lost until locating it in the morning.

It began to rain harder; thunder rumbled menacingly. In two minutes, we were drenched despite the poncho overhead. Rivulets of muddy water ran into our foxhole. The grunts there before us never considered rain when they dug in at the base of a hill.

The sound of falling rain drowned out all other noises. Occasional flashes of lightning lit up the sky. I tried to sleep while Howard took first watch, but frigid water came up to my ankles in the foxhole. I lay down in the mud outside the foxhole and wrapped up in a plastic ground cover. We were unbelievably miserable.

A grunt in the next fighting hole had rigged two ponchos into a rain shelter. His buddy was spending the night out at an ambush site, so he shared his shelter with us; besides, three shivering bodies pressed together might generate some badly needed warmth. Throughout the night, that exhausted infantryman groaned and moaned from one bad dream to the next, mumbling in his sleep, and flinging his arms about wildly. I was too uncomfortable to sleep anyway, but his carrying on did nothing to relax my taut nerves.

I fully realized for the first time how truly wretched the lot of the infantryman could be. Those men from 2/9 had been subjected to merciless elements for weeks, faced NVA mortars and artillery by day, and withstood enemy ground probes at night. They were constantly on the move; filthy; half starved; covered with open, running sores from dozens of infected insect bites and fungus patches; and always aware that the odds were against them returning home without being killed or wounded. Despite grueling hardships and a nagging sense of impending doom, all orders were carried out and rarely questioned; officers were addressed as "Sir," and sergeants were treated with respect by their men. I was filled with admiration for these Marines; they were true professionals; they would persevere.

Return to Con Thien

The coming of dawn was a blessed relief from those many hours spent shivering in rain-soaked clothing. In the misty morning light, I was able to perceive where we had stumbled to in the darkness. We were in a densely wooded area next to Yankee Station, about 400 yards from Con Thien's south gate. I never dreamed that Con Thien's bunker-encrusted hillsides could look so inviting. Spiraling columns of greasy smoke from burning "honey pots" told me we were home at last.

Two tanks were parked nearby, hatches closed, their guns facing to the west. I thought better of hiking the short distance to Con Thien because not a tree, bush, or depression existed along the way to conceal our movements from NVA forward observers. While retrieving my helmet lost in the darkness earlier, I gathered up all of my crewmen and told them to follow me. I then climbed aboard the closest tank and rapped on the loader's hatch.

"Whatever it is, we don't want any," said a gruff-voiced Marine as he opened the hatch, then stuck his upper torso out of the turret.

"Aren't you Doug Barney, Alpha's XO?" I blurted out.

"That's me . . . who the hell are you?" he asked hesitantly, eyes widening with surprise. After spending the night lying in the mud, I must have resembled a swamp creature on the loose.

"I'm Jim Coan, First Platoon. We met at Dong Ha just before Tom Barry took over First Platoon and you moved up to XO. Anyway, we had an unbelievable mess at the Washout yesterday. Three tanks and one retriever had to be abandoned. I have to get my men back to Con Thien this morning. Can you give us a lift over there?"

"Sure! Have your men climb aboard. I can't believe all the crap that's gone on in Alpha Company the last four days. Our captain's liable to lose his job over all this."

Without bothering to say goodbye to the infantry captain who had put us up for the night, I herded my seven gypsies over to Lieutenant Barney's tank. He explained, as his tank's diesel engine warmed up, that he had been sent out by our CO to take command of the few tanks left operational in Fifth Platoon until the remaining tanks got unstuck and the platoon commander could get his men reoutfitted and healthy. Apparently, several of his tank crewmen were suffering from mild trench foot after several days and nights spent out in the rain and mud.

We lurched forward and cruised over to the road, spraying chunks of mud behind us. The once rock-hard dirt road leading into Con Thien had been churned into the consistency and color of devil's-food cake batter by numerous tank treads chewing up the rain-saturated mud. I motioned at Doug Barney to let us off inside the perimeter near Sergeant Carter's tank. I jumped down, sinking in mud up to my ankles. The date was September 19. Four days had elapsed since we last set foot on Con Thien.

Before I could slog through the mud to reach Carter's location, his tank started moving toward the minefield gate. Carter indicated through sign language and shouting that his tank was being commandeered by an infantry company commander to go outside the perimeter and retrieve some bodies of Marines killed during the early morning while on patrol. After my experiences at the Washout, I instinctively disapproved of the tactical use of a single tank on such an operation. I yelled at Carter to stop so another tank could go along in the event he ran into trouble, but he was out of earshot and continued on along the path through the minefield.

With my little band trailing behind me, I hopscotched from one spot of firm ground to another. The rain, compounded by tracked vehicles, had altered roads into rivers of mud that made sizeable obstacles to cross on foot.

The tanker's bunker was right where I remembered it should be. Many new bunkers and trenches had been constructed in my absence, and many of the old, familiar landmarks had vanished, but there was no mistaking our huge, monolithic structure. I approached apprehensively, knowing I was going to have to pull rank to dislodge any squatters. Stepping purposely through the bunker doorway, I noticed a half dozen infantrymen sitting on our old cots, stirring cocoa and heating coffee. They totally ignored me.

"Who's in charge around here?" I barked. A few heads jerked in my direction, but no one said a word. "This is the tanker's bunker, and I'm the tank platoon leader. You'll have to find somewhere else to live."

That drew a response from one of the cocoa mixers. He stood up quickly and walked over to where I stood. "I'm Lieutenant Steppe, platoon leader here, and these are my men. We took over this bunker on the fifteenth of September when both companies at Yankee Station—Kilo and Lima—were moved inside Con Thien's perimeter. It's ours now; you tankers will have to live in your tanks—colonel's orders, buddy."

Good grief, I thought. The situation had really deteriorated in our absence. He had me dead to rights, though, because by all Marine Corps rules of possession, we were absent when his company moved into the lines, and his men needed the bunker worse than we did; therefore, it was theirs. We could live in our tanks, even if they were cramped. Without this bunker, the grunts had nowhere to call home, except their trenches. "All right," I said resignedly. "Then, we'd like to get our gear out of the corner over there."

My sudden change of demeanor appeared to catch the lieutenant off guard. "Umm . . . you can stay in here with me if you like," he said. "We'll be glad to share it with you and some of your men, as long as there's enough room."

I thanked him for his offer and explained that we had to return to Dong Ha to pick up two more tanks, but as soon as we returned, I would definitely move back into the bunker with him.

Our gear was piled haphazardly in one corner. A cursory examination showed it was all there, soaked and muddy, but untampered with. Even my portable radio was not bothered. That was a minor miracle, because Marines were notoriously light-fingered with the personal gear of outsiders. Lieutenant Steppe must have been responsible for keeping our belongings intact after a wall of muddy water had washed into the bunker and practically floated the contents away during that deluge of September 15 to 16.

Dean reiterated the story of the flooding to me as my crewmen sorted through packs and 782 gear. Trench lines and bunkers were flooded out all over the hill. Soaked, freezing men battled all day and into the night to divert the runoff and bail out trenches. Morale was at rock bottom because the constant misery of mud, rain, wind, and enemy shelling seeped into a man's very soul; only the close comradeship of other Marines enduring those hardships prevented men from going under. Conditions improved somewhat when the rain diminished, but much of Con Thien was still waterlogged. I could not help but feel fortunate to have spent those days and nights at C-2 instead of Con Thien.

The sound of a tank moving in our direction caught my attention. It was Sergeant Carter returning from his solo trip outside the perimeter. I waved him to a stop so I could ask why he had gone out there. As he climbed down from the turret and walked toward me, I noted the wild look in his eyes.

"What happened out there, Carter? . . . You look like you've seen a ghost," I said.

"I almost bought the farm, Lieutenant. A gook opened up on our tank with his AK and he barely missed me."

He explained that his tank and a nearby army "Duster" had been ordered to carry out a squad and help retrieve two Marines lying dead in the elephant grass outside the perimeter; they were part of a patrol sent out the previous night to set up an ambush site. An improvised explosive device of some sort had been detonated, killing the two Marines.

When Carter's tank and the army Duster arrived at the ambush site, the squad of Marines from I/3/9 and their company commander, Captain Conger, jumped down and began searching for the two murdered Marines. A lone North Vietnamese soldier hiding behind a shrub leaped to his feet and fired his AK-47 rifle wildly in Carter's direction. Before Carter could swing his main gun around and bring it into action, Captain Conger charged, killing the NVA soldier with a single burst from his M-16 rifle. Conger then continued his one-man attack, his rifle in one hand and pistol in the other, charging directly at the remaining NVA, killing all of them. The captain and his radioman then located the two mutilated Marines and loaded their weaponless, blood-drenched bodies onto the rear deck of Carter's tank. Carter was fortunate to still be alive and we both knew it.

When we had collected what was salvageable from our personal gear, I led my band of seven tankers toward the medevac LZ, where I hoped to hitch a helicopter ride back to Dong Ha. The tracked vehicle road in front of our bunker had been churned into a morass of semiliquid mud. We were in no mood to wade through knee-deep freezing mud after our adventure at Yankee Station the previous night, so we detoured left about 30 yards and located a shallow crossing bridged by empty, wooden artillery ammunition boxes. I crossed first, successfully, and turned to assist Bores, when, without any warning, a shrieking NVA artillery shell thudded flatly into the muddy road right where we had decided it was too deep to cross. KA-WHOOMP! A geyser of mud and shrapnel shot into the air; fortunately, only mud was sprayed at us.

We were immediately shocked back to the realities of life on Con Thien. "Run! Get the hell out of here, dammit!" We sprinted the remaining distance to the medevac LZ. While my panting tankers crouched outside of the Battalion Aid Station, I entered the darkened bunker to inquire about leaving on the next medevac chopper. A doctor and his staff of corpsmen were illuminated in the soft glow of candles and lanterns, quietly performing acts of surgery or first aid. Wounded men lay uncomplaining on stretchers with assorted life-preserving fluids and plasma flowing into their veins through glistening tubes dangling from bottles overhead. Men conversed in hushed, reverent tones within the surgical room atmosphere of the aid bunker. I whispered to a nearby NCO holding a clipboard, "Sergeant, when is the next chopper due in? I've got some men to go back to Dong Ha."

"Lieutenant, I'm afraid the only passengers leaving here today are WIA priorities and KIAs."

I was somewhat taken aback by his reply, but there was another possible way off The Hill—resupply choppers.

"What are our chances of hitching a ride out on a resupply chopper?"

"You might have better luck over there, but don't count on another bird for at least an hour."

"Well, thanks for your help." I headed dejectedly for the doorway. Things were not looking very promising. I loitered for a few minutes near the BAS to collect my thoughts. There had to be some way to finagle a lift back to Dong Ha.

A few yards outside of the BAS doorway was a disabled amtrac. Its bow hatch was lowered, and one could see several walking wounded waiting patiently inside to be medevaced. Some of the men appeared to be in shock; grimaces of apprehension strained their mud-smeared faces at each crashing report of our own 105mm artillery. They were only too aware of their vulnerability to a near miss or direct hit from an enemy shell. Conspicuous holes in the port and starboard sides of the vehicle reinforced their fears.

Piled carelessly in the mud by the BAS entrance were flak jackets, helmets, gas masks, canteens, and other gear for which the dead and wounded had no further use. Much of the gear was blood stained; jagged rents or holes in the various pieces of equipment attested to the destructive force of an exploding artillery or mortar shell.

That sickening, pungent odor of death filled my nostrils. I peered cautiously around a corner of the bunker and found six bodies laid out on stretchers, boot toes pointing skyward, covered from head to knees with muddy blankets. Dark, evil-smelling pools of gore swarmed with bloated flies and maggots lay beneath some stretchers. Two hard-rubber body bags lay nearby; they contained the mangled remains which only the morgue personnel at Dong Ha would have to see. I understood then why my request to ride out on a medevac was denied. We, the living, were the lowest priority.

Standing amid all that human suffering and death made me extremely anxious. "Sergeant Howard, have the men follow you over to the resupply LZ and wait for me. I'm going to see someone about boarding the next resupply chopper."

Located in a sturdily sandbagged enclosure adjacent to the resupply LZ were the Air Liaison NCO and Supply NCO. I again singled out a man holding a clipboard. "Say, buddy. What's the chance of getting a ride out of here?" I made sure my gold bar showed.

"Well, sir. Things are looking slim right now. Give me your name and I'll put you on the waiting list. See all those guys behind you? They're waiting to get out, too." I turned around quickly. At least a dozen Marines were sitting in foxholes, kneeling behind boulders, or pacing back and forth, all intent upon leaving Con Thien as fast as possible. I decided not to try to pull rank; that was not my style.

Howard was sitting despondently on the muddy rim of a foxhole near the LZ perimeter. "What's the story, sir?" His upturned face mirrored my own anxiety.

"No sweat, Sergeant Howard. We'll be on one of the next choppers out of this damned place." I hoped he could not detect the inner despair that threatened to come to the surface at any moment. We sat together on the edge of the foxhole, our legs dangling inside. My belongings were contained in a rubberized canvas bag and an AWOL bag, neatly placed on the ground beside Howard's gear. Everything I owned in the world was in those bags.

The sergeant smoked pensively and I gazed off at nothing, my fatigue-numbed brain yearning for rest. A shrill, screaming noise pierced the air overhead . . . then WHAMM!! A fountain of mud erupted 30 yards from us, next to the sandbagged Air Liaison enclosure. In my exhausted reverie, I failed to react instantly to the exploding artillery shell until something stung me sharply in the thigh. In one motion, I grabbed my leg and rolled into the foxhole.

"I got a Purple Heart! How about that!?"

"Let's see, Lieutenant. . . . W-where?" stammered a white-faced Howard.

"It's my leg." I slowly released the grip on my stinging thigh. But, to my utter amazement, no blood, no hole, nor anything amiss. *Damn, it was only a rock. Why couldn't it have been a little puncture worth a free ride to Dong Ha?*

Another shell came shrieking in—KA-RUMP!! Shrapnel whizzed viciously overhead; dirt splattered down on us. More shells arrived, shaking the ground violently. Howard's back muscles trembled as we clawed deeper into the foxhole. The world was erupting around us. Somehow, I faced certain death squarely, eyes open, my mind refusing to believe this madness was really happening.

Our own artillery opened fire, and, after a few minutes that seemed like an eternity, the enemy bombardment ended.

"Corpsman! Corpsman up!" That familiar, yet sickening, cry for help went up. I peeked cautiously over the edge of our foxhole and saw several fresh craters on the LZ. A man was stretched out in a prone position while two corpsmen tended his gory buttocks. The Air Liaison NCO and Supply NCO rushed by me toward the BAS with blood trickling down their faces and necks. They must have caught some shrapnel flush in the face from the first unexpected shell.

Sergeant Osborne was screaming hysterically for a corpsman. I could tell his voice anywhere. He was just out of sight behind some boulders; I had to stand upright to see what happened. A sharp tug on my arm by Howard pulled me back down. "Get down here, Lieutenant! You're no damned good to us with your head blowed off!"

"Somebody's hurt, Howard. I gotta go see who it is." Disengaging my arm from his grip, I leaped up from the foxhole and ran to the boulders. Two of my tank crewmen, Burnett and Irizarry, had narrowly escaped death when a shell struck 10 feet from them. They both had slight concussions but were otherwise unscathed. A mound of dirt separated them from the blast, and no shrapnel hit them. "Get these two men to the Aid Station!" I shouted at three Marines gawking nearby.

"Manchego's hit *real* bad, sir!" said Bores, pointing a trembling finger at a wounded Marine—one of my new replacements—being worked over by a corpsman about 20 yards away. I ran over there expecting to find one of his limbs blown off, or worse. The slender, quiet-spoken Mexican American lad managed a weak smile, but the gray pallor of his skin told me the seriousness of his condition; he was severely wounded by shrapnel punctures from head to toe.

After helping place Manchego on a stretcher, I returned to our foxhole. Howard was cursing softly to himself, examining the shredded contents of his duffle bag. Shrapnel had ripped through our personal gear during the shelling. My canvas AWOL bag had two jagged rents on each side, and the contents— shaving cream, portable radio, and homemade cookies—were demolished.

"It's a hell of a war, isn't it, Howard?" I said, as I sagged into a sitting position on the lip of the foxhole by the still-fuming sergeant.

"Sir, it's a gen-u-ine bitch!"

A resupply helicopter carrying a load of C-ration cases in an enormous cargo net dangling from its belly approached Con Thien from the south. That great, green bird was our salvation; we would surely get out now. The CH-53A Sea Stallion drifted in cautiously, maneuvering to place its net load of rations adjacent to the LZ. Engine noise from the giant rotor blades was deafening, almost stupefying.

My tankers crouched eagerly at the edge of the LZ, awaiting the helicopter's touchdown, so we could sprint over and climb aboard—the waiting list be damned!

Suddenly, the netted load was released. The huge helicopter lifted skyward, gracefully rotated 180 degrees, and was gone.

"Incoming!" someone cried. We scampered like rabbits to the nearest holes. More crashing, ear-splitting explosions rocked the earth; men trembled and prayed silently. The resupply chopper had evidently attracted the wrong kind of attention; NVA forward observers had the LZ zeroed in.

"Damn! Damn! Damn those lousy gooks! Sergeant Howard, take our guys to the nearest empty bunker and then meet me at the BAS. I've had enough!" I was infuriated by the indiscriminate shelling and frustrated by our predicament. Without tanks, we were useless. I had to get us out of there, one way or another. Back toward the aid station I sprinted. Halfway there, a string of incoming mortar rounds struck on my right at the base of OP-2, forcing me to flop head first into a mud-slicked depression. Then, a recoilless rifle round whizzed overhead, detonating harmlessly in the minefield.

At the medevac LZ, corpsmen were scurrying about in a state of semiconfusion. Several helicopters were due in from Dong Ha at any minute to extract the accumulated corpses as well as some of the high priority casualties.

Howard made it over to the BAS LZ a few minutes later, having located an empty bunker for my crewmen to wait out the incoming. In the meantime, I had checked on the condition of my three casualties. Manchego was inside the BAS bunker, his shrapnel wounds being dressed in preparation for evacuation. The two concussion victims were sitting morosely in the amtrac by the aid station doorway. I asked how they felt and both men nodded affirmatively, stating simultaneously, "We're okay, Lieutenant."

"Good. Come on with me, then," I said. "We're gonna get the hell outta here yet." The corpsman attending to the seriously wounded in the amtrac was glad to part with my two men; he would have more room for additional, higher priority casualties. "This is what we're going to do," I explained to Howard. "Go back and get our guys out of the bunker. When those choppers land, we'll help load the bodies, then climb aboard, if they'll let us. The first birds in will be picking up WIA priorities, so forget about getting a lift out with them, because all available space aboard will be occupied. When the wounded are all evacuated, they'll come for the bodies; that's when we go to work."

My plan was entirely ethical, but what I left unsaid was that we would be in a dangerously exposed position if the NVA shelled the LZ when those medevacs landed.

Crouched by the BAS, my group of tankers, minus Manchego, watched and waited as first one, then another UH-34D Marine helicopter descended to the BAS LZ. When all of the wounded were aboard and the last chopper lifted off the LZ, I said, "Okay, grab a stretcher with a body on it and stand by!"

The Third Battalion sergeant major, a burly, vociferous Marine with a completely shaved head, shouted instructions at everyone acting as stretcher bearers: "Move in fast and slide the stretcher through the door gunner's hatch, then duck out to the side so you won't bump into the stretcher behind you."

"Button your flak jackets and be ready to hit the deck if anyone yells incoming," I shouted to those tankers within earshot.

The drone of another approaching UH-34D helicopter grew louder as it skimmed ever closer, hugging the terrain. At the last possible moment, it lifted upward to barely clear some bunkers and settle with a bounce in the middle of the aid station LZ. I noted two large, slanted, white eyes painted on its nose. From the front, it resembled a demonic grasshopper about to land.[6]

A violent gust of wind from the rotors almost blew off my helmet. I glanced over my shoulder at the dead body on the stretcher I was carrying. The fierce prop wash had blown away the blanket and unveiled the corpse. What remained of a blood-splattered face frozen in agony stared up at me. Feeling shocked and revolted by that gruesome sight, I moved rapidly over to the chopper's flank so that Irizarry and I could slide our stretcher aboard. The door gunner was deliberately blocking the hatchway with his leg when we reached the helicopter's side. "We'll only take the ones in body bags," he said adamantly.

I retorted, "You take the poor bastard like he is! We're all out of body bags!"

"Sorry, Mac. That's my orders." With that, the chopper lifted off, and I was left fuming in the center of the LZ with an undraped, corpse-laden stretcher in my hands.

The next bird was due any moment. Irizarry and I retreated back to the BAS bunker, set our lifeless cargo down, and re-covered the corpse with a blanket; then, we hoisted one of the other stretchers containing a body bag and set it in position on the LZ so we would be ready as soon as the next chopper landed.

Miraculously, the North Vietnamese had not directed any shelling at the BAS LZ even though several helicopters had landed in succession. *Please, God. Just a few more minutes without incoming*, I prayed silently.

That sickening smell peculiar to dead bodies permeated my nostrils; my parched throat ached for water. Dried mud encrusted me from head to toe. A sensation in the pit of my stomach, which I knew as fear, threatened to boil upward and overwhelm me, but I fought it back, gripping the stretcher handles until my knuckles turned white. Visions of that mutilated face would haunt me forever.

The staccato throb of another approaching helicopter reached our ears. In an instant, it was skimming bunker rooftops and descending on the LZ. As soon as the wheels touched down, we sprinted over to it, slid the stretcher through the hatchway, and jumped inside the chopper before the door gunner could react. Together, Irizarry and I loaded another body bag aboard that two Marines thrust at us.

"We're going back to Dong Ha with you, okay?" I stated.

"Uhh, sure. Hang on!" replied the surprised door gunner; then we were airborne, hugging the treetops for a few minutes until we were far away from Con Thien. A feeling of relief surged through me. We were safe again, for the moment.

R&R in Dong Ha

We landed at Dong Ha next to a massive, sandbagged building named Delta Med. Howard and Bores were lounging comfortably under an awning when Irizarry and I arrived. "Hello, Lieutenant, I see you finally made it," said Howard, grinning smugly.

"Yeah, just barely. Say, how'd you guys beat us here, anyway."

"Hell, sir. There was room on that last load of wounded, so we jumped in with 'em. Nobody said we couldn't. By the way, Mister Coan, didn't you forget somethin' back there at Con Thien?"

"No, I don't think I . . . you're right! I forgot my bags!" The blood drained from my face in astonishment at my own gross stupidity. All of my personal gear was left sitting back at the LZ.

"Lieutenant, you can rest easy. I took your two bags with me. They're sitting right over there."

"Howard! If you were a girl, I'd plant a kiss on your mug right now." Good old Sergeant Howard. He had come through for me once again.

Moments later, another medevac landed, and my other three crewmen disembarked. They all possessed that peculiar, wild-eyed look of men freshly removed from combat; it was like the expression on people's faces as they climb out of a car that has just been involved in an accident. We waved at them and, when they spotted us, smiles of relief lit up their features at seeing they were at the right place. We were reunited once again.

What a motley gang! Irizarry wore a jungle slouch hat, cut-off trousers, and carried a .45-caliber submachine gun. I was covered with dried mud and had several days' growth of beard, as did the rest.

We watched in silence as corpsmen carried the cumbersome body bags across the concrete landing strip to a side building labeled MORGUE. Heaven only knew what horrors could be found over there. But I didn't wish to dwell on that; it was time for us to move on. "All those wishing to take a hot shower and eat some mess hall chow, follow me. The rest of you can stand out here sight-seeing all day."

The first duty to be attended to upon my arrival back in Alpha's company area was reporting Manchego's wound status to the company first sergeant. Some headquarters clerks practically recoiled in amazement, maybe even shock, when I entered their aseptic domain with my filthy, rank-smelling utilities and mud-encrusted boots. Those rear-area drones, so out of touch with the brutal realities of combat only a few miles away, were probably annoyed with me for tracking dirt over their nice, clean deck. As I finished reporting the facts concerning Manchego's wounds, the CO came into his office through a back door and slumped wearily into a swivel chair behind his desk.

"How'd it go last night, skipper?" I asked somewhat hesitantly.

"Well. . . ." He was momentarily lost in thought, glassy-eyed, as if not certain how he should respond to my question. "We got orders to leave all those vehicles and get outta there. Three tanks and one retriever." He shook his head back and forth slowly, sadly. "We were going to go after them first thing this morning, but there's an Arc Light strike scheduled for the Washout vicinity and the area is off limits. Can you believe that?"

"That means the road to Con Thien is closed, right?"

"That's what it means."

"So, we can't take two more tanks up to Con Thien. . . . What do you want us to do now, sir?"

Again, he was momentarily lost in thought. "Spend the night here, take a shower—you could use one—wash your clothes or whatever, and hop a flight back to Con Thien tomorrow. I'll figure out something on this damned mess." He rose abruptly, stalking out of the office, leaving me standing in the doorway.

I had wanted to say something to show I understood the burden he was carrying, that I knew this was a real strain on him, but it was his decisions, or lack of same, that brought this trouble down on his shoulders. And, of all the rotten luck, an Arc Light! That impending B-52 bomb strike in the Washout area had temporarily closed the MSR, so our abandoned armored vehicles would have to sit out there another night. I could just imagine all four vehicles sitting where we left them, burned-out hulks, turrets blown off by exploding ammunition, unrecognizable as the proud fighting machines they once were.

The captain did suggest that I spend the night there and return to Con Thien in the morning. I was grateful for the chance to wash my clothes, get a haircut, and put down a few cold beers. My crewmen would not return with me, however, because many of them had to be completely reoutfitted with clothing and 782 gear; they left almost everything they owned on the abandoned tanks at the Washout.

Throughout the rest of the day and into the evening, I was troubled by a peculiar longing to return to my platoon and Gunny Hopkins on Con Thien. It was a puzzling reaction because I so desperately wanted to be evacuated from there earlier in the day. Perhaps it was an instinctive need to be where I felt known, understood, and appreciated, or, possibly, it was a feeling of being in the way back in the company area. Whatever the cause, I avoided contact with the company commander and his staff, preferring instead to spend the evening writing to loved ones back home.

My family thought I was in Okinawa. I didn't want them to worry, so I deliberately misinformed them about where I was, what I was doing, and all. But I was facing a moral dilemma by choosing this course of action. If I did get killed, would it not be less of a shock if they knew I was in Vietnam, and they could prepare for that possibility? I lay awake tussling with the ramifications of both strategies: should I prevent them from worrying about me by allowing everyone to believe I was on Okinawa or let them know the truth. I finally decided I was going to be a survivor; I just couldn't allow myself to get killed; it was all very simple. They would find out I was really in Vietnam all along, when I walked off the airplane in Tucson in eleven months.

Marine tank crewman surveys antitank mine damage. Courtesy of the United States Marine Corps Vietnam Tankers Association (USMCVTA).

First Platoon of Alpha Company, June 1968, at Con Thien. James Coan on far left with hands on knees. Courtesy of James Coan.

Marine engineers building a "Dyemarker" bunker. Courtesy of David Smith.

USMC tank platoon moves out.
Courtesy of Jack Wilder.

Leathernecks of the Ninth Marines wait out a North Vietnamese Army (NVA) rocket-and-artillery attack against
the outpost at Con Thien in late 1967. United States
Marine Corps History Division/Department of Defense
(A193030).

Rat race winner. Courtesy of Larry Hogue,
USMCVTA.

Marine PFC R. L. Crumrine, operating in the Demilitarized Zone (DMZ) with the Ninth Marines on May 27, 1967, bows his head in anguish after learning that one of his best friends was killed by the NVA. United States Marine Corps History Division/Department of Defense (A188699).

Marine Infantry ride tanks on the road by Con Thien. Courtesy of the USMCVTA.

Lieutenant General Cushman, commanding officer of III Marine Amphibious Force, at Con Thien's command post bunker, October 1967. United States Marine Corps History Division/Department of Defense (A189454).

Lieutenant Coan aboard "The Believer" at Con Thien, 1968. Courtesy of James Coan.

Lieutenant Colonel Saul, CO of Second Tank Battalion, pins Purple Heart and Navy Commendation Medal on First Lieutenant Coan at Camp Lejeune, 1969. Courtesy of James Coan.

Marine artillery crew from the Second Battalion, Twelfth Marines, at Con Thien fire their 105mm howitzer at North Vietnamese units in the DMZ, October 19, 1967. United States Marine Corps History Division/Department of Defense (A421910).

A US Marine UH-34D helicopter from Squadron HMM-163 with "evil eyes." Courtesy of Robert Simon.

Staff Sergeant Howard as a Marine Corps recruiter. Courtesy of James Coan.

Sign posted by Con Thien's main gate entrance. Courtesy of John Wear, USMCVTA.

Reverse side of main gate sign. Courtesy of John Wear, USMCVTA.

Marines load casualties aboard an Alpha Company tank near Con Thien. Courtesy of Bob Stokes, USMCVTA.

Tank crewmen at Con Thien take a break from loading 90mm cannon ammunition aboard their tank. From left to right: Sergeant Davis, Corporal Trevail, Corporal Ingalls, and Lance Corporal McCartney. Courtesy of Lorena Taylor.

4.

HELL ON THE HILL

It was clear that what motivated these Marines to endure the daily hell of Con Thien was not victory or the chain of command, but their strong devotion to one another. They would risk all to be worthy of their comrades.

—Don North, "A Little Piece of Hell," *New York Times*, July 4, 2017

The situation at Con Thien was tense, even grim. No convoy resupply was possible. If weather conditions deteriorated into an early monsoon season, helicopter resupply would be sharply curtailed and the Marines would be forced to depend on supplies parachuted in from Air Force C-123 and C-130 aircraft.

Approximately twenty thousand NVA Regulars and Main-Force Viet Cong surrounded Con Thien on three sides. Dozens of artillery pieces entrenched in camouflaged caves and positions within the Demilitarized Zone (both northern and southern sections) leveled their sights on the beleaguered fortress. For purely political reasons, the US government chose not to allow US Marines to cross into the DMZ with ground forces and neutralize the enemy's guns and troops. Only air strikes and artillery fire were permitted to cross the boundary. Thus, the Marines on Con Thien were forced to dig in and hold on to the besieged outpost despite mounting casualties and increased opposition to these tactics from the American press, public, and many members of Congress. Concern was shared by all that history might repeat itself in the form of another military disaster like what happened to the French Army at Dien Bien Phu.

A Lesson Learned

The morning of September 20, I awoke at dawn and lay on my cot for a long while, staring up at the roof of Doug Barney's tent. Doug was still with the Fifth Platoon tanks at Yankee Station. I was going back to a hellhole where death was a twenty-four-hour reality. It was madness there. I felt compelled to reunite with my platoon—my "family"—but my stomach felt like a bowl of ball bearings when I thought about going back up there again to be shot at. I was filled with dread, but I had to go back. Call it what you may—duty, self-respect, pride—I had an obligation to myself, to my men, and to the Marine Corps; they were what mattered most. To not return was out of the question. After break-fast in the Ninth Motor Transport Battalion mess hall, one of our company clerks drove me to the main helicopter pad. There, I hailed a knowledgeable-looking staff sergeant in the operations shack and started to ask for informa-tion on departure schedules when he cut me off to ask first, "Where ya' headed, Lieutenant?"

"Con Thien," I replied tersely.

The sergeant's eyes softened for a brief moment, then he directed me to the proper waiting place and told me to stand by until the next flight was announced. Apparently, Con Thien had acquired a nasty reputation, because the other Marines waiting for a ride with me were tense and uncommunica-tive, each man preferring to sit by himself, absorbed in his own thoughts rather than interacting with those around him.

"All passengers for Con Thien, board this next bird approaching pad num-ber five. . . . Good luck," rasped a voice over the loudspeaker. Some men grum-bled; others paced nervously. I felt butterflies in my stomach as my palms grew slippery with nervous perspiration. A massive Marine CH-53A Sea Stallion helicopter settled gently to earth. I entered through its lowered rear ramp into a cavernous fuselage capable of carrying thirty-eight combat troops or twenty-four litters. It had no seats. Several men boarding with me carried bright red nylon bags labeled US MAIL; others only carried M-16 rifles; but we all wore helmets and buttoned-up flak jackets, whether we were privates or officers.

Within minutes after takeoff, the helicopter was cruising about 300 feet above the MSR to Con Thien. I looked out through a window as we passed over the Washout and spotted the tanks and retriever we had abandoned; they appeared exactly as we had left them. How strange it felt to be flying overhead, completely detached and indifferent toward the very vehicles whose abandon-ment necessitated my helicopter journey back to Con Thien in the first place.

The terrain from Con Thien to the Ben Hai River and beyond was pock-marked with thousands upon thousands of craters from bombs, artillery, and heavy mortars—truly unearthly, like looking at a close-up of the moon's sur-face. One couldn't help but appreciate the staggering amount of ordnance we

Americans had unleashed on the North Vietnamese in little over a year.

As we started our descent to the LZ, I could taste fear rising in my throat. I had this naked feeling, knowing that the enemy's eyes were on us, and knowing that, if the NVA opened fire, we would be trapped inside the chopper like flies in a bottle. The instant our helicopter landed, I was out of there as fast as I could make my legs move and then sprinted full bore away from the LZ.[1]

Halfway to my destination, I observed a battered, mud-coated tank sitting forlornly in an open area adjacent to the main road leading in from the minefield gate. The turret faced south toward Yankee Station. This was not one of my tanks because "The Believer" was painted on its gun tube and two grotesque, red and white eyeballs were painted on the front slope plate. I climbed aboard and rapped on the loader's hatch. A bearded, foul-smelling Marine responded to my request to come out of the turret.

"Who in the hell are you?" I asked incredulously.

"Nobody, sir. . . . I mean we were in the Fifth Platoon, but we got stuck in the mud a few days ago. Our tank wouldn't start, so they towed us here. We've been living in the tank since then. I'm acting tank commander."

"Do you have ammunition?"

"Oh, yes, sir. In fact, we're being used like a pillbox since we can't move."

"Get me a list of your crewmen and their serial numbers; bring the list to me. I'll be in that large bunker on the southwest corner of the perimeter. Just ask for me if you get lost. By the way, I'm Lieutenant Coan, the tank platoon leader on Con Thien. You belong to me, now."

"Aye, aye, sir. Comin' right over."

"Also, for Pete's sake, try using a little soap and water. You guys smell! There's no excuse for that." The man was embarrassed, which was a healthy sign, because it showed that there was some semblance of pride left in him. He and his crewmen must have been quite demoralized by their earlier predicament, and they stopped caring about anything—their appearance, the condition of their tank, or personal hygiene.

Some members of my platoon, including Gunny Hopkins, were in our old bunker when I walked in. "Mr. Coan! Am I glad to see you again!" exclaimed the gunny.

"Gunny, I hate to admit it, but it feels great to be back in this hellhole again.

Don't ask me what's happened the past five days—I'm still trying to figure it out—but I'm back to stay."

"Sir, the 3/9 brass had me a-runnin' my ass all over this hill—meetings, retrievin' tanks, and just general harassment. You can gladly have your job back."

Apparently, in my absence, life on Con Thien had been quite hectic for the gunny while doubling as platoon leader. He was only too happy to see some burdens of responsibility removed from his shoulders and placed back on mine.

Many crucial tasks needed to be performed, such as noting new tank locations, meeting the crewmen from Fifth Platoon whose three tanks were now assimilated into my platoon, listing serialized items on the new tanks, and taking inventory of ammunition stockpiles. I avoided reporting in to the Battalion CP. That formality could wait until my platoon was reorganized and administrative details were ironed out, I rationalized. . . . But I was wrong.

Many hours later, after evening darkness had descended, I relaxed in our bunker with the infantry platoon leader, Dean Steppe, and his grunts. I was bone weary, but the sight and smell of C-rations being heated restored my appetite. I hungrily anticipated a pleasant meal of beans and franks.

"The tiger leader is wanted up in the CP as soon as possible," said a begrimed radio operator from Dean Steppe's platoon.

I could see it was pitch black outside; what were once dirt roads had become rivers of mud.

The grease-slick path leading up the hillside to the CP was a genuine challenge to negotiate in the daytime, much less at night. "Radio them back and tell them I'll be there first thing in the morning."

"Aye, aye, sir."

My boots were off, and sleep was tugging at my heavy eyelids when the radioman returned and said, "Negative, sir. The CO says you'd better get your ass up to the CP *now*, sir."

I cursed the very day I signed up for Marine OCS as I fumbled under my cot for a pair of knee-length, rubber rain boots the former Alpha Company XO had given me. "Okay, by God. They want me, they'll get me. But it's going to be awhile before I can find my way up there. Tell 'em that, Marine."

"Right, sir," said the man, enjoying my displeasure immensely.

Many pitfalls awaited me: trigger-happy sentries (the evening password had not been disseminated to the tankers), yawning trenches and craters, unfamiliar artillery and mortar sections, and those damned maverick minefields within the perimeter. I was worried, to say the least.

I struck off blindly on what appeared to be the correct azimuth from my bunker to the CP. After traveling only 20 yards in that direction, I stepped off into deep, quicksand-like mud and immediately sank down to my knees. Cursing vehemently, I yanked and tugged, trying to get my right leg unstuck. At last, it pulled free—minus the rubber rain boot. There I stood, one boot on and the other sucked off in that quagmire, fuming at the complete and utter imbecility of the situation. To call the colonel and confess, "Sir, it's too dark and muddy to make it to the C P tonight," would be asking to have myself laughed out of the Corps. I stalked back to my tank, removed the remaining boot and both socks, rolled my trousers knee high, and grabbed a flashlight; light discipline be damned.

I was over halfway to the CP before my anger subsided and rational thinking returned. Going barefoot on Con Thien was sheer stupidity; sharp pieces of shrapnel, barbed wire, and tin lay strewn everywhere. I prayed nothing cut me, because it meant almost certain infection, if not worse.

After being yelled at twice—"*Douse that light!*"—I eventually arrived at a slippery path winding up the hillside to the CP. I slipped or fell about every three steps, and my flashlight got so muddy that it emitted only a pale brown glow.

At least thirty minutes after embarking on that hazardous trek, I finally climbed the wooden stairs at the base of the CP. Mud squished between my bare toes as I squinted into the doorway, blinded by intense light. Lieutenant Colonel Cook (promoted from major during my absence) and Major Gardner gawked in utter disbelief as I approached them, looking like some sort of prehistoric swamp dweller. From toes to thighs and from fingers to elbows, I was covered with mud; brown streaks striped my face and hair.

Whatever ass-chewing the CO had in mind to deliver for not reporting in as soon as I arrived on Con Thien was tempered, somewhat, by their realization that conditions at the base of The Hill, whence I had come, were unbelievably bad. They did gently chastise me for attempting to bring my vehicles back to Con Thien two days earlier without obtaining clearance from the Ninth Marines. I briefly recapitulated the incident at the Washout. They were unaware that my company commander was present at the Washout fiasco, and that I was following his direct orders that disastrous day.

As I was preparing to leave, Lieutenant Colonel Cook eyed my muck-covered limbs and said, "Don't forget, Lieutenant, you're attached to me now. You follow *my* orders."

"Yes, sir. I understand that. There won't be any problems in that regard."

The long, arduous sojourn back down the hill to my bunker ended finally. Numb with fatigue, I flopped down beside a water-filled shell hole, endeavoring to rinse off the caked mud. Trevail was sitting on his tank, chuckling good-naturedly at my disgruntlement. "Bathing by moonlight, sir? How delightful."

As much as I hated to admit it, the evening's ordeal had taught me a lesson on the evils of procrastination in the Marine Corps that would be long remembered. With most of the slimy mud washed off, I rolled down both trouser legs and staggered over to the bunker. Nothing short of an all-out assault on the lines would budge me from my cot that night.

The Battle at Phu Oc

Morning came much too soon for me on September 21, my first morning waking up on Con Thien since the fourteenth. One of Dean's men was brewing C-ration coffee, and its aroma was tantalizing; I literally hungered for some. I used the simple recipe for field coffee, and I in no time had enough to get my day started. My watch said 0700. It was strangely quiet; no guns, theirs or ours, were firing, which was odd. Remembering my struggle up to the CP by flashlight the previous night, barefooted no less, I made a hasty survey of my feet, looking for cuts. I saw none, luckily, then shook my head in disbelief at such impulsive stupidity.

The morning stillness was uncomfortable; it was too quiet. I headed for the place in the road by our bunker where my rubber rain boot got sucked off, hoping for a chance to find it in the daylight. What was formerly a hard-packed dirt road, capable of supporting tanks before the rains came, was a knee-deep, semiliquid river of reddish-brown mud. The rain boot was given up as irretrievably lost.

KA-KA-BOOM!! I flinched, almost diving into a nearby trench. It was our own artillery firing; the entire 105mm howitzer battery had opened fire simultaneously. Someone was getting a good morning salute. Then, the four-deuce mortars (4.2-in. or 107mm) opened up, followed by the 81s. I thought better of standing around staring at the mud and got back inside our bunker.

"Oh, Lord. I was dreaming my wife had made me breakfast and brought it to me in bed. I must have smelled chopped ham and eggs being heated up in here," said Dean Steppe as he yawned, stretched, and slowly sat upright on his cot, resting his boots on the damp, bare earthen floor. He sat for a long spell, as if in a stupor, staring at his hands, lost in deep thought.

"Here, Dean. Have some coffee. This'll help clear the cobwebs."

"No thanks, Jim. I'll be okay soon as I shake off my wake-up doom and gloom. Mornings are the worst. That's when I miss my wife and family the most."

"Yeah, I'm glad I don't have that problem. If I was married, it would be a lot harder for me being over here. . . . As it is, even my own family doesn't know I'm in Nam."

"Really?" Dean looked at me strangely for a moment. "You mean you don't *want* anyone knowing you're over here?"

"Yep."

"I don't know how you can do it, Jim. Those letters from my wife keep me going. Without her . . ." He broke off in mid-sentence, blinking hard, his eyes becoming moist. Then he sighed, "Well, I asked for this. Nobody had to twist my arm to make me join up. But I'll be one gloriously happy guy if I get home again in one piece—alive!"

"Amen to that, brother."

Faint booming sounds reverberated toward us from the north. "Here they come again! More incoming!" I reached down for my helmet. Some men crouched against the bunker wall sandbags, braced for whatever happened next. Heavy artillery crashed down around OP-3, east of us. More shells carried over OP-3 and landed out of sight somewhere in the densely vegetated area southeast of Con Thien. It seemed as if every gun tube on Con Thien was firing back. The racket was deafening. *Something big is up*, I thought absently. Then, more incoming artillery screamed down on Con Thien—WHAM! WHAM! WHAM! KA-WHAMM!—sounding like several heavy oaken doors being slammed shut hard.

"Lieutenant Steppe," said his radio operator urgently. "Get on the hook! It's the skipper!"

The lieutenant grabbed his radioman's handset just as a string of incoming mortar shells exploded out in the minefield. He nodded his head continuously, listening intently to what his CO was telling him, a frown spreading across his rugged features. "Aye, aye, sir," he signed off.

Dean stared hard at his platoon sergeant for a second, then they both nodded at each other, a silent message having passed between them. "Listen up!" shouted the sergeant. He didn't have to; all eyes were on him and Lieutenant Steppe.

"Okay, folks," said Dean urgently. "Some outfit stepped into the shit east of us over by Phu Oc. They got a tiger by the tail over there, and we're being put on alert. So, let's get with it." Dean and his men grabbed up their weapons without further discussion and shuffled out of the bunker.

I pulled a map out of my trouser pocket and hurriedly scanned it. The village of Phu Oc was roughly 2 kilometers east of Con Thien and 1 kilometer south of the Trace. I remained in the bunker studying my map. The tank crewmen were already in their tanks, buttoned up, no doubt, against the storm of incoming we were receiving. Gunny Hopkins and his crew were in A-15 just outside of our bunker; Sergeant Carter and his crew were 40 yards away in A-12. If something unexpected happened that morning, I reasoned, I would just place myself on A-12, my old tank. Meanwhile, I was feeling very much isolated and alone. I had no tank officially designated as mine on Con Thien. A-11 was abandoned at the Washout. Three Fifth Platoon tanks were sitting on Con Thien, however. As soon as the gunny and I could get things sorted out, one of those three tanks would become mine.

Later that morning during a lull in the incoming, Gunny Hopkins rushed into the bunker, breathing hard. "Wow, Lieutenant. A whole lotta shootin' is goin' on today!"

"Yeah, I know, Gunny. Some unit made heavy contact over to the east of us. They're really catching hell over there. At first, I thought some of the incoming was overshooting us by mistake, but it's no accident. The grunts were put on alert a while ago."

"Well, that explains all the jets makin' bomb runs around here this morning."

While the welcome lull continued, I went over to the gunny's tank and called my CO in Dong Ha. I wanted instructions on what to do with the Fifth Platoon tanks in Con Thien's perimeter. The captain informed me that my three tanks plus the three Fifth Platoon tanks were to be combined into one platoon under my command and still remain First Platoon. The Fifth Platoon tank numbers were altered as follows: A-51 to A-13; A-52 to A-11; A-54 to A-14; and my A-14 would become A-41. This gave me a total of six tanks to command, but A-54 was the "dead" tank sitting by the minefield gate, so we actually had five tanks operational in my platoon. The captain did not mention my two tanks (A-11 and A-13) abandoned at the Washout, but I assumed they would be retrieved and later integrated into Fifth Platoon.[2]

When I reentered the bunker, a host of faces greeted me: my band of gypsies from the Washout fiasco, plus some new men I'd never seen before.

"Well, I'll be damned! What a sight for sore eyes. How'd you men get back up from Dong Ha so fast? You must have pissed off the company gunny or something. I didn't expect to see you all up here for several days."

Gunny Hopkins was grinning from ear to ear. He also was happy to have us all together again. "They just couldn't handle all that easy livin' back in the rear, so they got to feelin' guilty and asked to come back. Now, ain't that what happened, gents?"

"Sure, Gunny, if you believe in Santa Claus," countered a smiling Sergeant Howard.

"Seriously, though, Gunny. I assume we're supposed to send the Fifth Platoon men back to Dong Ha today, if they can catch a bird out of here. We'd better spread the word."

"Already done. They're packin' up their gear right now. All we have to do is decide who's gonna be on those tanks."

Things were looking up. My returning crewmen were fully outfitted in new jungle utilities, and they all carried large waterproof bags loaded with spare clothing, toilet articles, and such, the noncritical items left behind when their tanks were abandoned at the Washout. I guessed that Sergeant Howard had cigarettes in his bag—several cartons, no doubt.

The gunny and I put our heads together and made crew assignments. I took over A-11 (formerly A-52) with DuBose, Irizarry, and a new man named Murphy on my crew. Sergeant Howard was given command of A-13 (formerly A-51), primarily because of my recommendation. He had strong leadership ability, maturity, and common sense; traits that would be wasted in a lesser job.

My crew set to work cleaning up the new A-11, oiling guns and ammo, while I completed an inventory of all serialized items. Considering the length of time exposed to dampness and rain the past several days, A-11 was not in bad shape. We inspected every round of 90mm gun ammo for rust and corrosion but found none. Incoming artillery, rockets, and mortars continued to strike sporadically on Con Thien, but not with the frequency encountered in the morning. Much of the incoming ordnance continued to land on or beyond OP-3, the opposite side of the perimeter from us, 200 or so yards distant.

The hour was 1600, CO's briefing time. Flak jacket snapped shut, helmet securely in place, and butterflies winging around in my gut, I struck off for the CP bunker behind OP-1, eating up as much ground as possible with each stride, but not too fast, because a bouncing helmet would make unwanted noise, and that would interfere with my ability to hear incoming. All senses fine-tuned, I negotiated the narrow path through the elephant grass and bounded up the mud-coated CP stairs into the bunker entrance. I was a minute or so late; all seats were taken, so I stood at the rear of the room taking notes.

After preliminary announcements, Major Gardner informed us of the tactical situation occurring east of Con Thien near Phu Oc. The Second Battalion, Fourth Marines, was conducting a search-and-destroy mission 2,000 meters east of us. At about 0800, lead elements came on a well-camouflaged, mutually supporting bunker system and were taken under enemy fire. The fight had lasted all day. Casualty figures for either side were not known, but one could assume logically they were high. Estimates of the number of enemy involved ranged from one battalion to an entire regiment.[3]

Some ominous implications came to mind. Were the NVA attempting to surround us and then lay siege to Con Thien? Did 2/4 stumble onto an enemy staging area that might be intended as a base for a night attack against Con Thien's blind side, the southeast? Many grim, serious faces were in that CP bunker. Mine was one of them. That abortive, company-sized probe from the north one week earlier was not the enemy's last hurrah. They still had designs on Con Thien. We might yet be in for a massive attack.

When I returned from the afternoon briefing, Gunny Hopkins and Dean Steppe were the only two people in our bunker; both of them were occupying cots—the gunny resting and Dean writing letters. They looked up at me expectantly, as if to ask, "Well, tell us, what'd you find out?" I was bursting with news; no more encouragement was necessary.

"That was 2/4 over there today. Lots of NVA are east of us. Looks like they were getting ready for something, but 2/4 pulled their covers."

"Yeah, because that thick vegetation over there is almost like a jungle," commented Dean. "It's the best direction from which to attack Con Thien. That vegetation grows right up to the outer perimeter wire over there. Why, they'd be comin' through the minefield before we even saw 'em."

"That minefield would put an awful hurt on them," I interjected.

The gunny rose to an upright sitting position, shaking his pointed index finger for emphasis. "Don't rest too easy believing that, Lieutenant. Them gooks has sappers trained to sneak through minefields. Why, I've heard stories of grunts goin' out to retrieve their claymore mines in the morning, only to find that they'd been turned around so's they faced *them* instead of towards the enemy."

"That's no bull, either," said Dean. "But every jet and gunship in Nam would be up here blastin' that jungle if they broke into the perimeter. They'd never get their reserves even close to the wire. Then it would be up to us to seal off the break and wipe out the ones who made it through the minefield."

I thought about that for a moment, imagining my six tanks buttoned up, each one a primary enemy sapper target, while we struggled for survival attempting to destroy darting, dodging enemy soldiers illuminated by swaying flares and the dancing light from other burning vehicles and structures. "I wonder how long we'd have to hold out before help arrived."

Dean pondered that briefly, then replied, "I think it depends on the distance our reaction force had to travel; plus, they might have to fight their way up to us if the NVA committed enough troops. We might not get help until the next day."

The gunny and I exchanged worry-laden glances; we both realized the odds against any tanks surviving until daylight with enemy sappers roaming the perimeter all night, tossing satchel charges and attaching shaped charges to the sides of our tanks. My stomach began to feel very tense.

"Well, we're not exactly alone up here," I said encouragingly, trying to inject a note of optimism into an otherwise pessimistic outlook. "There's 2/4 east of us and 2/9 south of us. Counting 3/9 here makes three battalions—a full regiment. And a regiment of US Marines could kick ass all the way to Hanoi!"

We all nodded in agreement; no dispute there. "And don't forget 3/26. They might be out there also backin' us up. They fought off that NVA regiment about a mile or so southwest of us ten days ago."

"I heard 3/26 caught 'em attacking across open rice paddies and clobbered the hell out of 'em," added Dean.

"I guess we just have to pray that 2/4 spoiled them gooks' chances for a surprise attack. As for me, gentlemen, I'm goin' to make sure our tanks is on the ball tonight in case Mr. Charles decides to come a-callin'." With that, Gunny Hopkins arose and started for the bunker exit.

"If he comes tonight, tell him we're not receiving any visitors . . . okay, Gunny?" I quipped.

The NVA Bush

It was my turn to have first watch that night, 2200 to 2400. I lay back on the cot prior to commencing my watch, gazing absently at nondescript shadows flitting back and forth across the overhead beams. Movement within the bunker gradually wound down. The only sounds were occasional whispers and the heavy, rhythmic breathing of a group of tired men sleeping. It wasn't long after the last candle flickered out and the last flashlight clicked off that I detected a faint rustling in the corner; then it grew louder. Rats were scrounging around in our trash box searching for discarded tidbits. My skin crawled at recognizing the source of those sounds. I grabbed a flashlight and aimed a beam of light at the corner; several pairs of tiny, gleaming eyes scurried out of sight. Everyone else in the bunker was sleeping, blissfully unaware of the four-legged intruders. I hated those disgusting creatures; something deep within me found them absolutely revolting.

When it was almost 2200 and time for my watch to begin, I exited the bunker and climbed aboard my tank, relieved to be free from hungry rats. A crewman was standing up in the commander's cupola, peering out toward the minefield with binoculars. It was Lance Corporal Murphy, the new man assigned to my tank. "See anything interesting out there, Murphy," I whispered.

Murphy was a personable, intelligent, thinly built Marine; he may have even gone to college at one time. He put the binoculars down quickly, almost sheepishly, as if he had been caught in the act of doing something illegal. "Maybe, sir. I mean, there's this bush out there that wasn't there this afternoon. Every time an illumination round goes up on our side of the perimeter, I scope in on the bush. I-I think it's moving toward us, little by little." An electric jolt of adrenalin surged through me as I recalled the gunny's warning earlier: *Gooks are trained to sneak through minefields.*

"Get down in the gunner's seat and traverse our gun tube at it. I'll look through the range finder."

We waited several agonizing, long minutes until another mortar illumination round popped overhead. The tank turret hummed as Murphy traversed left, right, up, and then down. Finally, the gun tube and turret stopped moving. "There it is, Lieutenant. My cross hairs are right on it."

I peered intently through the range finder, scarcely breathing, my heart pounding in my chest. A large, dense shrub was dead ahead of us, about 100 yards away. In the faint, flickering illumination flare light, its shape was barely discernable, but the more I stared at it, the more it began to resemble the vague outline of a crouching human covered with foliage. Then the flare went out and total darkness once more enveloped us.

I grabbed the handset from a PRC-25 radio strapped to the gypsy rack and contacted the infantry company manning our portion of the lines. "This is Tiger Leader. Be advised we have possible movement outside the southwest wire. Request illumination rounds, over."

"Roger, Tiger Leader. What do you see, over?"

"This is Tiger Leader. We think we've spotted a gook sneaking up to the wire. Request permission to fire, over." My tone of voice conveyed no nonsense urgency; every second counted.

After a brief pause, the operator came back with instructions to "wait one, over." I knew that the company was checking with battalion to determine if any "friendlies" were in the area. Several minutes dragged by. By this time, Irizarry and DuBose were wide awake, wanting to know what was happening. At last, the grunt radioman came back over the air to us. "Our actual says no friendlies are out there. You got permission, over."

"Roger, out." Seconds later, the distinctive *chunk* sound of our mortars being fired reached our ears. First one, then a second mortar illumination round popped high overhead, then gently floated down beneath a small, white, sway-ing parachute. "Let's get that sucker. Use the coax on him. Fire when ready." One long burst of .30-caliber machine gun tracers streaked toward the target, shat-tering the tranquil evening quiet. My binoculars were riveted to my eye sockets; I scarcely dared to breathe. Branches and leaves flew off the bush in every direc-tion. "Cease fire!" I shouted. The "infiltrator" was now a defoliated, denuded, once-healthy shrub; reduced to half its height with most of its leaves shot off.

"Murphy . . . guess what? We just killed outselves an NVA bush." After the snorts and giggles of my crew died down, DuBose commented, "Mighty fine shootin', Lieutenant. That poor bush won't ever sneak up on us again."

Before I could think of a good comeback, the PRC-25 handset crackled with a voice asking urgently, "Tiger Leader. What'd you hit out there, over?"

"This is Tiger Leader. Scratch one Communist bush. Go back to sleep, out."

Quite some time later, our portion of the perimeter finally settled down for the night. By then, my watch was over. I stepped down in the turret and reached over to pat Irizarry, but he was already awake. We exchanged places: he stood on the TC's seat and rested his elbows on the outside of the cupola; I placed my bed board across some ammo storage boxes on the turret deck, folded a blanket into a sleeping pad and placed that on my bed board, then lay in a fetal position with my head beneath the main gun breech. Covered up with a poncho liner, I felt warm, dry, and secure; sleep was not far away.

Surviving under the siege conditions at Con Thien was becoming more dif-ficult with each passing day. Perhaps it was only my imagination, but the inten-sity of enemy shelling attacks seemed to be increasing. I noticed more medevacs flying in and out the past two days than ever before. I was weary, physically and mentally fatigued from the stresses of leadership and from straining to be alert for incoming missiles. But the worst thing about the so-called siege was the cer-tainty that each new day would only bring more of the same.[4]

The "Doomsday" Device

I was up early the next day, perhaps because I was curious to see the NVA bush we had blown away. There it was, barely recognizable in the gray morning mist. I suppressed a chuckle and walked around behind our bunker, squish-ing through ankle-deep mud, and paid a visit to the urinal, a brass shell cas-ing buried two-thirds of its length in the ground and filled with gravel. While conducting my business there, I casually surveyed the terrain around our bunker, pockmarked by several fresh craters. Some of those incoming rounds were landing closer than we realized. So far, none of the bunkers on our portion of the perimeter had received a direct hit from an enemy projectile, but sooner or later someone's luck might run out. I didn't wish to dwell on that ghastly possibility any longer, so I switched my attention elsewhere.

The road by our bunker was still an impossible morass of chocolate mud. Tracked vehicles—tanks, amtracs, Ontos, and "dusters" (US Army M-42 light tanks mounting twin 40mm Bofors antiaircraft guns)—were responsible for the abysmal road conditions on Con Thien, but they had missions to perform, and their routes of travel were channelized on the roads by necessity. Tracked vehicles could not roam where they pleased throughout the conclave because wire communications would be continuously in need of repair. It was difficult enough to maintain communications in the face of all that enemy shelling without having to contend with tracked vehicles chewing up the commo wire every day.

The stubble on my face was growing uncomfortable, so I brought my shaving gear outside the bunker and set it up on the sandbagged blast wall immediately in front of the bunker hatchway. Water rationing was in effect, and all personnel were instructed to shave only every third day. Bathing and washing clothes were luxuries that Con Thien's water shortage would no longer permit.

My mind was elsewhere that morning as I hacked away at three days' growth of beard. My flak jacket and helmet were off, but within arm's reach. I never heard the lone artillery round that came in; it must have just cleared our bunker before detonating in the nearby road with a loud BLAMM! An enormous geyser of mud exploded straight up. Had the ground been hard, I definitely would have been a casualty because the round landed only 20 yards from me. I finished shaving inside the bunker, in spite of my shaking hands.

My tankers did not go out on road sweeps anymore since the Washout fiasco. We whiled away the hours talking about home, girls, food, hunting, and automobiles. Some men played rummy, poker, or solitaire; others read books, wrote letters, cleaned weapons and equipment, and ate C-rations. Periodically, a sharp report from the guns in our artillery battery would jar the bunker, but it was a comforting noise, something one adjusted to rapidly.

What I could never grow accustomed to was the piercing scream incoming enemy rockets made before crashing into the earth—a sound unlike anything imaginable. Nothing could ever condition a person to hear that hideous sound and not be alarmed. Knowing that the scream preceded by only seconds the deadly arrival of a 9-foot-long rocket weighing 125 pounds always made my heart leap into my throat.

The afternoon briefing at the Battalion CP was routine except for one piece of bad news I accidentally stumbled on. Before the meeting started, I was standing in the rear of the CP bunker, absently surveying the haggard, grimy faces of those present to determine if any attached unit leaders I knew had not shown up for the briefing. One familiar face was absent: the sergeant in charge of amtracs. I asked a Marine NCO next to me, "Where is that sergeant from the amtracs unit?"

The NCO's face clouded over momentarily; then, he dropped his head and stared at the floor. "You didn't hear what happened?" he said softly.

"No, I haven't heard anything; what happened to him?"

"He was killed instantly a few days ago by a direct hit on his amtrac. He was sitting on top, and an arty round landed right on him."

"Oh, my God!" I spat disgustedly. The news seared through me, almost making me ill. The man had been a friend to me and my platoon, hauling tank ammunition from the LZ, and sharing his allotment of C-ration heat tabs with some of my tank commanders. It must have happened while I was marooned at C-2, or the news would have reached me sooner.

A shroud of depression enveloped me during the briefing; little of what was said seemed to matter anymore; the dead Marine's smiling face kept reappearing before my eyes.

Later that evening, the Battalion S-3 sent word down via messenger that a tank was needed to go outside the perimeter wire and escort some engineers and a bulldozer returning from the northern sector of the minefield. A late afternoon mortar attack had pinned them down out there before dark. They were extremely vulnerable, ripe for an ambush.

I wanted to send two vehicles out, but the platoon was critically low on fuel. Gunny Hopkins' tank had the most petrol, plus he was familiar with the route, having gone out over it twice. He volunteered to go without any hesitation.

The gunny's tank had only been absent for a matter of minutes when a tremendous explosion outside the perimeter shattered the evening's serenity. The tank engine stopped; my heart skipped a few beats thinking that the gunny had detonated a powerful antitank mine. Moments later, the engine cranked over and A-15 continued out of earshot on its mission, much to my relief.

When the gunny and the engineers returned, their route home illuminated by flares shot up from our 60mm and 81mm mortars, I was curious to learn what caused that mighty blast outside the perimeter.

"What the hell was that explosion out there, Gunny? It sounded like a five-hundred pounder goin' off. Then, I didn't hear your engine anymore. I thought for sure you were a goner."

"Yeah, Lieutenant. Well, sir, we came pretty close to buyin' the farm that time. It was some kinda command-detonated booby trap; maybe an unexploded bomb from an air strike, I don't know. The gooks set it off a little too soon. It like to scrambled our brains for a second."

"A doomsday device of some sort?"

"Right! And you know that new man on my crew?" I recalled seeing him, a lanky, fair-haired lad, new to Vietnam but bursting with bravado and swagger. He wasn't afraid of anything—just ask him. "When that blast rocked our tank, he bolted right outta the gunner's seat screaming, 'Let me out! I'm outta here!' I had to boot his ass back down into his seat, all the while yellin' at my driver to get the god-damned tank movin' and get us the hell away from there!" The normally even-tempered gunny was upset, but more so at his crewmen who nearly panicked than at his brush with eternity.

"How are they now, Gunny . . . they still shook up?"

A smile played briefly across the rugged, wrinkled features of Gunny Hopkins's face. "That new boy looks like a whupped puppy dog, ears all droopy and his tail curled down between his legs. He got all the starch washed right out of him tonight."

I felt a bit sorry for the new man. He was cocky in an offensive way, but even he did not deserve such a rude awakening to his own human frailties. I suspected that, with his inflated ego punctured and both feet more firmly on the ground, he might yet make a good tanker—the gunny would see to that.

Preventive Maintenance (PM)

The dampness and high humidity were not really that aversive, because the weather was cool, but one could easily forget how corrosive the elements were on metal surfaces. I was slightly shocked the following morning when I pulled my .45-caliber pistol out of its shoulder holster and gave it a cursory inspection. I didn't expect to find rust, but there it was, a faint, dark-orange stain on the barrel . . . *RUST!* . . . *Oh, my God!* Visions of a beet-red drill instructor choking with rage flitted across my mind. RUST! The unforgiveable sin to a Marine. Like a man who suspects for the first time he has body lice, frantically inspecting every square inch of his body for more signs of the abominable critters, I checked the pistol over thoroughly, inside and out, all the while looking over my shoulder to make certain no one else happened on my evil secret before I had a chance to erase the evidence. A little cleaning solvent followed by a light coat of oil rectified the problem, but I was still annoyed at myself, anyway. *Officers should know better!* I made a vow right then to check my own pistol for rust every day.

I placed a routine call on the radio to Dong Ha from A-11. Alpha Company Headquarters had no messages for us. I switched frequencies to monitor the grunt company on our side of the perimeter, partly out of boredom, but primarily because it helped me to stay informed about what was happening with the infantry that day. The following exchange of dialogue was heard:

"And, tell your Six Actual to report over here ASAP, over."

"Roger dodger."

"Listen up, *Marine!* You'd better start using proper radio procedure or you're gonna find your ass in hot water! Do you roger THAT!"

"Roger dodger. . . . Out."

God love anonymity. It allowed a few free spirits to remain unfettered by military conventionality.

All of my vehicles were in need of refueling. As long as we weren't required to go out on road sweeps or rescue missions, we would be all right, but I decided that it was time to think about having several barrels of diesel fuel flown in to us; we might otherwise encounter the unexpected and find ourselves in a bind. At the afternoon briefing, I brought up the fuel situation of my tanks. The CO agreed that my concern was warranted, because no one knew when the Washout would be repaired; it might be weeks before the

MSR was reopened to Con Thien. A priority resupply mission was ordered for us by the 3/9 Battalion S-4. The "hoped for" arrival time was September 24, the following day.

After the briefing, I undertook an excursion on foot around the lines to see how my tankers were getting along. The footing was as muddy as ever, and the danger of enemy shells dropping out of the sky was a constant source of apprehension. I instructed each tank commander to make certain that all personal weapons, tank weapons, and ammunition received preventive maintenance every day because prolonged exposure to moist air was fatal to polished metal surfaces . . . as I had learned the hard way earlier.

Those three tanks transferred to us from Fifth Platoon were especially in need of PM. To reinforce my point, prior to departing from each bunker, I gathered a tank commander and his crew around me and reiterated what had happened to Sergeant Howard's tank that afternoon.

Around 1400, Sergeant Howard and his crew were on the perimeter's north side, replenishing their load of ammunition on the new A-13. They were exposed and quite vulnerable because all the crewmen, except Howard, were outside on the ground, breaking open wooden cases of 90mm cannon ammunition, and carrying the bulky, cumbersome rounds from an ammo storage berm over to their tank. An NVA mortar crew observed that lucrative target and lobbed several rounds in around A-13, pinning the crewmen down outside their vehicle.

An infantryman on the lines pointed in the direction where he thought he detected white puffs of mortar tube smoke rising. Howard, who had been left by himself in the turret, traversed his main gun in that direction, knocked the safety switch off, aimed his gun sight at the NVA mortar position 800 meters away, and fired. The round was a trifle high. All he needed was to lower the gun a few degrees and blast away for a certain bull's-eye, but he could not! The main gun was jammed by a section of shell casing stuck in the chamber.

A considerably upset sergeant jumped out of the turret and clambered into the driver's compartment, pulling his tank out of danger behind OP-2. After almost an hour of labor, he and his crewmen managed to loosen the piece of cartridge casing with a hammer and chisel and tap it into the turret with the tank's "rammer staff," a long metal pole used for swabbing the main gun bore.

It was too late, however, to go back after that enemy mortar crew; they vacated their firing position right after that first cannon round zipped overhead.

Howard had assumed that, when he instructed his new loader the day before to PM the main gun breech, he would remove the round from inside the chamber, clean and oil the shiny metal surfaces on the breech, check for rust spots on the shell casing and projectile, and replace the round. His loader got lazy and failed to do this, merely going through the motions of wiping down the breech. After so many days and nights of rain, moisture, and constant dampness, the shiny metal casing containing the explosive propellant rusted to the inside of the gun chamber sufficiently to cause the cartridge extractor to rip the shell casing in half when it attempted to extract the empty casing from the chamber.

No serious damage was done to anything except Howard's trust in his loader, who was soon demoted to gunner on the crew. No official action was taken against the errant crewman, because we considered the chewing out by his deeply angered tank commander and the subsequent castigation by his fellow crewmen to be sufficient punishment. He was well aware that goofing off had endangered his life as well as the lives of his cohorts. Anything more would have been overkill.

The rest of the evening before sunset, a prodigious amount of activity took place among my tank crews. They were cleaning and checking their guns and ammunition with a zeal unlike anything I'd witnessed since back in tank school.

The "Willie Peter" Incident

Morning on the twenty-fourth found me lying on my cot, feeling lethargic and unmotivated. I was mentally flat. The day was going to run its course with a minimum of help from me. I had been a platoon leader for two weeks—two stressful weeks—and I wanted no part of any more stressful situations that day.

"What kind of C-rats do we have left?" I asked one of Dean's men sitting on a cot by the bunker entrance.

"Chopped ham 'n' eggs and ham 'n' 'muthas.'"

No way was I going to have ham and lima beans for breakfast, or for any other meal if I could avoid it. "I'll take chopped ham and eggs, thanks."

I needed a shave. My bristly face was itching—a sure sign. When water rationing went into effect, we rigged the plastic tarp covering our bunker so that rainwater could be collected and then funneled into an empty 40mm ammo can; thus, we had plenty of water in the aluminum can. I heated some for shaving, then washed dirty socks, T-shirts, and jungle utilities in the remainder. A directive issued previously by 3/9 stipulated that no *drinking* water would be used for washing clothes; nothing was mentioned about catching rainwater for that purpose.

My spirits were still low; this time the shave and clean clothes did not have such an uplifting effect. I needed time to think, to pull myself together—uninterrupted. A-11 was empty; my crewmen were all in the bunker. I grabbed a box of letter writing paper and climbed into my tank, securing the cupola hatch above me, then dropped the commander's seat down and allowed myself to sit back and relax.

A small Gideon's Bible was in my letter box. I hadn't opened it before, being only a casually religious person by nature. Thumbing randomly through the pages, scanning the Psalms, my eyes came to rest on Psalm 56:

> Have mercy upon me, O God; for man would walk over me.
> Daily would my enemies devour me; for many are they who proudly
>   fight against me.
> In the day when I am afraid I will have confidence in Thee.
> In God I trust, I will not fear; what can man do to me?

No sense worrying about it. Take it one day at a time; that was going to be my watchword. I was going to face each day as it came at me and not dwell on the misfortunes tomorrow might bring. I copied the words from Psalm 56 in my pocket memorandum book and turned the page corner down for future reference. Somehow, the message in that Psalm struck close to home; it gave me comfort. I was no longer alone in the Con Thien lion's den.

Seated comfortably in the tank commander's seat, I swiveled around and gazed absently through the vision blocks. My attention was drawn immediately to the 105mm artillery battery behind me, buzzing with activity. Some Marines unloaded wooden crates of ammunition; others cleaned the guns; a few filled sandbags. An artillery battery was no place for lazy men, because those "cannon cockers" always seemed to be doing something, whether or not they were carrying out fire missions. I often wondered if they ever slept; they shot continuously around the clock with only an occasional respite from firing.

The faint, throbbing sound of an approaching helicopter caught my ear. It was a CH-53 "Jolly Green Giant." Dangling underneath the chopper's belly was a huge cargo net filled with red and white 55-gallon drums.

"Hey, it's here," I shouted over to the bunker. "They're bringing in our diesel fuel!"

The tankers exited from their bunker to observe the arrival of our precious fuel. The giant helicopter hovered low over the LZ for a moment, released its cargo net, and climbed rapidly away to the south. The pilot apparently did not care to be in close proximity to those fuel drums if they received a direct hit.

Sergeant Howard already had his vehicle started and on the way to the LZ before I could return to the bunker and notify Gunny Hopkins to supervise the refueling process. The gunny instructed all tank commanders to proceed one at a time to the LZ; work rapidly and don't waste time loitering around there. We did not want to attract the wrong kind of attention.

When one tank was finished refueling, it left the LZ and was replaced by a second. This operation was risky business; NVA forward observers must have seen what we were doing. For some unknown reason, they waited until just before the last tank, A-12, was ready to leave, then they rained an artillery barrage down on the LZ. Fortunately, all of the crewmen managed to scramble into their tank and roar away without becoming casualties.

Later in the day, I felt an urge to stroll down to the LZ and examine the area in which we had refueled our tanks. Empty fuel drums were strewn all over, many riddled with shrapnel holes. Ordinarily, if that were a noncombat situation, I would have seen to it that the empty drums were stacked neatly in one area to await pickup; however, while on Con Thien, my personal philosophy was that the less time one spent exposed in the open, the better one's chances of surviving. S-4 personnel could collect the drums and load them into a cargo net whenever they wanted them picked up.

On the return leg of my journey, I passed next to a perimeter strong point on the trench line near my bunker. Corporal Hodge, my platoon maintenance man, and two other grunts from 3/9 were talking excitedly about something. Hodge turned to me as I wandered over and said, "Say, Lieutenant, is it true that . . ." when an incoming mortar shell exploded nearby with a loud BAMM! and cut him off in mid-sentence. I dove head first into the nearby trench. The other three Marines piled in the trench with me. Another round landed closer, about 20 yards away along the trench line. Two seconds later, another shell exploded 15 yards away; a fourth round was even closer.

An NVA mortar crew was walking mortar rounds in our direction along the trench line. Terror wrenched my guts; I was trapped in that trench. My only chance for survival was to stay put; it was too late to reach the bunker.

Sss-BAMM! Another blast showered us with mud and debris. I was sure the next round was going to land right on us. My mind was crystal clear as I detached myself from the insanity of it all and glanced around for one last look before being blown to pieces. Hodge was trembling; everyone was hugging the earth and praying. The next mortar shell struck a few feet away, between the trench line and our bunker.

Bright, whitish globs rained down on us like sleet. "My God! They're shooting 'Willie Peter' at us!!" screamed Hodge. That terrified me even more. "Willie Peter" (white phosphorus shells) exploded into thousands of particles that ignited on contact with the air and burned with an intensity that could sear nasty holes completely through a man's flesh.

Numb with fear, I resisted the impulse to jump and run to the Battalion Aid Station, but only because nothing was burning me. Several white globs rested on my sleeve. Peeking cautiously over the edge of the trench, I saw that the ground nearby was heavily coated with white foam. A shrapnel-punctured aerosol shave cream can lay nearby.

"That's what it was!" I shouted, pointing to the can. "We got sprayed by shaving cream, Hodge, you ding-a-ling!"

The sudden release of tension did it. All four of us, doubled up in convulsive laughter, howling, shrieking, and rolling on the ground. Several worried-looking Marines stood outside their bunkers staring as us, no doubt believing they were witnessing a simultaneous nervous breakdown by four of their comrades.

As word of the "Willie Peter" incident passed along the line from bunker to bunker, it was obvious that many men on the southwest portion of Con Thien's perimeter were having their first good laugh in weeks.

I inspected our bunker. One mortar round had struck on a corner of the roof. Fortunately for the men inside, it was not a large-caliber mortar round; otherwise, the exploding shell would have done more than merely knock sand down on them and tear up a few dirt-filled ammo boxes.

A stabbing clutch grabbed onto the pit of my stomach while standing there, imagining what *could* have happened to me and the others in the trench. A person could get killed anywhere on Con Thien, depending on where fate chose for him to be when a blindly fired enemy projectile arrived at its detonation point. Then, recalling my personal vow earlier in the day, I shook off those distressing thoughts and forced myself to think about something else, anything else.

The Sword of Damocles syndrome was repressed after a short while (as it must to preserve one's sanity), and we set about heating our evening meal. Conversation was sparse; most minds were preoccupied with private thoughts. I did not dare think of home that evening, because the longing to be safe from danger or fear once again was almost overwhelming.

My crew was scheduled to spend the night on the lines. Just before dark we cranked over our tank engine and moved noisily to our assigned position on the south rim of the perimeter, 50 yards away from our bunker. Soon afterward, a little Ontos chugged over near us and pulled into its night position. Used for infantry support in Vietnam, the Ontos was intended to be a tank killer, as it mounted six 106mm recoilless rifles. Together, we faced silently toward the south, poised in readiness for whatever the enemy had in store that night for Con Thien.

Murphy's Ordeal

I assumed last watch at 0400. The predawn stillness was in such sharp contrast to the cacophony of sound experienced during daylight hours that it was disquieting. One could almost hear NVA sappers creeping stealthily through the elephant grass toward the minefield. Time ticked by endlessly. Mosquitoes whined about my head, incensed by the greasy, pungent-smelling insect repellant doused liberally on my exposed face and hands. An occasional flare popped overhead, bathing the surrounding terrain with faint, yellowish light.

The first hint of grayness in the early morning sky meant that 0600 was close at hand. My watch would soon be over and I could close my leaden eyelids for a few hours of sleep without concern for an NVA ground attack. The enemy rarely moved in the open during daylight.

My crewmen were all slumbering peacefully in their cramped positions within the turret: Murphy was on the turret deck, curled up in a blanket;

Irizarry was slumped forward in the gunner's seat, snoring softly, his forehead pressed into the gunner's rubber headrest pad. I stood on the tank commander's seat so that my upper torso protruded out of the cupola hatch for better all-around night vision.

After my last SITREP at 0600, I slid my binoculars into a leather carrying case hanging inside the turret, closed the cupola hatch above me, and eased my tired body down into a sitting position on the tank commander's seat. A journey to dreamland was all that really mattered. Sleep, the blissful opiate of the weary, enveloped me as soon as I placed my forehead against the range finder headrest. The new day, September 25, would just have to wait a few hours before it could be officially recognized.

A crashing, thundering barrage of large-caliber artillery shells jolted me back to my senses. The scream of incoming rounds mingled with ear-shattering explosions. *This has to be a nightmare,* I thought at first, but it wasn't; that horrendous racket was all too real. Our tank rocked and shuddered from near misses. My first instinct was to lock all hatches, but I quickly remembered an old-time tanker's advice: *Close your hatches, but never lock them when you're being shelled, because a direct hit will clobber everyone inside the turret if the concussion is not permitted to escape.* I watched in awe through my vision blocks as exploding shells blasted a pattern of destruction across the length and breadth of Con Thien. We were so damned helpless; I wanted to retaliate, but we faced friendly troops to the south, and we had no way of knowing where the NVA guns were located. We couldn't do anything but sit tight and take the pounding. I glanced at my watch—0745.

Round after round shrieked overhead; they seemed to be coming in from several directions at once. Not a single man could be seen out in the open. Survival meant hugging the bottom of a trench or crouching inside a bunker and praying for the bombardment to lift.

"Sir, Murphy isn't here," said Irizarry worriedly.

"Where the hell is he?" I asked, realizing for the first time that he was missing. "DuBose!" I shouted into the driver's compartment. "Where's Murphy?"

"I-I haven't seen him, Lieutenant."

Murphy must have climbed out of the turret while we were all asleep; he could have been almost anywhere. There wasn't anything we could do but hope he was able to reach shelter.

Still the bombardment continued. Shells exploded viciously everywhere on Con Thien. A chill came over me as the possibility of a massive ground assault flashed into mind.

"Stay alert! This could be the one we've been waiting for," I said to no one in particular, pulling down hard on my .50-caliber machine gun charging handle to chamber a round. "Where is Murphy, damn it!"

A shrieking rocket whacked into the mud beside the tank. I waited . . . no blast occurred; it was a dud.

To my left, a direct hit blew a bunker to pieces; sandbags and lumber flew in all directions. A Marine scrambled up from amid the shambles of his former shelter and dove head first into a nearby trench. *Now, that has to be a miracle,* I thought.

As suddenly as it began, the deluge of enemy rockets and artillery subsided. The silence was profound; no one dared breathe lest the hellish ordeal resume again. I surveyed Con Thien's battered hillsides, expecting to find every bunker and privy on the hill smashed. A pall of smoke hung in the air and obscured much of The Hill from view, but, incredibly, practically every structure was still standing despite that tremendous show of firepower by the NVA.

The loader's hatch flipped open suddenly and Murphy wiggled through, dropping down on to the turret deck.

"Where the heck were you, Murphy?" I asked, noticing dried remnants of shaving cream on his eyebrows, nose, and ears.

"I was shaving, standing behind the tank. That first salvo came in before I could duck. I-I think I got hit in the back, Lieutenant. Anyways, I dove under the tank and sweated it out from there."

Murphy was pale and trembling. I did not dare ask him what he thought when that dud rocket screamed into the earth beside him.

"Let's take a look at your back," I said gently, turning him around. . . . *Good God!* I almost blurted out. His entire lower back and trouser seat were soaking wet with blood. A piece of shrapnel had apparently penetrated just below his belt, dangerously close to his spine. With the shock of all that incoming, he had felt little more than a sting.

"How bad is it?" he mumbled weakly.

"Hmmm . . . it's only a scratch. It missed the spine. You'll be okay. Button your trousers and we'll run you over to the BAS."

Murphy's eyes grew large when he saw my blood-covered fingers. Suddenly his knees buckled and he collapsed on the turret deck. "My legs . . . they're *paralyzed!*" he cried.

The chalky pallor of his skin told me he was lapsing into shock. The emergency situation demanded fast action, not convincing arguments. "Crank 'er up, DuBose!" I shouted. "Get us to the BAS fast!"

Our dormant diesel engine roared to life, and DuBose propelled the tank through the muddy terrain leading to the aid station 50 yards away. Numerous casualties were being funneled through the BAS bunker entrance. Small groups of stretcher bearers congregated outside the entrance, catching their breaths before sprinting back whence they had come.

Irizarry and I struggled to hoist Murphy up through the loader's hatch, but try as we might, we could not seem to get him into the proper position to push him up out of the turret. Our situation was growing more precarious by the moment. Our tank was halted in spongy clay outside of the BAS, and we were slowly sinking into the mud. Soon, we would be so bogged down another tank would have to tow us free. That would surely interfere with medevac choppers attempting to land on the BAS LZ. *Somebody could die because his emergency evacuation was delayed,* I feared.

I grabbed Murphy's knee and squeezed it hard. "Did you feel that?"

"I think so."

"Then you aren't paralyzed if you could feel that. Now, get those legs moving, Marine!"

Murphy's "paralyzed" lower limbs began probing for a toe hold. His face was a mask of fear and pain as he pulled himself up through the loader's hatch. The last I ever saw of him was his blood-soaked trouser seat as he stumbled through the BAS entrance.

We drove back to our previous position on the perimeter and parked, staying buttoned up as we did not want to get caught outside the tank if another all-out bombardment was due that morning. After rinsing Murphy's blood off my fingers, I called in a spot report on his wound to company headquarters back in Dong Ha, requesting a replacement ASAP. After what we had just experienced, I didn't want to spend any more time than absolutely necessary minus one of my crewmen. Whatever the NVA had in store for us, I needed to be prepared.

A few enemy mortar rounds hit along the crest of OP-1, where Mike Company was dug in, but their effect was minimal compared to the furious counterbattery fire being rained on enemy artillery positions in the DMZ by our artillerymen at C-2, Cam Lo, Camp Carroll, Dong Ha, and Gio Linh. Salvo after salvo whooshed overhead, headed north. Then, Con Thien's 105s opened fire.

Activity that had ground to a halt during the sudden enemy shelling attack was resumed all over The Hill, but now everyone moved quickly in a crouch, never lingering for more than an instant in any unprotected spots. Ammunition had to be distributed, positions repaired or strengthened, phone wire relaid, and the wounded treated and evacuated. The humming activity in itself was a morale booster. Watching the hillsides come alive again with purposeful activity made us believe in our hearts that we could take anything the NVA had to dish out. We were there to stay.

Battalion staff at Con Thien estimated that we had received over 1,000 rounds of artillery, mortars, and rockets that day. This display of firepower must have cost the enemy heavily because, during the bombardment, many heretofore carefully concealed artillery pieces were spotted by circling aerial observers, who, in turn, directed numerous air strikes and counterbattery fires against the newly disclosed enemy gun locations.[5]

Kentucky Windage

Early in the morning of September 27, I awoke to find myself sitting upright on my cot, breathing heavily, my heart beating wildly. It must have been a bad dream, but I was unable to recall any details.

Everyone else was asleep. I swung my mud-encrusted boots off the cot and walked outside to make use of the urinal at the rear of the bunker. The tube reeked of stagnant urine in the predawn mist. I longed for a bath to wash the week's accumulation of scaly grime from my body, but we were still rationing water.

KA-KA-BLAMM!! The sharp report of our entire artillery battery opening up startled me. I squished back through the ever-present mud and reentered the bunker. I dropped a lighted heat tab into my tin can oven and heated water for some C-ration instant coffee. Orange and blue flames from the chemical heat tab danced brightly inside the darkened bunker.

I stared into the flames entranced, warming my hands and contemplating my present station in life. In spite of the burdens of responsibility I had to bear, the nagging fear of death that lurked in my subconscious, and the unending hardships, I felt strangely comforted to be crowded together in a damp, musty, dimly lit, sandbagged bunker with men I respected, who could always be depended on, who would stick by each other until the end. The feeling of camaraderie we shared acted as a soothing balm to quiet my apprehensions.

About midmorning, I climbed aboard A-11 and called Dong Ha to inquire as to the whereabouts of Murphy's replacement. The radio operator read me a message from Alpha's XO, informing me that three men were arriving that morning as replacements: one for Murphy; one to replace DuBose, who was rotating stateside very soon; and a third Marine to replace Corporal Sanders, who was also rotating home.

"How about that, DuBose," I shouted into the driver's compartment from inside the turret. "You're going back to the world."

Silence. . . . Then DuBose climbed hastily out of his driver's compartment and scurried around the turret until he was peering through the cupola hatch, his anxious face inches from mine. "That cain't be right, Lieutenant. Ah've got twenty-three days left in this hole . . . plus a wake-up."

"Aren't you Lance Corporal Delta, number three niner three niner?"

"Yes, sir."

"Well, that's you, pardner. Pack your bags and say goodbye. You're goin' home."

With one loud rebel yell, DuBose sprang to the ground and vanished inside the bunker. He wasted no time getting his things together. As soon as the three replacements arrived at our bunker, easily distinguishable by their new equipment and clean faces, DuBose said his goodbyes hurriedly and struck off for the resupply LZ to catch a chopper out. His quiet competence and sense of humor would be missed, but barring some unforeseen calamity such as a helicopter crash, I took satisfaction in knowing my earlier promise to him had been realized; he was walking away from there on his own two feet, not being carried out in a body bag.

Gunny Hopkins and I put our heads together once again to make some personnel switches within First Platoon. With Sanders gone from Carter's tank (A-12), a dependable corporal was needed there. Irizarry was seen as the best man to move, so that left me with three slots to fill on my tank. Sergeant Davis, a fairly recent arrival temporarily assigned to Gunny Hopkins's tank, was moved to my tank; Hodge and Minch were moved to my crew from Weicak's tank. A few other minor changes were made to accommodate the newest arrivals, and we were set once again.

Late that afternoon, Weicak ambled up to the bunker, leaned in, and spoke casually, "Uhm . . . Lieutenant? My tank fired two HE rounds this morning at an FO position a few miles northeast of here."

"Okay, Weicak. Thanks for letting me know." I jotted down the information and made a mental note to call in a routine spot report that evening on Weicak's expenditure of ammunition. I was eager to get to the CP for the afternoon briefing at that moment and saw no need to make another spot report right away concerning such a routine action.

The sky was gloomily overcast as I made my way rapidly on foot to the CP. More rain appeared to be in the offing. While climbing the wooden stairs extending from the CP, I noticed a few VIP civilians standing at the top of the stairs, surveying the activity on Con Thien. One civilian was a woman, a French journalist with extensive experience in covering the Vietnam War. Another person in that group was David Douglas Duncan, a US Marine Corps Reserve lieutenant colonel, who was on special assignment from *Life* magazine to do a photographic essay on Con Thien.[6]

Apparently, Con Thien was attracting a lot of attention back in the States. One of my crewmen observed what happened earlier in the day when a cameraman from a major American television network was filming close-ups of critically wounded Marines being carried into the aid station. One particularly distraught litter bearer standing nearby threatened to punch out the cameraman if he did not stop filming casualties, but other Marines intervened in time and strongly urged the offended cameraman to go make his movies elsewhere.

Our briefing commenced with the usual introductory comments by the battalion commander, Lieutenant Colonel Cook. Then, to my complete surprise, he said, "Congratulations are in order for the excellent shooting by one of your tanks this morning, Lieutenant Coan. They knocked out an FO position with only two rounds fired from their main gun."

I was caught off guard momentarily, thinking it must be a mistake. Surely, someone in the platoon would have brought it to my attention. Then, it occurred to me that Weicak's tank must have been responsible, only he did not inform me of the incident until late in the afternoon, and, on top of that, he never mentioned actually destroying the FO position.

On returning to my bunker after the briefing, I was met by a runner from 3/9 bearing a message that Local Train Alpha Six was trying to reach me. I feared that it must be urgent because my CO at Alpha Company had never called me before. I immediately climbed into A-11 and switched on the tank radio. The dialogue went as follows:

"Local Train Alpha Six, this is Local Train Alpha One, over," I said.

"Local Train Alpha One, this is Alpha Six!" said the captain heatedly. "I want to know why no report was made to us back here about the target your people engaged this morning. I was congratulated by some brass at battalion headquarters today on your tanker's good marksmanship and didn't even know what in hell they were talking about, over!"

"This is Alpha One . . . no excuse, over."

"Look, Alpha One, I want to know what's going on up there! Why aren't you making incident reports like you were ordered, over!"

I repressed the urge to ask him to visit Con Thien if he wanted to know what was going on; instead, I answered: "This is Alpha One. We had a failure to communicate in my unit today. We'll get it straightened out, over."

"This is Alpha Six! You'd better get your men on the stick up there! . . . OUT!"

I was burning hot; unfair criticism such as that really hooked me. He was chewing me out when he should have been offering congratulations. I asked the gunny to gather all the tank commanders together at my bunker where they were counseled on the evils of being tardy in reporting ammo expenditures to me. I attempted to not take out my anger at the captain on my men, but that proved to be a difficult task.

Later that same evening, I learned the full story from Sergeant Howard of what had actually happened in the morning to precipitate that chain of errors that subsequently led to my chewing out by the captain. A North Vietnamese

FO team had occupied an abandoned church nestled between two hills approximately 3,500 meters northeast of Con Thien. They were using the church steeple as an observation post for adjusting artillery, mortar, and recoilless rifle fire on Con Thien.

Our own artillery and 4.2-inch mortars attempted unsuccessfully to destroy the FO position. Some brass from the Ninth Marine Regiment were watching that futile shooting exhibition from one of the OPs. An anonymous senior officer in the group suggested that perhaps the tankers should have a chance at the target. Weicak's tank was chosen because the building could be observed from Weicak's northern perimeter location. A runner was sent to ask Weicak to deliver fire on the heretofore unscathed target.

Lance Corporal "Charlie" Brown, the dozer tank operator who had stayed with my two tanks at C-2 prior to the Washout fiasco, was the "new" gunner on Weicak's tank. He had joined my platoon as a replacement several days earlier. Weicak elevated the main gun tube and ranged in on the target, then Brown applied some "Kentucky windage" and adjusted the gun tube's deflection and elevation a fraction. The entire 3/9 CP group plus the "brass hats" from Ninth Marine Regiment watched as the first round blasted out of the main gun tube and arched toward the building, striking slightly over the target. Twenty seconds later, a second round blasted out of the gun tube and streaked toward the FO position, exploding squarely in the middle of the building, disintegrating it completely, and presumably wiping out the NVA FO team.

I understood, then, why those spectators were impressed; that was mighty fine shooting on the part of Weicak and his gunner, "Charlie" Brown.

Monsoons Revisited

We had reached the end of September. Drizzling rains had saturated everything in the past forty-eight hours. Plastic tarps glistened and Con Thien's soggy laterite clay oozed rivulets of fresh rainfall that filled foot prints, shell craters, and trenches. Muzzle blasts from our artillery and mortars seemed oddly distant and muffled by the dense cloud layers overhead.

Our bunker was waterproofed, so we weren't overly concerned about the rain; however, my heart went out to those grunts in the trenches, standing watch at night in frigid, ankle-deep water. The infantrymen on the lines draped themselves in ponchos and shelter halves to ward off much of the precipitation, but when your trousers are soaked to the knees and your toes squish around inside your wet boots, there's no way to dispel the misery that penetrates to your very soul.

My morale matched the ceiling visibility—low. Something drastic was needed to perk me up. I filled my steel pot with some rainwater that had been collecting in the folds of our bunker tarp since the new rains commenced and balanced the pot on an empty C-ration can containing a lighted heat tab. In a few minutes, I had a basin full of warm water, and none of our precious drinking water had to be tapped in the process. First, I took the luxury of brushing my long-neglected teeth. Next, I rinsed several days' worth of accumulated grime from my face and scalp, lathered up, and scraped my beard off by feel, as no one had a mirror. The remainder of that scummy water was used to bathe my armpits, crotch and moisture-wrinkled feet. The bath was completed with a liberal dousing of my feet, crotch, and armpits with medicated powder. A stopgap measure, at best, but even that small amount of attention to personal hygiene was sufficient to heighten my sagging morale immensely.

I waited until almost noon before bothering to step outside the bunker. The rain had ceased temporarily, but the sky remained darkly overcast and forbidding. Numerous muffled thuds reached my ears; our B-52s were dropping bombs out in the DMZ again. Then, I heard the dreaded scream of an incoming artillery shell and ducked inside our bunker; the round exploded over near the medevac LZ, right by my path to the CP.

Lieutenant Steppe laughed when I came barreling in through the doorway. A few seconds after that first shell, another incoming artillery shell just missed our bunker with a sharp KA-BLAM!! Dean's mirthful expression quickly vanished.

The enemy was taking advantage of the weather to fire on us at will, being quite aware that our forward observers and air support were severely hampered by decreased visibility.

"I wonder if people back home know we're sittin' ducks up here on Con Thien, because a bunch of chicken-shit congressmen won't allow us to go out after those damn gooks shootin' at us from the DMZ!" Dean mouthed off to no one in particular.

"Don't forget those reporters and photographers flocking in here like pigeons at a city park," I replied. "They know we're here."

"They send reporters to cover car wrecks, fires, and homicides, don't they? . . . Sure, and they get nice, juicy pictures of dying or suffering victims and slap them on page one. That sells newspapers. But as far as caring about what we're going through, cheering us on and all that—forget it! We're on our own up here, one for all and all for one." Right or wrong, what Dean had to say stirred up some strong feelings among us.

I climbed aboard A-11 to call Dong Ha, but the atmospheric conditions rendered my efforts futile; I gave up the idea. The remainder of that dreary afternoon, except for an hour spent at the CO's briefing, was passed inside the turret of A-11 writing letters home.

With each succeeding day, I was becoming more and more leery of staying in my bunker during daylight hours. I was convinced that most of Con Thien's bunkers, including mine, were not constructed well enough to withstand a direct hit by enemy rockets or artillery shells. The odds were high that, sooner or later, one of the bunkers on our portion of the perimeter would receive a direct hit, killing or maiming everyone inside. I did not want to be caught inside our bunker if and when that awful fate was realized.

After sunset, we were sitting inside the bunker telling sea stories and reading by candlelight when a loud blast rocked our bunker. Shortly afterward, an enemy AK-47 ripped off a long, staccato burst of automatic gunfire. Our own mortar crews reacted quickly; within seconds, their mortars were going Chunk! Chunk! as they lobbed illumination rounds over the western perimeter.

"That explosion might have been a 'Bangalore torpedo,' Lieutenant," said my worried platoon sergeant.

"I think you're right, gunny. We better man our tanks until we find out what's up."

I led the way to A-11 and scrambled aboard; the other three crewmen were right on my heels. Hoisting a pair of binoculars, I scanned the flare-lit terrain to my front. A gaping hole had been blown in the outer perimeter wire, but no NVA were discernable in the vicinity of the breach.

Some enemy soldiers were able to sneak up to the outer wire under cover of a shroud-like fog blanketing Con Thien that night. They pushed a long pipe stuffed with explosives under the perimeter concertina wire. That "Bangalore torpedo" vaporized a swath through the wire almost 10 feet wide. The subsequent enemy automatic weapon's fire was intended to draw our return fire toward the breach, I surmised, perhaps to have us reveal the locations and concentrations of our automatic weapons on the western perimeter. If that was the case, no one fell for the ruse.

An alternative motive for the enemy's strange action might have been that they were merely harassing us, trying to jangle our already taut nerves. If that was indeed their underlying motive, they were successful. My hands trembled noticeably as I supported the binoculars between sweat-slicked fingers; my heart pounded from navel to Adam's apple.

Eventually, all flares burned out and no more were catapulted skyward. Blackness closed in around us once again. We prepared to spend the night in our tanks in the event Mr. Charles had any more surprises in store for us later.

Mud, Blood, and Rats

Early morning fog had reduced our visibility dangerously as I strained to see through the mist enveloping Con Thien during my watch. Mortar illumination rounds popped overhead periodically, but they helped naught, for the gauze-like curtain of moisture was impenetrable to human eyes. The only function flares served that night was to detect infiltrators actually in the minefield; we were unable to see past the outer wire. An entire NVA regiment could have formed up 50 meters from the outer wire and we would have been none the wiser.

The blessed hour of 0600, October 1, finally arrived. Not a hint of enemy activity had occurred on my watch. I retired to the confines of the bunker, crawled onto my cot, and fell soundly asleep. It was midmorning before I was ready to face the new day.

After breakfast, I exited from the bunker to see if the monsoon-like weather was going to remain with us. Amazingly, not a cloud could be seen; the sun beamed brightly in the sky as if it had not rained a drop in the past seventy-two hours.

An O-1 "Bird Dog" cruising high above Con Thien attracted my attention as it began to circle purposefully in one area about 1,000 meters to the west. Bird Dog was an appropriate name for the diminutive spotter plane. Two Marine Corps F-4 Phantom jets then came streaking inland from the South China Sea. A drama was unfolding and I had a front-row seat.

As the two jets circled menacingly, high above us, the spotter plane flew on a straight, level course for a moment, then dove at an angle toward the ground, releasing a white smoke rocket to mark the target. The Bird Dog pulled up and banked away sharply as the two jets swooped down in single file and passed over the white-smoked target area without releasing any ordnance. Then, the gray-painted Phantom jets banked around for another pass. The lead jet zoomed in low, spraying its guns in long bursts at the target, followed seconds later by the second jet, which decelerated so noticeably on reaching the target that it almost appeared to be floating. Two long, shiny, tear-drop shaped metal canisters of napalm tumbled crazily earthward and erupted violently on impact into a billowing, mushroom-shaped cloud of red-orange flame and greasy-black smoke that boiled at least a hundred feet up into the air. I felt no remorse for any NVA trapped in that inferno; they had been trying to kill me for weeks.

Moments later, the jets made another run over the target area, firing their guns in BURRRRP-BURRRRP-BURRRP fashion. I guessed that the napalm had flushed their prey into the open and the jets were going after them. The Bird Dog floated over the target area as the two jets circled out of range. A red smoke grenade was lobbed from the Bird Dog's cockpit toward the napalmed area. The previous white-smoke rocket must have been obliterated by the napalm, and the pilots had asked for another marking.

I couldn't see anything except shrubs, trees, and smoke, but I assumed that the target must have been NVA troops who had moved in close to Con Thien during the preceding days and nights of limited visibility.

Again, the jets descended on the target area. The first plane released two Mark 81 250-pound Snake-eye bombs. Braking fins on the bombs unfolded and slowed their descent long enough to allow the low-flying jets time to roar out of range of their own detonating bombs. WHAMM! WHUMP! Concussion thumped my eardrums. Brown columns of earth erupted into the air, and boulders, trees, and other debris rained back down. The second jet dropped two more Snake-eye bombs right in the midst of the smoke lingering over the target area. I still felt no pity for my tormentors. After several more bombing runs, their payloads expended, the two jets then climbed away out of sight.

A pall of smoke hung in the air over the target area. I was thankful that we were not subject to attacks from enemy aircraft. Artillery and rockets were bad enough, but for sheer, awesome, destructive capability, nothing the NVA possessed could begin to rival American airpower.

Throughout the air strike, I was conscious of the comradeship I felt toward the Marines piloting those Phantom jets. We had experienced OCS at Quantico, and we shared a common enemy in Vietnam. I knew that if I was in trouble somewhere, and an aircraft with the block letters MARINES printed on the fuselage was summoned to the scene, I could depend on that pilot to render assistance, even at the risk of being shot down.

A Marine carrying a bright-orange, waterproofed mailbag approached me and said, "Sir, this mailbag came in on one of the resupply choppers from Dong Ha this morning, and it's addressed to First Platoon, Alpha Company, Third Tank Battalion. Is it yours?"

"It's about time we got some mail up here. Thanks, Corporal." I carried the mailbag over to Gunny Hopkins, and we sorted the mail out for pickup by the respective tank commanders. No sooner was the sorting task completed than Sergeant Howard lunged through the bunker entryway, obviously upset. His face was flushed and deep furrows creased his sweaty forehead.

"Skipper! Piggy Bores got hit!"

"Oh, God, no!" I blurted out. "How bad is it?"

"He got it in the hand, sir. A big piece of shrapnel nearly sheared the knuckles off the back of his hand. He's gonna be medevaced out. Damn, I hate to lose him. He's the best crewman I got."

"He was getting short, Howard. He would've gone home in a few weeks anyway," said Gunny Hopkins.

"Well, anyway, I need a replacement, and if he's half as good as Bores, I'll be entirely satisfied."

Howard left abruptly. I made a mental note to call in a casualty report at the next opportunity. Bores was our fourth casualty; he, Manchego, and Murphy were medevacs, but Weicak's facial wound was treated locally and he remained with us.

When it was time to depart for the afternoon briefing, I buttoned up my flak jacket, pressed my steel helmet on, and exited the bunker after listening by the doorway for a moment to gauge the extent, if any, of enemy shelling activity. My very survival depended on this ritual. It was akin to looking both ways before crossing the street.

A half dozen members of the press corps milled about on the porch as I entered the CP bunker. The CO's briefing was abbreviated because the colonel expected some general officers from Third Marine Division to visit that afternoon.

Word was passed during the meeting that no more slugging of press photographers would be tolerated. On at least two and possibly three occasions the past week, AP/UPI photographers were in the act of snapping pictures of dead and seriously wounded Marines when close friends of the victims became enraged at what they considered violations of decency and assaulted the photographers. I could not condone this behavior, but I understood the complicated, deep-seated emotions causing such raw, pent-up fury to be unleashed on those news media outsiders. One particular photographer among us we tolerated, even encouraged. He was David Douglas Duncan, a retired Marine lieutenant colonel, easily recognizable in his camouflaged utilities with camera equipment dangling from straps hung from his neck. He was one of us, not an outsider. He got down in the bunkers and trenches with the men and lived their daily existence with them. We trusted him. His film captions would be accurate and fair; he would treat his camera subjects with dignity.

I selected a route back from the briefing that gave a wide berth to the unpleasant sights and smells of the BAS. My route entailed crossing the barren medevac LZ, but we had not received any incoming for a few hours, so I felt reasonably secure.

A half dozen steps out onto the LZ, I heard the sss-WHAM! sound of an incoming mortar round; it struck to my left at the base of OP-2. I was nakedly exposed—not the slightest depression on the LZ to hide in. My only chance was to reach shelter in the aid station. Sss-BAMM! *That one was close!* I sprinted 10 yards to the BAS bunker but slipped and fell in the mud before reaching the doorway. Ssss-WHAM!! I lay where I fell, panting heavily, nauseating fear rising once more in my throat. Seconds dragged by until a few minutes had passed. No more incoming landed. *Maybe it's over,* I thought, looking about me. Then, to my absolute horror, I realized that my left arm, from elbow to fingertips, was resting in a puddle stained red-violet from the stagnant blood of some recently departed corpse awaiting evacuation.

I could stand it no longer. With a mighty lunge, I jumped to my feet and ran the rest of the distance back to my bunker. Revulsion threatened to make me gag as I rinsed the gore from my arm. A few of Dean Steppe's men had seen me run into our bunker with the bloody arm and thought I was a casualty. When they learned where the blood came from, they looked even more disgusted than I felt.

Being the last one awake in the bunker that night, I blew out the one remaining candle before lying back on my cot. Not ten seconds after the candlelight was extinguished, I heard rats crawling around on the bunker floor, fighting over food scraps and rummaging through empty ration boxes. Their noises filled me with loathing. My scalp prickled as I groped in the darkness for my flashlight and shined it at the floor. A cat-sized rat's gleaming eyes were frozen momentarily in the flashlight's beam, then the disgusting creature vanished underneath a cot across the room.

When it was quiet once again, I snapped off the flashlight, hoping the rats would go away. A minute later, they resumed their noisy, quarrelsome search for food, totally undaunted by my dislike for them.

I lay very still, my imagination working overtime, and recollected some tales circulating around Con Thien of men having fingers or toes gnawed in their sleep by ravenous rats. My God! How I detested those rats. They were known to crawl all over prostrate bodies of sleeping Marines in search of food.

The bane of humanity—rats, mosquitoes, flies, and ants—resided in abundance on Con Thien. A wave of disgust washed over me. I hated that bunker, the rats, the insects, the shellings, the death, the blood, the mud, the rain, the misery, and the boredom, so much that I wanted to scream, "Let me out of here!"

I jumped up from the cot, grabbed my flashlight, and stalked out of that oppressive, stifling bunker. A cool, refreshing breeze washed over me as I gazed up at the star-sprinkled sky. It was peaceful outside, soothing to my pent-up, hyperactive state of mind. I made a promise to myself right then to sleep in my tank whenever possible. It was cramped and uncomfortable, but we had no rats with which to contend.

Unrolling a blanket, I stretched it out on the rear deck of A-11. My flak jacket was folded into a pillow, and I wrapped up in my poncho liner. Despite a horde of bloodthirsty mosquitoes that dive-bombed my head with a vengeance, I drifted off to a sound sleep after vowing to move into the tank first thing in the morning.

Lost on the Lines

The next morning, I collected my precious few belongings from inside the bunker—canteens, .45-caliber pistol and shoulder holster, map case, diary, and waterproofed sleeping bag cover containing blankets, poncho, poncho liner, writing gear, and shaving equipment—and carried the gear to my new mobile home, A-11. The cot was left behind. Living inside the tank with three other men was going to be crowded, but it was dry, warm, and, most importantly, free of rats.

A-11 rested in its firing slot like a kneeling elephant. Not a sound did I hear, nor even feel the slightest vibration when walking on it. Fifty-two tons of homogeneous steel may as well have been a gigantic boulder. Sergeant Davis, one of three recent additions to the crew, had a tarp rigged over the opened TC hatch to keep rain from dripping into the turret. From the looks of the heavily overcast morning sky, we would be putting the tarp to use again before long.

"Anybody home?" I inquired, pulling the tarp to one side.

"Yessir. Come on in, Lieutenant," answered Davis.

My flak jacket stayed on, even inside the turret, but my steel helmet was stowed along with my waterproofed gear bag in the gypsy rack on the back of the turret. "Well, you got yourselves a new bunk mate. The rats in that bunker finally got to me last night." None of the men winced or appeared disgruntled when they learned of my intentions; hopefully, my almost continuous presence in the tank from that day forth would not be a burden to them.

While heating a C-ration breakfast of beans and franks on the turret deck, I conversed with Davis; Minch, the gunner; and Hodge, platoon maintenance man and driver, who usually sat in the driver's compartment isolated from the rest of us.

The original snow-white enamel finish of our turret interior was so streaked and smeared from mud-caked boots and hands the past few weeks that I was ashamed for anyone to look inside the turret. The turret deck itself was covered with mud. Davis agreed that it needed cleaning because machine gun ammo stored in deck containers, as well as 90mm tank gun ammunition resting on the turret deck, was vulnerable to corrosion caused by moisture.

The entire crew embarked on a cleaning campaign that lasted over three hours. After a break for lunch, we broke out all machine gun ammunition and thoroughly cleaned and oiled the belts, bullets, and the guns themselves. It was repetitive, boring work, but morale picked up noticeably when the chore was finished. Davis suggested cutting up an ancient, moth-eaten blanket and laying it on the turret deck as a rug; we all agreed it was an excellent idea.

The day passed quickly. We swapped some war stories and talked of our plans when we got home (not if, *when*), but mainly we listened to Davis, a wiry, fair-skinned redhead with gold-rimmed eyeglasses, who loved to talk, especially about his Mexican American wife and her cooking. "She makes enchiladas and tostadas that would have you drooling as soon as you got a whiff of the stuff. And her huevos rancheros . . . heavenly, just heavenly!"

"We'll just have to make do with plain old C-ration chopped ham and eggs in the meantime, right, Minch?" I said, giving him a wink.

Davis, with a sly grin, reached back behind the radio set and pulled out a small canvas bag. With deliberate ceremony, he slowly produced from the bag a glass bottle of red Tabasco sauce. "Not quite," he said. "A few drops of this stuff on your C-rats and you'll think you're back home again."

"Good show, Davis. Now, how did you get that hot sauce . . . or shouldn't I ask?"

"No problem. I'm a barber. I got my barber tools with me." He produced a manually operated hair clipper and a pair of barber's scissors from his canvas bag. "I usually cut hair for free, but I will accept small tokens of appreciation, such as this gift of hot sauce from the cook at Ninth Motor's mess hall."

He was a unique character, outgoing and talkative; the complete opposite of my new gunner, Minch, who was a heavily built older man, reserved, close-mouthed, perhaps even shy. When subjected to enemy shelling, Minch's voice and hands trembled, and he chain smoked Camels, staring glassy-eyed at the turret deck. But there was something solid about Minch, despite his nervous exterior, that told me intuitively he was good people, that he would do his job well when the chips were down.

The weather turned foul late in the day, then drizzled steadily all evening. We chose to wait out the precipitation inside our cozy—but certainly not drip-free—tank. It seemed that every alternative we experimented with to stem the drips, from lining hatch seals and periscope mounts with rags to draping pon-chos over the hatches, was a failure.

About 2100, it occurred to me that I had neglected to learn which tank had SITREP responsibility for the night on our segment of the perimeter. The gunny was in his tank about 75 yards away; this required an excursion over there on foot to make certain one assigned crew was prepared to stand watch that night.

I climbed through the turret into the blackest night I had ever seen, like being locked inside a bank vault with the lights out—impossible to discern any shapes or forms in the blackness. A howling wind turned the falling raindrops into liquid pellets that peppered my face and ears as I headed in the general direction of my former bunker. Once back on familiar territory, I reasoned, it would be simpler to find my way to the gunny. Placing one foot cautiously in front of the other to avoid stepping into an unseen crater or trench, I leaned into the blowing wind, wrapped my flapping poncho tightly around me, and fine-tuned all senses to lead me in the right direction.

Several minutes passed as I inched along in blind-man fashion, confident that I was making headway. I heard voices to my left, clearly audible, as if they were only a matter of yards from me, but that was impossible because I was supposed to be behind the lines moving south; any voices should have been on my right. Momentarily disoriented, I halted in my tracks to contemplate this alarming development.

A mortar illumination flare popped high above OP-2. I crouched down quickly and froze; my worst fears had been realized. In the faint flare light, I perceived, to my utter horror, that I had strayed directly in front of a machine gun position, only a few feet from the wire-encircled minefield! The voices I heard were those of two Marines standing watch, manning the machine gun position. Fortunately for me, they were reminiscing about home rather than keeping alert to detect infiltrators in the minefield.

I stayed crouched, fearing even to breathe lest my presence be noted. I alternately cursed and blessed the slowly fading flare that had stopped me just in time from possibly wandering into the minefield wire, yet had me danger-ously silhouetted in front of two machine gunners who would fire without a second's hesitation if they observed me. Only NVA sappers would be where I was on a night like that.

My gut clenched with fear as I struggled to remain perfectly still in the 30-knot winds. The machine gun barrel glistened evilly in the eerie flare light. I waited in an agony of apprehension, fearing that at any second the gun would explode to life and spray instant death in my direction.

At long last, the flare burned out. I waited until the machine gunners again appeared engrossed in their conversation, then slowly retraced my steps. My pounding heart threatened to burst open my rib cage as each stride brought me closer to safety. Finally, I reached my tank and almost embraced the iron monster. *Safe!* Another flare popped over OP-2, and I ran the entire distance to the gunny's tank before the light faded away.

The two machine gunners on watch must not have been able to see me through the curtain of rain and mist that descended on Con Thien that night. I understood then how the NVA could sneak up on us undetected and plant Bangalore torpedoes in the perimeter wire.

I did not report the incident to Lieutenant Steppe because I was thoroughly embarrassed by it. In fact, I did not even relate my experience to anyone in my platoon. Their trust in my judgment might have been irreparably damaged if they knew they were following a lieutenant into combat who got himself lost on the lines at Con Thien one dark night and almost paid with his life for that error.

Morale Problems

The Third Battalion, Ninth Marines, had occupied Con Thien for nearly a month. The knowledge that the grim reaper lurked nearby, waiting to claim more victims, hung over every man's head as his own personal Sword of Damocles. Weeks of living with skin, clothes, and everything one possessed coated with grime and mud; the grinding misery of men forced to live in waterlogged trenches; the abominable rats and mosquitoes; unrelenting boredom laced with moments of profound terror; and, most unbearable of all, the nagging fears that one tried to force back into the recesses of one's subconscious, fears that one could very likely be blasted to pieces today, tomorrow, or next week—this made Con Thien a living hell.

Sergeant Rock (not his real name) was a large-framed, powerfully built Marine. He was coarse, yet handsome, in a rugged way that many women find appealing and lesser men envy. He led his squad by virtue of the unanimous respect he garnered from his peers for his bravery under fire, his aggressiveness, and his physical toughness.

After several weeks spent with Dean Steppe and his men in our bunker, I began to notice an increasing amount of tension and irritability being displayed by Sergeant Rock and the others. At first, a sharp word from the platoon sergeant or Dean was sufficient to squelch any brewing squabbles. By the end of 3/9's stay on Con Thien, morale had slipped. It eventually reached its lowest point one damp afternoon, early in October.

Sergeant Rock had taken to badgering certain individuals in his squad to ease his own frustrations at their expense. Most of the squad members accepted the sarcasm and abusive language because he was their physical superior and, more importantly, because he outranked them. It was an indicator of Rock's basic immaturity to behave so poorly, but Dean Steppe let it pass, hoping the problem would rectify itself once Rock and the others like him were able to vent their pent-up emotions against a live enemy, face to face in a firefight. Men such as Rock were not mentally equipped to huddle in bunkers and take a pounding from unseen enemy guns day after day, watching their fellow Marines get killed and maimed without being able to strike back.

Enemy shells rained on Con Thien sporadically all morning, and casualties were so numerous that the BAS had no room for all of them. By noon, the shelling began to slacken; then, it ceased altogether. My frazzled nerves welcomed a breather. I climbed out of A-11 to survey the damage, if any, and check on the condition of my other crews. I was about 15 yards from the old bunker, when angry shouts and vehement, guttural cursing sounded behind me. Sergeant Rock and a black Marine were throwing haymakers at each other, scuffling in the mud, simultaneously struggling to disengage themselves from the grasp of near-frantic comrades only too aware of the consequences if an officer or senior NCO happened on the scene. This was a serious fight, however, and both men broke free of their friends and tore at each other with all the ferocity that weeks of pent-up adrenalin could give. It required a half dozen men to restrain them. The two Marines had been feuding for several days, and it did not take much imagination on my part to deduce that Rock's rural southern upbringing was probably a contributing factor in triggering the melee.

Both men were herded somewhat sheepishly over to where Lieutenant Steppe waited with hands on hips, every inch the disgruntled officer poised to chastise two members of his flock for going astray. Sergeant Rock and the other Marine stood before their lieutenant, heads bowed and panting, glaring at each other with darting, sideways glances. I wondered what Dean would say. . . . *What would I have done?*

Lieutenant Steppe asked them to explain themselves, and all of the pain, frustration, and fear of the past month spilled out. After the recriminations and denials were exchanged, Dean said, "Well, what are you two going to do to settle this? Are you going to shake hands like men and forget this thing, or are you going to make me refer this to the CO?" The two men looked first at Lieutenant Steppe in surprised relief; then, they slowly, resignedly, faced each other and extended an arm, gripping each other's right hand. They exchanged their apologies in the quiet, dignified manner universal among good men. Dean excused them, and they trudged back to their own bunkers, thankful that they were led by a wise, understanding officer who did not have to adhere to the book in making all decisions. The episode was terminated then, to my knowledge, but it was clearly evident that 3/9 was growing stale. They were due for rotation soon, or serious morale problems would manifest themselves as 3/9's "time in the barrel" mounted.

5.
RETURN OF THE WALKING DEAD

Something almost always went wrong somewhere, somehow. It was always something vague, unexplainable, tasting of bad fate, and the results were always brought down to their most basic element—the dead Marine. And you knew that, sooner or later, if you went with them often enough, it would happen to you, too. . . . And the grunts themselves knew: the madness, the bitterness, the horror and doom of it. . . . It took no age, seasoning, or education to make them know exactly where true violence resided.

—Michael Herr, *Dispatches*

On October 8, Third Battalion, Ninth Marines, turned over tactical control of Con Thien to First Battalion, Ninth Marines. The Marines from 3/9 had served their time in the barrel. It was imperative that they be relieved without delay. The attached units left behind—tanks, Ontos, amtracs, engineers, and artillery—were less than pleased at the prospect of 1/9 taking up residence on The Hill in place of 3/9. The First Battalion, Ninth Marines, and particularly B/1/9, had acquired the unenviable reputation of being jinxed. That unfortunate battalion acquired its notoriety after being decimated in the infamous "Marketplace Massacre" three months earlier. Deservedly or undeservedly, their peers had labeled them a hard-luck outfit, and a common expectation shared by those left behind on Con Thien was that 1/9's run of bad luck would probably continue.

That morning could prove interesting for all hands because troop concentrations moving to and from Con Thien would certainly make tantalizing targets of opportunity for the NVA FOs in the area. Several hundred yards of open grassland lay between Con Thien and Yankee Station.

Menacing, gray-black storm clouds hung low on the horizon, meaning that another monsoon deluge was threatening to drench us. I left A-11 and headed for Gunny Hopkins's tank to confer with him on the morning's scheduled activities. The ground was still muddy in spots; I was not exactly thrilled at the prospect of more rain. As I came abreast of my old bunker, it occurred to me that this was probably the last time Dean Steppe and I would see each other, so I made a detour and entered the bunker to say goodbye.

Dean was intently studying a map with some of his men, probably his squad leaders, while several radio operators lounged nearby. I sat inconspicuously on a cot, out of the way of things, waiting for Dean to finish before interrupting him. The Marine closest to me spoke quietly, almost whispering to another man beside him, but I was within range to overhear him state, "You know that 1/9 is replacing us? They're the same jinxed outfit that got wiped out at the Marketplace last July."[1]

"Yeah," replied the other man knowingly. "Bravo 1/9 got their butts kicked *really* bad."

"What do you mean, jinxed?" I interjected, intensely curious about this new wrinkle.

"That's the word on them. They step into shit wherever they go. If somethin' *can* go wrong, it *will* go wrong with them poor bastards."

I was caught up short for a moment. I'd never heard of such a thing. That had to be a rumor, one of those unfortunate innuendos circulated around about another unit, probably undeserved, unconsciously intended to make the rumor-spreader feel better about his own unit at the expense of another. I discounted the jinxed label; we were all US Marines; we endured the same boot camps and OCS programs. *Why,* I wondered, *should a Marine Corps infantry battalion have a reputation that negative, just because they had one disastrous encounter with the NVA a few months earlier?*

Dean concluded his briefing and rose to his feet. "Okay, let's move out," he instructed his men quietly—no John Wayne stuff; no pep talks.

"Dean . . . good luck, buddy," I said, a tinge of emotion creeping into my voice. His intense, serious eyes met mine for a long moment, then he abruptly lowered his gaze as he picked up his pack and rifle and stepped out—no goodbye—not a word.

How strange that two men who had endured so much together could not find words to express their feelings when it came time to say goodbye. Perhaps it was a defense mechanism; we had both experienced the profound sorrow of losing friends in Vietnam. Unconsciously, we must have realized the odds were high that one or both of us would be killed or mangled before our thirteen-month tours in Vietnam were completed.

I continued my journey on over to Gunny Hopkins's tank and climbed aboard. The gunny assured me that all tank crews were fully alert and were monitoring the grunt frequency on their PRC-25 radios. I asked him to please keep an eye on a sturdy little bunker near him that had belonged to one of our tank crews when I first arrived on Con Thien but was commandeered by the infantry on September 15 when Kilo and Lima Companies joined 3/9 within the perimeter. When 3/9 departed, we would reclaim ownership of the four-man bunker, which faced Yankee Station to the south. As for the larger bunker on the southwestern perimeter that we formerly shared with Dean Steppe, it was rat infested, leaky, rickety, and zeroed in by NVA FOs, so 1/9 was welcome to it. I asked Gunny Hopkins to see that we retained the cots and tarps from the old bunker, however, because they originally belonged to the tankers; we could put them to good use in that new four-man bunker.

The monotonous drone of spotter planes circling high above Con Thien like vultures seeking out carrion, and salvos of artillery smoke rounds spreading a curtain of dense, grayish-white smoke between us and the DMZ, indicated that the show was about to begin. I strode back over to A-11 and climbed down in the turret. No one knew for certain what to expect that morning, and I was not about to be caught outside of my tank if the NVA risked everything and greeted the fresh troops from 1/9 with a rocket, mortar, and artillery salute.

A second smoke screen was laid between Con Thien and the mountains, 6,000 meters to the west. NVA rocket sites were known to exist on Hill 174, one of the places screened by the dense smoke.

A steady fusillade of 60mm, 81mm, and 4.2-inch mortar fire was lobbed at known or suspected enemy positions within a 2-mile radius. Artillery pieces at Dong Ha, Camp Carroll, Cam Lo, and C-2 boomed off in the distance as they delivered a continuous stream of H&I fire that whooshed menacingly overhead.

The actual troop exchange went off without a hitch. Obviously, the enemy was keeping close to the ground. As the last man from 3/9 humped along the road bypassing Yankee Station, that dreaded BOOOOM! BA-BOOOM! sound reached us from the north; NVA heavy artillery (130mm or 152mm) was firing in our direction.

I ducked down in the turret shouting, "Look out, incoming! It's big stuff!" We braced instinctively, but for naught; several shells screamed overhead, landing in the vicinity of Yankee Station. The shells weren't meant for us on The Hill. NVA gunners were risking being pinpointed in order to clobber the rear of 3/9's southward-bound column. A few more shells screamed overhead and struck near the MSR east of Yankee Station. I prayed silently for those poor bastards exposed in the open. What tragic irony to have survived Con Thien with all of its horrors, only to fall prey to the enemy's last parting shots, completely out of sight of Con Thien.

Our spotter planes reacted quickly to the enemy fire; within minutes, two US Marine A-4 Skyhawk jets began making bomb runs in the part of the DMZ where the shelling originated. We had no way of knowing if the NVA guns were knocked out, but all shelling from that area ceased immediately.

The entire Third Battalion, Ninth Marines, was gone. They had endured enemy shelling for four weeks, but never once was the thought of abandoning Con Thien seriously entertained. Their mission was to hold Con Thien, and that they did; however, their success did not come lightly. The battalion of infantry from 3/9, plus all attached units, suffered the loss of 27 killed and 683 wounded.[2]

Mike Company, led by Captain Breth, bore the brunt of the NVA shelling attacks. M/3/9 was dug in along the base and across the crest of OP-1, dangerously exposed and quite vulnerable. They were mortared frequently, sniped at by recoilless rifles, and hit repeatedly by almost every caliber of artillery in the NVA arsenal.[3]

That 3/9 gave better than they got, there's no doubt. For every shell that landed on Con Thien, ten or more were fired back at the enemy. B-52 strikes, air strikes, naval gunfire, and dozens of artillery pieces blasted away relentlessly at the 20,000 NVA hiding in and south of the DMZ. The actual number of enemy casualties will probably never be known, but it is safe to state that the attempted siege of Con Thien had cost the enemy dearly so far.

The replacement of 3/9 by 1/9 progressed smoothly. Perhaps it was only our imagination, but Con Thien was quieter and more peaceful that day than any of us could remember. Quite possibly, the heavy suppressive fire from our big guns and the added aerial surveillance were keeping the enemy gunners back in their caves and hiding places.

Minch, Davis, and I were content to just sit inside of A-11 and wait. Time would tell. I fully expected that once the heat was off, our antagonists would initiate 1/9 to the realities of life on Con Thien. The unknown factor was when, not if, Charlie would open up on us; therefore, I chose to keep a low profile inside our tank until something happened.

"I guess when 1/9 gets settled in, we'll have to get acquainted all over again and find out how 1/9 does things," said Minch, staring blankly into a tin can cup full of C-ration cocoa he was stirring with a plastic spoon.

"They do things all screwed up," said Davis.

"What do you mean by that?" I asked.

Davis pushed his gold-rimmed spectacles up on his nose and leaned forward, as he always did to make his point. "Everything they touch turns to shit. They're jinxed."

"Come on, Davis; don't believe that. I heard somebody else say that today, but I just can't buy it."

"Believe it, Lieutenant, it's true. So help me, God, it's true! You ain't been in Nam long enough to know. 1/9 takes more casualties than anybody else. That's why they're called the walking dead!" Davis was leaning forward in the tank commander's seat, both hands gesturing excitedly. He was wound up and nothing could derail him from his argument. "Bravo 1/9 got wiped out this summer at the Marketplace, a mile or so northeast of here. Some of our tanks had to go out and get the bodies. Those tankers spent the night out there in the boondocks with dead grunts lyin' all over the rear decks and sponson boxes of their tanks. It spooked the hell outta everyone, especially when you had to stand your night watch sticking up outta the cupola, knowing there was a bunch of corpses within arm's reach. You didn't dare look back if you heard somethin' behind you."

"Okay," I countered. "That could happen to any outfit. It was just bad luck, that's all."

"Exactly, Lieutenant. That's what 1/9 is all about—bad luck."

"Well, we're stuck with 'em—bad luck or no bad luck. Let's quit talking about this jinxed stuff; it's not helping anybody's peace of mind hearing that crap. . . . Pass me some hot sauce for the chopped ham 'n' eggs, Davis."

"Okay, Lieutenant . . . but you'll see . . . you'll see."

Lightning Never Strikes Twice

The morning of October 10 dawned clear and sunny, a superb start to what was a special day, my one-month anniversary. I had been on Con Thien thirty days. While basking in the morning sun outside of our new four-man bunker on the southern perimeter, a distinctly familiar voice from the past shouted behind me. "Hey, Ice Cream!" It was one of my old classmates from the Basic School at Quantico, Second Lieutenant Ted Christian.

"Warthog!" I yelled back, pleased to see an old friend, so cruelly nicknamed "Warthog" by his peers at Quantico because of his stocky build, pug nose, heavy eyebrow bones, and thrusting lower jaw. He'd played fullback on his college football team and he basically had no neck—his head seemed just to rest atop his shoulders. He had a slow, deliberate manner of speaking, his words heavily accented from a rural West Virginia upbringing. But his looks and mannerisms were deceiving, as I soon learned at Quantico. He was a decisive, quick-thinking Marine officer—a natural born leader. Ted was given an infantry officer military occupational specialty (MOS) after the Basic School at Quantico and shipped over to Vietnam immediately.

"Ice Cream Man! How the hell you been? Never thought I'd see you again. It shore is good seein' a familiar face up here." A broad grin brightened the homely features of my former classmate. We had endured much together at the Basic School in those many grueling months of training, and a warm bond had formed between us. He occupied the room across the hallway from mine at the bachelor officers' quarters. In retaliation for his nickname, he labeled me "Ice Cream" because my last name was pronounced "cone," but that nickname never took hold, fortunately, with anyone else but him.

"Well, you're lookin' at the new XO of Alpha Company. I just moved up today! No more friggin' patrols, and no more walking the damned lines at night."

Ted had been a platoon commander with A/1/9 throughout the terrible summer of 1967 while I was still attending tank school at Camp Pendleton. He had escaped unscathed so far, and the odds of him continuing to survive the war had just improved markedly. He was the officer in charge of company administration; his perilous platoon leader's job belonged to another newly arrived second lieutenant who would be expected to prove his worth in the same manner as Ted: through bravery under fire and excellence in administering the platoon's functions, from commonplace routines to life or death crises.

"Somehow Ted, it seems appropriate that you would be doing well in the grunts, with a nickname like . . ."

"Yeah, okay, Ice Cream Man."

"I have to admit, though, you never struck me as the infantry type when we were back at Quantico."

"Well, it ain't too bad, if you don't care about living." He forced a laugh, but it rang hollow, as often happens when people make light of death, especially their own.

"What's this stuff I hear about 1/9 being jinxed, Ted?"

His eyes narrowed as he pursed his lips and inhaled sharply; he almost winced. No further response was really necessary. I had struck a nerve. An uncomfortable silent minute passed as he deliberated in his mind how to respond.

"Bravo has had more than its share of bad luck," he replied seriously, "and now they've got mostly new guys, and new guys make dumb-ass mistakes. But the rest of 1/9 is okay. We got us a number one CO, Colonel Mitchell. That crap about being jinxed really bugs me, Jim. Our guys hear that and it hurts their damned morale."

Ted stared into his cup for a long moment, then deliberately changed the subject. "I guess you heard about 'Duke' Jory and 'Spanky' Dineen?"

"I heard they bought the farm."

"Yeah. . . ." He shook his head back and forth slowly, as I did, thinking about the last time we saw our friends alive.

"Remember Tom Barry? I took over this tank platoon after he got two 'Hearts' in two weeks up here. This is a bad place, Ted."

"We been here a couple days now and it don't seem so bad like everyone said."

"Well," I replied, hoping to convince him otherwise. "It was *real* bad for a whole month. For some reason, the gooks have slacked off the past few days. Don't let your men get careless, Ted. Take it from me as someone who has been here for a while. This place is like living on a bull's-eye. The whole damned hill is ground zero!"

Ted stood up. It was time for him to be on his way. "Got to let the rest of

Alpha see their new, hard-chargin' XO in action. Thanks for the coffee, Jim."

"Sure, Ted. I'll be sure to stop by your place and see how the other half lives." I could tell that he didn't take me too seriously about how perilous it could be on The Hill. He would have to find out for himself, experience a few close calls, then he'd know.

I went over to A-11 and climbed aboard. The crew was industriously hard at work under Sergeant Davis's prodding, pulling preventive maintenance on our vehicle. I joined in and went to work on the .50-caliber machine gun, taking it out of the tank commander's cupola so it could be stripped down and cleaned. This was dirty work, but, once the chore was finished, I had that feeling of satisfaction one receives when a job is done right, plus, I felt more secure knowing the timing mechanism on that weapon was reset correctly.

After a lunch of crackers with peanut butter and a can of sliced peaches, I took advantage of the lack of enemy activity to go check in with my other tank crews around the perimeter. I was curious about the condition of that unmanned tank by the main gate. The former Fifth Platoon tank with the dead engine was sitting there like an outcast member of the herd, stoically awaiting its fate. I inspected it thoroughly, expecting to find equipment either missing or damaged, but it was in fairly good shape, considering that it had been left unattended in the rain for so long. The hatches were securely padlocked and that would keep the inside of the turret reasonably dry.

Sergeant Howard's tank was nearby. He could be depended on to watch over the abandoned tank. I approached his position on the perimeter and found Howard and his crewmen laboring like Welsh coal miners, tunneling with pick and shovel into the side of a small, steep-sloped hill.

"What's this, Howard? You goin' underground?"

"Right, skipper. We're gonna have the best damned bunker on Con Thien, ain't we, boys?" A chorus of affirmative responses told me his crewmen were thoroughly enjoying their task, loving the chance to put their long-dormant muscles to good use. They had several support beams at hand, so it appeared they need not worry about a cave-in.

"Say, Howard. I want you to see to it that no one messes with that abandoned tank down by the main gate. You're closest to it. If you see anyone on it, shoo them off."

"Already done, skipper. We put the word out to the grunts that it was booby-trapped and that some experts from Third MAF were bein' flown in to disarm it. Nobody's come near it since."

I had to laugh at that. Howard had a genius for arriving at simple solutions to complicated problems. "You do good work, Howard. I'll be back later to see your finished cave project."

Sergeant Carter's tank was near OP-3, 100 meters northwest of Howard's position on the southern perimeter. I struck off in that direction, intending to follow a straight path, thereby reducing my exposure in the open. I was in the vicinity of the resupply LZ when I noticed Ted Christian standing outside of the adjacent Alpha Company command bunker, chatting amiably with some other officers. I walked over to say hello. Ted introduced me first to a robust, blond-haired, blue-eyed giant of a man; he was the battalion chaplain. I also met the Alpha Company commander, Captain Ryan, who was dressed in new utilities and wore unscuffed jungle boots, a sure sign he was a rookie.

We made small talk about the weather, lack of incoming, and Ted's recent promotion. None of the three had their flak jackets or helmets on, whereas my flak jacket was buttoned and my steel pot was firmly situated atop my head—dare I walk in the open on Con Thien any other way? In due time, they would not be so careless.

I pulled Ted aside and said, "Ted, this place is like living on a bull's-eye. The gooks have every inch of this place zeroed in. Flak jackets and helmets at all times—that's the best way to stay alive up here—and you and a lot of your men aren't wearing theirs."

He dismissed my concern with, "Ahh, this place ain't so bad. We've been in a lot worse. We haven't seen nothin' yet to be that concerned about."

I suddenly experienced a strange sensation while standing there with Ted and the other officers; it was a premonition that something awful was about to happen. I'd learned on Con Thien to pay attention when that strange feeling of dread came over me; it was usually followed shortly by some dangerous event such as incoming enemy ordnance. I excused myself from Ted's group, unable to give any reason for departing so suddenly, and hurried away from the A/1/9 CP toward my bunker. I thought to myself that something must be wrong with one of my tank crews and that I'd better look into it, no matter how ridiculous

I felt afterward about leaving a group of fellow officers in mid-conversation because a feeling of fear had suddenly washed over me.

I was approximately 10 yards from my tank when WHOOOSHH-BAMM!! A sharp explosion socked my eardrums. I dove head first into a nearby trench. A greasy-black cloud of smoke hung in the air back where I had been chatting with Ted, the chaplain, and Alpha's CO only seconds earlier.

With ringing ears, I jumped up from the trench and ran to A-11, scrambled up onto the turret, and dropped inside, covering my ears to stop the ringing noise in my head. Gradually, the ringing ceased, and I heard that sickening cry for help, "Corpsman! Corpsman!" Someone had been hurt by that unexpected, solitary enemy projectile.

A handful of navy corpsmen bearing stretchers sprinted by me in the direction from whence the urgent cries for assistance had originated. I was unable to determine the nature of the emergency from my position, because numerous bunkers obscured the view. One round of incoming was usually followed by another, and I was not about to run over and see what had happened. Several others could not resist that temptation, however, and at least a half dozen men rushed after the corpsmen to see what havoc the mystery blast had wrought.

I was staring through my cupola vision blocks at the cloud of smoke gradually dissipating over the LZ, when a ball of flame erupted about 10 feet off the ground, right where the first shell had exploded, with that same ear-slapping sound. I determined then that it had to be an airburst from either a recoilless rifle round equipped with a VT fuse, or an antiaircraft gun leveled to fire horizontally. That same greasy-black cloud hung in the air like a shroud of death.

I knew, even before the panicked cries for more corpsmen went up, that the second round had caught some spectators and corpsmen out in the open. Again, several brave corpsmen answered the calls for help and, without any hesitation, left the safety of their bunkers to render aid. A stream of stretcher bearers now ran from the BAS to the scene of the two airbursts. I observed four casualties, then quit counting; I could not bear to watch any longer. Those green troops from 1/9 had paid for their ignorance of the enemy's modus operandi. Never again would they congregate in the open when "Charlie" was shooting at them.

From prior experience, I knew it would be foolhardy to venture out of the tank until some pattern to that unusual shelling could be established. I waited for almost an hour, but no more shelling occurred. As I was climbing out of the turret, a runner arrived at my bunker with word that the CO of 1/9 was holding a briefing at the CP at 1600 for all battalion staff, including attachments.

The meeting time approached rapidly. I buttoned my flak jacket, pressed on my steel pot, and departed on the dreaded hike up to the CP. My route carried me past three blanket-draped bodies lying on stretchers outside of the aid station bunker entrance, boot toes pointing skyward. I glanced absently at a wristwatch on the left arm of one corpse. The black stretch band of the watch was identical to mine. *Ted Christian wore a watch like that, but . . . could it be him?* I wanted to walk away from there and forget what I had seen, but my intuition would not let me rest without checking into the matter further.

I walked into the BAS bunker and asked the nearest navy corpsman to step outside with me a moment. I pointed to the corpse whose arm rested on the ground outside of the blanket and asked, "Who is that man?"

The corpsman shook his head. "We don't know; he didn't have no dog tags on when they brought him here. He was with a group of guys who took a direct hit down by the LZ earlier."

"Let me take a look . . . I think I know who he is." I reached down with trembling hands and drew back the blanket covering his face. It was Ted, his ashen face frozen in that instantly recognizable mask of death. Those two airbursts must have detonated right over the A/1/9 CP. Had I lingered there another few seconds with Ted, the chaplain, and Captain Ryan, I might have also been killed.

I mumbled some barely audible words to the corpsman, informing him of Ted's identity, then walked off in a daze, mechanically placing one foot before the other in the direction of the CO's bunker. *First Tom Dineen, then Duke Jory . . . and now Ted Christian—dead!*

I was in a mild state of shock on reaching the CO's bunker porch at the head of the stairs. Lieutenant Colonel Mitchell, the commanding officer of 1/9, was standing in the bunker entrance greeting attached unit leaders as they arrived for his briefing. He nodded warmly toward me, expecting, no doubt, to exchange a few typical military greetings.

He noticed my obviously stricken expression and asked, "Are you okay, Lieutenant? You don't look well."

"Sir," I replied weakly, mustering every ounce of self-control I had left. "Lieutenant Christian got hit bad. I just came from the BAS and he's dead."

The colonel's face went pale. He spun abruptly on his heel and vanished into his private bunker quarters. Several minutes passed, then, the battalion XO appeared and gravely announced to all within earshot that the briefing was postponed until later that evening. He had just called the BAS and was informed that, in addition to Lieutenant Christian, a corpsman and another Marine were killed. Captain Ryan was in critical condition, and the corpsmen were working frantically to get him stabilized for emergency medevac before dusk.

A commanding officer expects to lose good men in combat; that knowledge is inherently present every time he gives an order. But the loss of a fine, young officer like Ted was a tragedy to all who knew him, and the colonel was no exception.

Still in shock and grieving over what had happened, I made my way back to the BAS to learn the details of Ted's death. Inside the aid bunker, I saw corpsmen working frantically to save several casualties, all caused by those two airbursts that exploded out of the sky without warning like bolts of lightning. The chaplain had been near Ted when the first airburst exploded, but, through some miracle, he came away unscratched. He recognized me standing by the doorway and walked over. "Don't worry, Lieutenant," he said. "I was able to reach Lieutenant Christian in time before he died."

"*In time?*" I said loudly. "He's dead and you got to him in time?" The chaplain recoiled as if struck and backed cautiously away from me.

My thoughtless, irreverent outburst had embarrassed us both. Feeling tears welling up in my eyes, I turned and ran out of the BAS toward my tank. On the trail leading from the BAS was a pile of human brains. I was simultaneously outraged and sickened, only vaguely conscious of the mortar shells striking behind me as I ran.

I climbed into A-11 and sat there alone, seething with a half-crazed rage for many minutes. Soon, my anger subsided, only to be replaced by profound sorrow at the loss of my friend. Many, many thoughts passed through my mind: the reaction of Ted's fiancée and family to the news of his passing; our experiences together at Basic School; and the brief encounter we had shared that very morning.

I had to talk with someone. Sergeant Howard, the tank commander who had been through everything with me at the Washout fiasco, was nearby; he was acquainted also with Lieutenant Christian. His tank crew was putting some finishing touches on the new bunker they had dug into the side of a hill when I approached. Howard knew immediately that something terrible had happened when his eyes met mine; he ordered his men to stop working and take a break elsewhere. I crawled into a far corner of his bunker and slumped down, staring blankly at the flames in the tin can oven while he heated some water for C-ration coffee. Soon, the sorrow and pain of the afternoon could not be restrained any longer; I poured forth the story of Ted's tragic passing, stopping often to swallow a little coffee whenever the tide of my emotions rose too high. At that moment, Sergeant Howard was not a subordinate under my command; he was a friend.

Shortly before dusk, I headed back to rejoin my men at our bunker. The battalion S-4, Captain Radcliffe, was appointed the CO of Alpha Company after the loss of Captain Ryan. I noted that Captain Radcliffe, accompanied by the company gunny, made a tour of the company lines to console his men as needed, reassuring them that things were well in hand. The men who had gone through the summer fighting alongside Lieutenant Christian were shocked by his loss—visibly upset. And with Alpha's CO and XO both wiped out, those men needed a steadying hand. With a consoling word here, a pat on the back there, Captain Radcliffe and the gunny met personally with every man in the company before dark. After he departed each position on the lines, I noted that every man he had contacted was wearing his flak jacket and helmet.

For thirty days, I had not even dared to consider the possibility of someday being rotated off Con Thien. Later that same evening, however, I swore that I would commence making inquiries regarding our chances of being rotated, before some freak accident or tactical blunder killed me or some of my men.

The TPQ Bombing Incident

Quite often during the siege of Con Thien, the nocturnal quietude was rudely interrupted by the unsettling sound of several bombs landing with muffled thuds in the distance. When I inquired as to the source of those bomb runs, I was informed by a captain in the battalion CP that the bombs were carried by a solitary A-6 Intruder jet fighter-bomber that was locked in by radar operating in conjunction with a computer and controlled from the ground. This sophis-ticated weapons system, labeled TPQ, was designed to correct the plane's air-speed, altitude, and heading, thereby directing the plane unerringly over the target area. Known or suspected enemy artillery positions and troop concentra-tions were the primary targets of these nighttime bombing missions.

Those of us on the ground rarely paid much attention to TPQs, but I became a staunch proponent of their tactical worth when I personally observed a secondary explosion in the DMZ resulting from a TPQ the night my tank was engaged in fending off the ground assault on Con Thien's northwestern perimeter.

The day after Ted Christian's death, Con Thien's bustling activity had slowed almost to a halt as the blackness of night again enveloped The Hill. My crewmen and I lounged comfortably inside our cozy bunker, reading books or writing letters home. Several strategically located candles provided just enough light to see, barely avoiding eyestrain. I was totally absorbed in a paper-back version of Steinbeck's classic, *East of Eden*.

"Say, Lieutenant, how do you spell bravery?" asked Hodge.

"B-R-A-V-E-R-Y," I spelled slowly, keeping my head buried in my book.

Hodge chewed on the tip of his tongue, almost sweating as he concen-trated intently on a sheet of lined tablet paper smeared with faint, reddish-brown dirt stains from his grimy fingers.

"How do you spell courage . . . C-U . . . ?"

"C-O-U-R . . . Okay, John Wayne. What kind of bull shit are you spreading around over there, anyway?"

"Awww, Lieutenant," he protested weakly. "You weren't supposed ta be . . ." He halted in mid-sentence as a low-flying jet screamed overhead, followed immediately by four shattering blasts that shook our bunker violently.

For several seconds, we all stared open-mouthed and wide-eyed at one another. Davis spoke first, "Christ Almighty! What in hell was *that!*" He bolted through the bunker entrance, followed by the others. The Hill was strangely quiet, as if everyone on Con Thien had stopped at once to listen. The faint, fading whine of a rapidly departing jet aircraft reached us from far away.

"That was a TPQ, I think. But it was very close."

"It was closer than that," said Hodge, as several mortar illumination rounds popped open over by OP-2. "Them bombs hit *us!*"

Rumors began to fly around the perimeter that four bombs had accidently landed inside our own lines north of OP-2, burying many men in their bunkers. My first thought was, if any doubts still lingered in anyone's mind that 1/9 was jinxed, and we really had been bombed by mistake, this deplorable incident should erase those doubts permanently.

I remembered that Weicak's tank was located on the northeastern portion of the perimeter and sent Minch over on foot to ascertain the status of Weicak and his crew. Minch reported back within fifteen minutes and informed me that although moderately shaken up, none of the tank crewmen required medical attention. The lead bomb of the stick had missed Weicak's tank by 50 meters. Weicak, who had been standing at a urinal outside his bunker, was knocked flat on his back. The other crewmen were all inside the tank; they suffered only jangled nerves.

Many men congregated in small gatherings, speaking in hushed tones, asking each other how such a blunder was possible. Mortar illumination flares popped steadily overhead, bathing the northern half of the perimeter in an eerie, yellowish glow, as hastily formed rescue teams and corpsmen combed the smashed bunkers and trenches for casualties.

Word was passed around the perimeter for all units to assume full-alert status. If the NVA became aware of the calamity that had befallen the northern portion of Con Thien and mounted an attack from that direction, we would have been hard-pressed to repel such an assault.

"Hey, tankers!" shouted a bare-headed Marine as he jogged toward my tank. "You got any axes, crow bars, or ropes we can borrow? They bombed us by mistake, and we got some dudes pinned inside their bunkers."

"How the hell did that happen?" I asked.

"Christ, we don't know! Four bombs landed on the northern perimeter. Lots of bunkers got collapsed. And to top off the whole mess, one bomb landed in the middle of an old minefield within the perimeter, and it scattered dozens of mines everywhere. It's the damnedest predicament you ever saw."

The magnitude of that disaster surpassed my worst fears. We loaned the man a shovel and some rope, not really caring if they were returned or not.

I thought of taking my tank over there to assist in some way, but it was dark, and we might have run over someone inadvertently in all that confusion, compounding the tragedy. Just then, a bulldozer engine rumbled to life, easing my mind because the smaller, more compact dozer would be ideal for clearing away rubble or lifting heavy beams.

We remained on full alert throughout the night, sickened, upset, and finally angry, but unable to pinpoint a deserving target for our wrath. Did the radar operators err? Was the computer fed faulty information? Was it pilot error? Whom could we blame? Gradually, yet almost simultaneously, a scapegoat was divined: 1/9 itself was the cause; they were jinxed, and nothing could alter that fact in our minds. Marines serving with 1/9 were ultimately doomed; that's why they were called the "walking dead."

The following morning, while walking over to the CP bunker for a meeting with Lieutenant Colonel Mitchell's staff, I happened across a gruesome sight outside the aid station bunker. Stretched out on the ground, face up, were the uncovered bodies of three Marines contorted by rigor mortis. I regretted it afterward, but morbid curiosity forced me to stare at them. An agonized expression of horror was frozen on their mask-like faces . . . as if they might have been buried alive.

A preliminary tally for the TPQ bombing mishap was relayed to us that morning: three killed and twenty-one injured—not as bad as it could have been, but, and everyone agreed, it should *never* have happened!

6.

THE SIEGE IS BROKEN

Anybody who is anybody can get shot—five hundred Marines on this hill cain't be wrong.

—David Douglas Duncan, *War Without Heroes*

Unbeknownst to most of us at Con Thien, engineers and Seabees worked for many days in the mud and rain to construct a steel bridge spanning the Washout. They labored hard to complete the project in record time so that Con Thien would no longer be isolated from vehicular traffic. Every day counted.

The bridge builders were in constant danger of attack because the enemy was cognizant of the bridge's strategic importance; therefore, a detachment from BLT 2/3 was assigned the task of securing the vulnerable Washout area.[1] When finally finished, the bridge was a masterpiece of combat engineering, sturdy enough to support our 52-ton tanks.

The siege of Con Thien was broken on the date that the bridge over the Washout was successfully completed. The main supply route from Dong Ha to Con Thien was reopened to truck convoys; no longer were we totally dependent on helicopters for our resupply. However, even though the MSR was once again a viable traffic artery and the siege was technically lifted, we still existed under siege conditions at Con Thien; the mental attitude was that of men besieged. The fierce struggle for control of our precious piece of real estate was not over yet.

A Failure to Communicate

The morning of October 12 passed without the usual worrisome presence of enemy shelling attacks. That prompted speculation among our foxhole theoreticians that the NVA had finally given up their plans to force us off Con Thien's blood-soaked hillsides. A blistering enemy mortar barrage rained down on us shortly before noon, however, thoroughly quashing any hopes we might have entertained that the 20,000 NVA troops around Con Thien were gone.

In the early afternoon, I was summoned by messenger to report to the CP bunker. The S-3 told me to have two tanks ready to escort some amtracs back to Dong Ha that afternoon. My first reaction was one of incredulity. Did he not realize that the Washout was impassable? What about the order disseminated two weeks earlier that forbade any tanks from leaving a defensive perimeter without the commanding general's explicit permission? I could envision another repeat of the Washout fiasco because, to my knowledge, the MSR had not been swept for mines in nearly a month and the culvert had yet to be repaired.

I strongly objected to the major's order and left no doubt in his mind how I felt. He was unaware of the order curtailing tracked vehicle operations, just as I suspected. He dismissed me curtly by saying, "You just have your tanks ready to leave at 1400, Lieutenant. I'll get clearance from Division."

I stalked out of the CP, determined to enlist the backing of my CO in warding off what I feared would be another disaster at the Washout. Atmospheric conditions were playing tricks on radio communications that day and, try as I might, it was impossible to make radio contact with Dong Ha on a tank radio or the auxiliary PRC-25.

The situation called for some planning so we would not be caught flat-footed if we had to send out our tanks. I sat down with Gunny Hopkins to determine which two tanks were able to make the hazardous journey. All six tanks were hurting. Batteries were low, fuel was limited, and all of the tanks were critically in need of engine overhauls. Sitting for weeks on end in the rain and mud, without being driven and without being cared for properly (impossible to undertake while under siege), had been fatal to all but one tank in the platoon—mine. The other tanks either would not start or were suffering from major engine malfunctions, which hampered their operational ability so severely that they would be more of a liability than an asset in escorting amtracs to Dong Ha.

A runner from the CP said that I was wanted back up at the command bunker right away. The S-3 and another staff officer were waiting for me when I arrived. They were obviously annoyed at my gall in demanding earlier that they clear the proposed departure of my tanks from the perimeter with the commanding general.

"Lieutenant, get your tanks ready to move," said the major abruptly. "We got clearance from Division to move your tanks."

"I can't do that, sir," I protested. "All of my tanks are down except one, and my superiors will not permit one tank to leave the perimeter without another tank being along in case they run into trouble." This was a bluff on my part, because 1/9 had operational control over my platoon, and, technically, they could deploy it in almost any manner they chose. I was attempting desperately to buy time until I could reach Dong Ha by radio.

The S-3 did not swallow my story. "Lieutenant! We cleared this with the general. You will provide the *one* tank, then, as an escort. A mine sweep team and a squad of infantry will go with them. Now, get that tank ready!"

I was beaten. To refuse his direct order would place me in more trouble than I wanted. "Yes, sir. But if any of those vehicles are lost trying to ford the Washout, don't try and pin the blame on me!" With that irrational outburst, I spun on my heel and exited the bunker, choking with anger, frustrated at not being able to forestall what I feared would be another Washout fiasco.

Sergeant Davis was not exactly gratified to be chosen as tank commander on this mission. I explained to the reluctant tanker that I was given a direct order to send one tank with the amtracs but was refused permission to go along. If I had protested the order any more, I told him, a charge of insubordination might have resulted.

The other three crewmen stared at me in bewildered resignation as A-11 maneuvered into position ahead of the two amtracs. If only they knew how concerned I was for their safety. I was left standing by the minefield gate as the caravan chugged toward Yankee Station then disappeared over a crest of high ground to the southeast.

I resolved then and there to discover some means of informing my CO of what was happening. While walking dejectedly back to my bunker, I observed a communications antenna rising high above the artillery command bunker. If any radio set could reach Dong Ha, it had to be the one connected to that antenna, I reasoned, and set a course for that bunker.

A sympathetic Marine first lieutenant, probably the artillery battery XO, listened patiently to my plight, then consented to allow me the use of his radio. I switched the frequency to 36.8 and took the handset from the seated operator.

"Local Train Alpha, this is Local Train Alpha One, over," I said.

"Local Train Alpha One, this is Alpha. Go ahead, over."

"This is Alpha One. It's important that I speak with Alpha Six Actual ASAP, over."

"Roger, Alpha One. Wait, over."

I was pacing back and forth in place, eager to warn the captain of Davis's situation. I also wanted to absolve myself of any blame for what I knew was a serious error in tank tactics: sending one tank out alone on escort duty.

"This is Alpha Six, over," came the slightly irritated voice of my captain. I assumed that he was probably grumpy over being pulled away from a hot meal.

"This is Alpha One. Be advised that one of my tigers was ordered to leave here by itself, against my objections, to escort some 'seals' (amtracs) to 'tent city' (Dong Ha). I tried to prevent it, but the boss here gave me a direct order. What now, over?"

"This is Six. Don't worry about it; you did all you could at your end. I'll alert my Actual and stay on top of it, over."

"Roger, Alpha Six. Thanks much, out."

I was somewhat relieved because I had covered myself, but concern for my tank crew's welfare still weighed heavily on my conscience. I thanked the "arty" lieutenant for allowing me the use of his radio. "No sweat, buddy. Anytime you need it, you're welcome to it," he replied.

Later that evening, I tried reading a paperback novel, but jarring blasts from the nearby artillery battery, and my own preoccupied mind, made concentration impossible. I had to know if Davis had arrived safely in Dong Ha. Leaping up from my cot, I stalked off toward the artillery bunker and was again granted permission to use their radio.

The captain himself acknowledged my preliminary call procedures. That was unusual for him to be standing by the radio; he must have been planning on contacting me. His voice was heavy with concern as he said, "Roger, Alpha One. We have Sergeant Delta here. His tiger is in such awful shape, however, that we are going to do some work on it tonight and in the morning before sending it back. Sergeant Delta informed me that his beast was your healthiest one. If that's so, you must be in sad shape up there, over."

I could scarcely believe my ears. I had been sending messages for over a week that our tanks badly needed overhauling. He was finally aware of the deplorable situation we faced. "This is Alpha One. That's affirmative. We are hurting up here, over."

"This is Six. We'll be contacting you about that at a later date. Sergeant Delta will be returning tomorrow, out."

I was overjoyed to learn that my tank crew was safe in Dong Ha. I could still picture in my mind the look of dismay on Davis's face as he departed. At this very moment, he was likely leaving the Ninth Motors mess hall, stuffed to the bursting point, and heading for a hot shower—the lucky bastard.

Relief on the Way

Shortly after dawn on the morning of October 13, I awoke feeling restless, unable to sleep. I was all alone in my new, compact, four-man bunker, because Sergeant Davis had taken my crew (plus one man from A-15) to escort the amtracs into Dong Ha.

The crisp morning air was invigorating as I exited my bunker and observed the hillsides of Con Thien gradually stirring to life. A few men were already performing routine chores, signaling the start of another day. Thin columns of greasy-black smoke spiraled skyward from numerous privy "honey pots" being burned with diesel fuel. The unmistakable report of our 4.2-inch mortars, firing from within their sandbagged parapets near OP-3, shattered the morning stillness with their characteristic, siren-like whistling noise as each mortar round shot skyward.

I reentered the bunker, placed a lighted heat tab into a tin-can oven, and started another day on Con Thien with a breakfast of chopped ham and scrambled eggs, instant coffee, and canned fruit. Staring vacantly at the bunker wall across from me, I was lost in thought when a solitary explosion rocked the southern portion of the perimeter. I flinched reflexively, then quickly disregarded the sudden blast as the work of our engineers clearing duds from within the perimeter by detonating them in place. I must have missed the "Fire in the hole!" warning that was usually shouted prior to blowing up a dud; besides, it was too early in the morning for the NVA wake-up call.

Moments later, a barrage of large-caliber artillery shells screamed down around me; mud and shrapnel slapped against the bunker. Terror overwhelmed me as I lay prostrate on the bunker floor, convinced that my time on this earth was ended. The next salvo would surely kill me. Trapped in the tomb-like bunker and unable to run from danger, every nerve in my body crawled, demanding that I do something . . . but nothing could be done.

Seconds passed into minutes—minutes spent scarcely breathing for fear that the nausea brewing within me would boil up. Then, at last, the shelling stopped; a few moments of eerie silence followed. *No cries for corpsmen.* . . . *That's good,* I thought. The clenched grip in my guts began to let go as a feeling of relief washed over me.

Our own 105mm artillery opened fire, cannonading the enemy gunners. Salvo after salvo whistled northward. After several minutes without any return fire from the enemy, I surmised that Marine gunners had successfully suppressed the enemy fire. We had at least an hour before any more NVA gun batteries blasted away at Con Thien. By then, our spotter planes would be circling overhead.

I was convinced that we were gaining the upper hand in this insane struggle between faceless enemies. The volume of enemy incoming had peaked in late September; thereafter, each successive day brought fewer enemy shells down on the defenders of Con Thien. Instant death or dismemberment was still a constant threat, but the breathing spells between shellings were growing longer and more frequent with each passing day.

The sun was warm and bright in the noon October sky as I made contact by radio with my company commander in Dong Ha. Besides informing me that Davis was returning that morning, he requested that I release Gunny Hopkins to return to Dong Ha for a few days. I signed off and made a straight path to Gunny Hopkins's hootch, knowing that he would be happy to learn the good news. "Pack your bags, Gunny. You're going back to Dong Ha for a few days . . . captain's orders."

The look of astonishment on Gunny Hopkins's face soon spread into a wide-eyed grin. "You don't have to say it twice. I'm on my way!" Not five minutes later, it seemed, the gunny was jogging gleefully over to the main LZ with his pack under his arm.

After making the rounds of my other tank crews, I arrived back at my bunker in time to observe a giant CH-53 helicopter landing at the resupply LZ. That bird was the gunny's transportation back to Dong Ha. Thirty seconds after touching down, the king-sized helicopter revved up its mighty engine and lifted slowly off the LZ with its human cargo destined for Dong Ha.

The giant chopper was approximately 100 feet over the LZ when it pivoted 180 degrees in place and started heading south. Just then, I heard *whoosh*-BAMM! A bright, red-orange fireball exploded just behind the tail rotor, buffeting the chopper with such concussion that it made the tail dip. The imperiled chopper then rolled violently to the left, almost going into a fatal nose dive. Somehow, the pilot righted his craft, gunned the engine, and climbed rapidly out of danger.

I watched the horrifying scenario unfold before my eyes, knowing my platoon sergeant was aboard, yet unable to do anything but thank God for sparing his life. The VT (proximity-fused) shell must have been fired from the same mysterious, high-velocity, flat-trajectory weapon that killed Ted Christian a few days earlier. I made a mental note to relay my observations to the staff of 1/9. Something had to be done about the mystery weapon before it eventually knocked a helicopter out of the sky over the LZ.

The familiar clanking sound of an approaching tank reached my ears; Davis was returning. He was grinning broadly as A-11 pulled to a halt beside our bunker. I thought it was unusual for him to be in such high spirits on his return to Con Thien; the opposite reaction would have been more understandable.

"Say, Lieutenant. We made it back okay."

"Yes, I can see that. Guess you found a good fording site at the Washout."

"Fording site? Hell, no. They've got a damn steel bridge built up over the Washout that can support our tanks with no sweat at all!"

"A-a bridge? . . . You're kidding."

"That's the honest truth, Lieutenant. We could all pack up and leave today if we had to. That bridge is there to stay."

"Why the hell didn't someone tell me this before?" I said, starting to grow angry at the failure of 1/9 to communicate such vital information.

"Well, I don't know about that, but the captain said we'll be relieved tomorrow morning by the Fifth Platoon. We're going to Charlie-Two."

I could hardly believe my ears. *Oh, thank God! We were going to survive Con Thien after all!*

"Davis, are you sure, now? This isn't a rumor, is it? Did the captain actually tell you that we'd be rotated tomorrow?"

"Yes, sir! And he said for you to notify the grunts so's they'd know about it."

I ducked inside the bunker to grab my flak jacket and helmet before running up to the CP with the news of our impending rotation. The battalion staff needed such information far enough in advance to make necessary arrangements for a mine sweep team and road security to be available on October 14. I wanted no more failures to communicate ruining my platoon's golden opportunity to vacate Con Thien.

Attack on the Washout Bridge

Last minute details such as which tanks would leave and which would remain, which crewmen would be rotated, and so forth, occupied all of my time. Needed engine replacement parts were flown in by helicopter, along with two tank mechanics, in order to have those tanks selected for rotation in operable condition. We would have to limp away from Con Thien, it appeared, but at least we were getting away from The Hill under our own power.

A major nuisance during those complicated, predeparture hours was 1/9 itself. It seemed that when merely staying alive was of primary importance, as it was when 3/9 occupied The Hill, I rarely had battalion-initiated problems to contend with. I was left alone to function as best I could under the circumstances. But, when the shelling intensity began to slacken, as it did in early October, 1/9's staff started to pay more attention to attached units, and tanks, naturally, were impossible to ignore.

Requests for my tank crewmen to participate in sandbag-filling and trench-digging details were annoying, but not intolerable, and criticism of my men's personal appearance and lack of bunker police was irritating, but, again, not totally unwarranted. What really upset me was the staff officer who toured the perimeter that afternoon enlisting extra bodies from all attached units to stand watch in the trenches that night with the infantry. I flatly refused to cooperate with the officer in that misadventure. I told him, "We have only one man awake on each tank at all times during the night; however, it takes four men to fight that tank if we ever got attacked. That's why we have four crewmen assigned to each tank, not three. If it only required three men to drive and fight a tank effectively in combat, that's how many crewmen would be assigned to each tank!"

I was adamant, refusing to back down on my stand in the face of much per-

188

suasion by the staff officer. As he was also a lieutenant, I was able to say "No," and there was not much he could do about it. I fully expected to be called on the carpet later by the major for my failure to cooperate . . . again.

The evening of October 13, I heated up what I hoped would be my last supper on Con Thien. I was all prepared to depart from the perimeter at 0730 the following morning with my three unhealthiest tanks: A-13, A-15, and A-41, plus the immovable "pillbox" abandoned by the south gate when Fifth Platoon ran into difficulties in the mud during the mid-September deluge. My other two tanks, A-11 and A-12, were in the best condition; therefore, they would remain behind at Con Thien and be assimilated into the Fifth Platoon.

After supper, several of us sat quietly inside the bunker. We weren't having boisterous farewell celebrations, and no one seemed compelled to reminisce about our previous days spent weathering the hellish storm of enemy shell-fire. The prevailing, though not verbalized, attitude was that we were not safely away from Con Thien yet. Anything could happen in the ensuing twelve hours.

Stretched out comfortably on my cot, I attempted to read a paperback novel by flickering candlelight, but my thoughts kept wandering. *Did I forget anything? What will happen tomorrow? Everything has to go off well.* Visions of steaming hot showers, clean uniforms, and mess hall–cooked food awaiting us at C-2 flitted in and out of my thoughts. Gradually, my eyelids grew heavy; sleep was close at hand.

WHAMM! I was jarred out of my somnolent state by a crashing explosion in the minefield. As I fumbled wildly in the impenetrable blackness for my flak jacket and helmet, an ungodly shriek followed by another earthshaking explosion made my spine crawl. . . . *Rockets!!*

I was completely alone. The others, seeing that I was drifting off to sleep while reclining on my cot, must have quietly snuffed out the candles when they vacated our bunker. I had no idea what time it was.

Rockets screamed down on us at ten-second intervals. Those huge 122mm projectiles were nine feet long and weighed 125 pounds. This knowledge, plus the psychological trauma induced by their terrifying scream, had me almost immobilized with fear. I was torn between two risky alternatives: remain inside the flimsy, darkened bunker without benefit of human accompaniment and risk succumbing to the panic threatening to overwhelm me, or take a calculated gamble that I could sprint 30 yards, clamber atop my tank, and drop inside the turret in less than ten seconds of elapsed time before another rocket would surely come crashing down nearby, filling the air with whirring chunks of lethal, white-hot, jagged shrapnel.

I dropped to my knees and peered out through the bunker doorway; not even a silhouette of my tank was discernible in the darkness. Each rocket seemed to land closer than the last one, the explosion shaking the bunker floor violently, socking my eardrums with concussion. After each explosion, shrapnel whizzed viciously overhead and clods of mud rained down on the bunker roof. *What irony to get killed my last night on Con Thien!*

Panic welled up in my throat. My pounding heart threatened to burst from its rib cage. *This bunker is a trap. Fate's going to steer the next rocket right down through the bunker roof, blasting it and me into charred, broken flesh, sandbags, and lumber.*

I remembered that Psalm. The words poured forth from memory as I spoke them aloud: "Have mercy upon me, O God. . . . In God I trust. . . . I will not fear."

Another rocket came in with a deafening shriek. Then, silence. . . . *A dud!* Several seconds later, another missile shrieked in . . . no explosion. Those rockets were either duds or set on delayed fuses. A mortar illumination flare popped over the minefield, revealing the location of my tank. I knew I had to escape from the confines of that accursed bunker, the shrapnel be damned. Searing hot breaths burned my parched throat; sweat trickled down my armpits. *Wheeeowwww*-BLAMM!!

With a mighty lunge, I leaped out of the bunker and sprinted across open ground toward A-11. *Go! Run! . . . Ten seconds to make it inside my tank!* Halfway there, another rocket screamed over my head, forcing me to drop face down in the mud. The earth heaved beneath me; chunks of falling debris smacked down on my back and legs. *That was not ten seconds, you gook bastards!* I lay there gasping, feeling naked and vulnerable: a sacrificial lamb at the altar of fate.

Another rocket screamed in and . . . nothing—another dud. I scrambled up the slope plate of my tank and pounded desperately with bare fists on the unyielding steel loader's hatch atop the turret. "Let me in, goddammit!" My frantic plea went unanswered; the hatch stayed sealed. At that precise moment, another rocket struck close by, just missing the tank. The tremendous blast blew me off the turret, slamming me down on the rear steel deck of the tank. I lay there stunned for many seconds, unable to function, like a prizefighter knocked to the canvas, struggling to shake off mind-fogging cobwebs before being counted out.

Soon regaining consciousness, I realized that my position atop the tank was untenable. I located someone's steel pot in the gypsy rack (mine was blown off by the near miss) and banged it down on the loader's hatch. Seconds later, the hatch popped open and I dove headfirst into the turret, knocking Minch and Davis against the breech. I mumbled an apology to the two startled crewmen, then sprawled panting in utter exhaustion on the turret deck, swimming in my sweat-drenched flak jacket, unable to put into words the terror I had just experienced. My nerves were shot.

Meanwhile, Howard had cautiously maneuvered his tank in the darkness over to the southwest corner of the perimeter. One of his crewmen, Corporal Baker, had detected a rocket launching site near Hill 174, approximately 6,000 meters to the west.

A sharp KRAACK! sound of a tank cannon firing compelled me to look out through the cupola vision blocks. There was Baker, silhouetted by flare light, standing atop the turret of A-13. He was peering through a pair of binoculars in the direction of Hill 174, attempting to follow the tracer-lit flight of his tank's projectile so that he could adjust his main gun onto the NVA rocket launching sites. Our own artillery appeared dazed, unable to respond with counterbattery fire. Howard's tank was the only weapon on Con Thien returning the enemy fire. The sight of one of my men recklessly exposing himself like that in the face of enemy rockets filled me with admiration for his bravery. I felt something less than courageous at that moment.

After the fifth round fired by A-13, the enemy rocket fire ceased. Several more minutes of quiet passed before I dared to open the cupola hatch and expose my upper torso. Those dreaded cries for corpsmen were coming from all over the southern portion of the enclave. An involuntary shudder coursed through me as I recalled the moments of dreadful terror I underwent during the rocket barrage.

Something of major consequence was occurring in the vicinity of the

Washout, 1.5 miles south of Con Thien. A terrain drop-off on the reverse slope of Yankee Station, coupled with a thick growth of semitropical vegetation standing between our position and the Washout, prevented us from seeing what was actually happening. Muted sounds of battle, bright flashes, and glowing red tracer bullets streaking off into the night sky indicated that a furious battle was being fought there.[2]

The underlying purpose of that prolonged rocket attack became obvious. The NVA were likely assaulting the Washout bridge, which meant they wanted to prevent the Marines on Con Thien from organizing reinforcements to come to the aid of the beleaguered bridge defenders. That was an alarming development, especially to my tank crewmen and me. We had been counting the hours until 0730, when we could exit through Con Thien's minefield gate for the last time and receive clear sailing to C-2. If the vital Washout bridge was damaged that night, or, even more disheartening, captured by the NVA, it would be some time before we could leave Con Thien.

I was barely fit to command after my previous ordeal, and nagging concern over the security of the bridge did nothing to bolster my condition. Thirty-four days of constant strain had taken their toll. Physically and mentally I was dangerously overfatigued, drawing on hidden reserves of stamina and will power that I never dreamed were there in order to assure the safe and orderly departure of my platoon on October 14. Any delay whatsoever would be a crushing disappointment.

The unmistakable drone of "Puff the Magic Dragon" (US Air Force AC-47 gunship) was heard circling the area west of the Washout bridge. That was an encouraging indication the attack on the bridge had failed, and that the NVA assault troops were withdrawing to the west whence they had come. We could not visibly detect the gunship itself, but, periodically, a stream of tracer bullets would pour down from the heavens like a giant tongue of fire. The awesome Gatling guns mounted on each AC-47 gunship could hose down an area the size of a football field with a short burst. First, a concentrated stream of tracers shot earthward like molten lava exploding from a volcano fissure; then, the buzzing of the gunship's weapon reached our ears with a *BRRRRRRR-RUUUUP!* followed by the distant drone of "Puff's" twin engines. Flares were dropped regularly, either by the gunship itself or by a sister ship, thus main-

THE SIEGE IS BROKEN

taining constant illumination over the target area and casting an eerie glow on the night.

A runner from 1/9's CP suddenly appeared beside the tank and asked, "Where's the tiger leader?"

"Right here, Marine. What's up?"

"Sir, the major says to tell you the bridge is secure. You leave Con Thien in the morning as planned."

"Hallelujah!!" I shouted. "Tell the major 'aye, aye, sir' for me." I was ecstatic. My worst fears had not materialized—the bridge was still ours.

The Last Day

Sleep did not come easily that last night on The Hill. After a long, restless night, I was awake early, brewing a steaming hot cup of cocoa when the morning sun finally showed its face on the horizon. Gunny Hopkins would have been an invaluable asset to me that day, but he was back at Dong Ha. None of the other NCOs in the platoon could even attempt to fill the gunny's shoes. The whole show rested squarely on my shoulders.

Minch and Davis gathered together all of their belongings and left to join the tank crews they were assigned to ride out with. I was left alone in the bunker with Hodge, the platoon maintenance man and driver on A-11. He was not leaving with us because he was a relatively recent addition to the platoon. In the eyes of Alpha Company staff, his limited experience was more appreciated on Con Thien than it would have been back in the rear.

"Hodge, don't let it get you down." The obviously depressed young Marine sat on his cot, staring down at the bunker floor between his boots. "You'll be rotated out of here in a week or so and then you'll be easin' it in Dong Ha with the rest of those candy asses back in the rear." I wanted to cheer him up; it was not like the jovial, uncomplicated southerner to behave in such a downhearted manner.

"Sir . . . It's not that. I know they'll pull me outta here 'fore too long. It's just that I really wanted to stay in this platoon. I liked serving with you and these guys, and it just won't seem right being in another outfit after what we went through together and all."

I was touched—so much so that my eyes grew moist at the man's honest, heartfelt statement of affection and regard. "Hodge, I promise I'll talk to the captain today about making you First Platoon's permanent maintenance man. How's that sound?"

"Sir, that would suit me just fine," he said, with a broad grin starting to crease his features.

"Okay, how about going over to Alpha-41 and make sure that crew is up and ready to go when we start forming up. They might need a little help from you to get that tank started." Hodge left the bunker much elevated in spirit, reassured that I would do everything possible to keep him in First Platoon.

I was going to leave Con Thien on Howard's tank. Rather than sit by myself and worry over what might possibly go wrong, I walked over to his bunker to pass the time until our departure. As anticipated, the good sergeant had prepared a steel pot full of boiling hot water. I brewed some C-ration instant coffee and cupped my grimy hands around the tin can cup to ward off the morning chill. Nothing remained for me to do except to wait impatiently as the minutes dragged by.

Howard scurried around his bunker, cursing first at one crewman, then cajoling another. He resembled a harried sheepdog rounding up its flock.

A light ground fog had drifted in during the predawn hours, dampening the air and creating an eerie backdrop for our departure. With a growing sense of excitement, I watched as our infantry escort and engineer mine sweep team began congregating sleepily by the fog-shrouded minefield gate. Since the time was only 0710, they were probably as anxious as we were to get underway before "Charlie" delivered his usual good-morning salutations.

Howard ordered his driver to crank up the engine on A-13. The turbo-supercharged, 12-cylinder diesel power plant hummed for a few seconds in characteristic fashion, then coughed to life with a deep-throated rumble, sounding quite healthy. *One down, two to go.*

Moments later, a black cloud of diesel smoke belched forth from the rear of A-15, which was some distance away, indicating that Davis had successfully started Gunny Hopkins's tank and would be joining us momentarily at the minefield gate. *One to go.* I paced back and forth nervously. Hodge still had not returned. A-41 was in deplorable condition; anything might have gone wrong.

After several more minutes passed, I could not wait any longer and sent a runner to tell the tank commander we were waiting on him and to get his tank down to the gate, ASAP!

Seconds dragged into minutes, and still no word. It was 0735 and the sergeant in charge of the mine sweep detail approached worriedly, not wanting to seem impatient, of course, but he was concerned over the delay. "We're ready to go anytime you are, Lieutenant."

"Okay, Sergeant. I can't leave until everyone is down here. Give me a few more minutes, okay?"

"No problem. We'll meet you out at Yankee Station."

I still had no word on A-41's condition and was ready to jog over there myself to see what the problem was. Then, Hodge came running up to me shouting, "Sir! Alpha-41 is dead; she won't start!"

Oh, Christ! Wouldn't you know it. Something would screw it up at the last second. "Let's go over there and slave start the damned thing, Howard."

A-13 lurched up the path and came to a stop alongside of A-41. The slave cable from our tank was hooked into the receptacle in the driver's compartment of the other tank. We waited impatiently for a few more minutes until the dead engine purred to life and then roared mightily.

"Okay! Let's get the hell outta here!" I shouted. We still had to hook up a tow bar to the dead ex–Fifth Platoon tank, A-14, that was sitting unattended between the gate and the LZ. I felt certain that we had caused enough commotion with the three tanks starting up and moving around the perimeter that the NVA would begin shelling Con Thien at any minute. I wanted to be long gone when the fireworks started.

A-41 was following A-13 through a gap in some concertina wire near OP-3, when A-41's right rear sprocket snagged onto a loose strand of barbed wire. Before the driver knew what was happening, his sprocket became hopelessly entangled; he was dragging 10 yards of wire behind him. I looked back just then, saw what calamity was befalling A-41, and gestured frantically to the tank commander to look behind him. Both tanks halted immediately and we dismounted to survey the damage. Ordinarily, in a situation like that, which was not uncommon with tracked vehicles, the driver of the ensnared tank would take a pair of wire cutters and snip the wire loose, one strand at a time; however, we were pressed for time and the tank commander knew it. He attempted to tear the wire loose by having his driver run the tank back and forth in place.

This tactic only created a worse problem; he soon had a beehive-shaped roll of concertina wire wrapped around the rear sprocket.

I was beside myself with frustration. We could not wait an hour or two for that crew to cut the wire loose; our mine sweep team was standing by at Yankee Station, and they would not delay their departure much longer. If we severed the main strand of wire dragging behind A-41 and proceeded on to C-2 with that enormous, beehive-shaped mass of barbed wire protruding out from the sprocket, it was certain to become entangled in the barbed wire paralleling the narrow road through the minefield. Then, we would be in real danger of taking incoming if some sharp-eyed NVA forward observer noted our predicament. I made a snap decision. Sergeant Carter's tank, A-12, was located about 100 feet away. I ran over to Carter and grabbed him by the arm. "Your tank is going in place of 41. Get your crew ready to roll . . . now!"

"B-but—yessir?" he replied, somewhat taken aback by my agitated demeanor. I was almost frothing at the mouth over the plight that had jeopardized our safe exodus from The Hill. Carter's crew tossed their personal belongings on top of their tank, then roared over to join us. Our disgruntled infantry escort and mine sweep team paced anxiously in place out at Yankee Station, obviously wondering how anything as uncomplicated as getting four tanks on the road could be so complicated. I glanced at my watch—*0815!*

Someone from the CP was on the radio and wanted to speak with the tiger leader. I tried explaining what the delay was, but he wanted no excuses. He cut me off abruptly, saying, "Lieutenant, if your tanks aren't out of here in five minutes, you aren't going at all today, because we have more important things for our people to do than have them sit around on their dead asses out at Yankee Station while your tanks rearrange half the perimeter wire down there!"

I was too flabbergasted at first to even respond. A long moment of silence ensued at my end of the conversation before I snapped through clenched teeth, "We're leaving here now—*out!*"

I could feel my temples throbbing with that special ache that meant a migraine headache was about to follow. The pain in my skull matched the shooting pains in my stomach, as I felt the twinge of my shriveled adrenal glands straining to push me just a little further.

Our tow cables were hooked up to A-14; we were almost ready to leave. I remembered the advice Lieutenant Colonel Chaplin had given to me before I came up to Con Thien. He told me that I had better *make* my men wear flak jackets and helmets at all times, because tankers sometimes think they are made of steel like their tanks. Looking back at the column of tanks behind me, I was pleased to note that all the crewmen I could see had their flak jackets buttoned securely. They'd learned their lessons well.

Howard dropped down into the gunner's seat of A-13; I assumed the tank commander's position standing upright in the cupola and gave the command to our driver to move out. We lurched forward, towing the disabled A-14. *Five more minutes,* I told myself. *All we need is five more minutes to be out of here . . . alive!*

We were long overdue for our morning "salute" from the NVA gunners. I fully expected a salvo of enemy shells to crash down around us at any second as our armored caravan crawled forward at its agonizing snail's pace through the minefield to join up with our mine sweep team at Yankee Station. A tingling sensation on the back of my neck told me to duck down inside the turret; only a direct hit could get me then. But pride, fear of losing stature in front of my men, or both, forced me to stand upright in the tank commander's cupola. Perhaps it was also defiance, my personal gesture of contempt directed at any NVA FOS who might be observing our departure.

At last, the interminable journey across the flat, open terrain stretching from the minefield to Yankee Station ended. We were safe! We had run the gauntlet without mishap. All of my bottled-up fear, anxiety, and tension drained away with one mighty sigh.

I took one last look at Con Thien's battered hillsides as we approached the bend in the road that would take us around to the rear of Yankee Station. Con Thien had not changed; it appeared almost the same as when I had first glimpsed those cratered, debris-strewn hills from that point on the road thirty-four days earlier. The only change had been within me. I was no longer the same untried, inexperienced second lieutenant who had arrived there on September 10, lacking in expertise and uncertain of his own capabilities. I was a veteran—a man who had learned the ways and means of coping with the insanity of war, and a man who knew and appreciated, as only those few can who have come close to forfeiting it, how very dear and sweet life can be.

Subtly, yet undeniably, the horrors of Con Thien, combined with the pressures and responsibilities of command, had placed a severe strain on my physical and mental faculties; however, I had met those challenges and emerged a wiser, more competent leader. Not one member of First Platoon had suffered death or injury caused by any lack of judgment on my part. I thanked God for that blessing.

As our rolling stock of limping, ailing iron monsters pulled out of sight of Con Thien and headed straight for the sturdy, green girders of the Washout bridge that loomed before us, I realized then that Con Thien's fate was no longer in doubt; the enemy siege had failed. We had absorbed a fearful pounding, but never once did the thought of abandoning Con Thien to the NVA ever cross our minds. I also knew that none of us who had spent "time in the barrel" there would ever forget those hellish days and nights under siege on that isolated Marine outpost below the DMZ.

EPILOGUE

Little did we suspect, that long-awaited morning of October 14, 1967, that my platoon had not seen the last of Con Thien by any means. I would spend a total of six more months on that red clay bull's-eye before my thirteen-month tour in RVN was completed. Through a rotation policy conceived at Third Tank Battalion, the First, Second, and Third Platoons of Alpha Company were rotated every thirty days from C-2, to C-2 Bridge (the Washout), and back to Con Thien again. This procedure worked well for me until the first week of March 1968, when my platoon was sent back to Con Thien with instructions to plan on remaining there for an indefinite stay of up to ninety days. First Platoon was still operating out of Con Thien when I departed Vietnam in September of that year.

Of course, being at Con Thien was never again as perilous as it was during those abominable days in September and October 1967, when, every day without letup, hundreds of enemy rockets, mortars, and artillery shells rained down on Con Thien's miserable, mud-caked defenders. When my platoon rotated up to Con Thien for the last time in March 1968, we had shower facilities (cold water only), electric lights in specially constructed "Dyemarker" bunkers, fresh milk and fruit rationed daily, and, most important, the incoming had slacked off to a mere dribble; weeks passed without a single enemy shell being aimed our way.

On May 5, 1968, my platoon sergeant and I were standing on my tank, watching an air strike being carried out in the DMZ. An NVA FO must have spotted us because a solitary incoming mortar round barely missed the tank, wounding us both. Gunny Thomason was hurt badly and was medevaced. I only got a piece of shrapnel in my wrist, not considered serious enough to medevac me, but serious enough to receive a Purple Heart. (Twenty years later, when no longer able to grip a pen or shake hands without sharp pain in my thumb joint, I had the shrapnel surgically removed.)

The second week of July 1968, the entire Ninth Marine Regiment conducted a massive sweep around Con Thien as part of Operation Thor. All three tank platoons from Alpha Company were involved. My tank platoon was assigned to work with 2/9 during the weeklong operation. Of particular note was the fact that all elements of the Ninth Marine Regiment roamed throughout Leatherneck Square, crisscrossed the Trace, and operated throughout the southern half of the DMZ with little enemy contact. This would not have been possible in the fall and winter of 1967/68, when patrols were certain to be challenged by the enemy if they strayed more than a few hundred meters north of Con Thien's outer perimeter wire.

I was particularly impressed throughout Operation Thor by the depth and extent of the enemy fortifications north of Con Thien. We destroyed hundreds of bunkers and staggering quantities of arms, ammunition, and equipment caches. We also discovered extensive trench line/tunnel systems—some exposed, some camouflaged—that one must assume were manned by many thousands of NVA soldiers during the siege of Con Thien.

At the termination of Operation Thor in mid-July 1968, I was finally pulled out of the field and assigned to fill the post of executive officer of Alpha Company, Third Tank Battalion in Dong Ha. In conjunction with the responsibilities of the billet, I was required to make excursions out in the field to ascertain the needs, morale, and so on, of our various deployed tank units.

While returning from what I knew would be my last trip up to Con Thien (my rotation date for heading home was only a week away), my memory was stirred by the sight of a burned-out, rusted tank retriever hulk sitting forlornly in the underbrush about 100 yards west of the Washout bridge. Untold numbers of Marines and soldiers must have noticed that once-proud derelict as they rode over the bridge spanning the Washout. I wondered if any of them were curious to learn how that retriever happened to be abandoned there, of all places. I knew the whole story by heart, of course; that abandoned tank retriever was a lasting monument to the comedy of errors I subsequently labeled the "Washout fiasco."

When my tour of duty in Vietnam ended, I took stock one day and tallied the number of friends and associates who served with me overseas who did not make it home again. The total was sixteen. Twice that number were wounded.

○

As for some of the Marines mentioned in this book, Gunnery Sergeant Hopkins moved into a Third Tank Battalion staff billet shortly after he departed Con Thien—no more getting shot at. His dream was to retire from the Marine Corps in two years, return to his home in West Virginia, and get a job driving a truck for a local brewery. Knowing him, I have no doubt that he realized his dream job.

Canadian Albert Trevail served with me all during my RVN tour, rising to tank commander soon after Con Thien. I submitted his name once for a Bronze Star when, during a tank/infantry assault in the DMZ, he bravely left his tank, ignoring the enemy mortars striking nearby, and single-handedly hooked up a tow cable to another tank stuck down in a 2,000-pound bomb crater. Thanks to his courageous actions, we were able to continue in the attack without further delay. He was grazed in the face by an AK-47 bullet on another occasion yet refused evacuation until all casualties were carried to the medevac LZ. I put him in for a meritorious promotion to sergeant and he received it. He extended for two more tours in Vietnam, stayed in the Corps, and retired after twenty-two years as a master sergeant. I contacted him in 2002 when I heard he was living near me in Northern California. He was teaching computer science classes at a local high school.

After I took over command of Lieutenant Tom Barry's tank platoon, he was transferred to Third Tank Battalion at Quang Tri where he spent the remainder of his Vietnam tour as a staff officer. The MACV policy at the time mandated that any officer who received two Purple Hearts for their wounds would be reassigned to a safer position in the rear area. My belief, though not officially verified, was that because Marines who received three wounds were sent home, pulling them out of harm's way after two "Hearts" was an attempt to keep from depleting the junior officer ranks any more than they already were.

Sergeant Paul Carter transferred to another platoon and soon became a platoon sergeant after leaving Con Thien. He was later wounded by ricocheting bullet fragments during a firefight in Leatherneck Square and evacuated.

Sergeant Howard eventually became my acting platoon sergeant after Gunny Hopkins left: then, several months later, Howard was transferred to another platoon. I only saw him once again in Vietnam; however, while perusing a Marine Corps recruiting pamphlet ("Life in the Marine Corps") several years later, I came across a photograph of Staff Sergeant Howard, intently counseling another Marine, doing in real life what he so often dreamed of becoming—a Marine Corps recruiter.

When Ken "Piggy" Bores was wounded and evacuated, I never imagined

I'd see him again. In 2001, I attended a USMC Vietnam Tankers Association reunion in Minneapolis. As I walked through the door of the local VFW where we were holding a business meeting, someone shouted "Mr. Coan!!" It was "Piggy." He ran over and gave me a welcoming bear hug. We've stayed in touch ever since.

During my ten months in the field as a tank platoon leader with Alpha Company, I served with five platoon sergeants. Gunnery Sergeant Hopkins was kept back in the rear after Con Thien and given a staff NCO billet; Sergeant Howard became acting platoon sergeant and acted in that capacity until Gunnery Sergeant Thomason replaced him. Thomason was wounded and evacuated after he and I were wounded by that single NVA mortar round. Next was Staff Sergeant Woodard. He was only at Con Thien two weeks when he took a limping tank back to the rear for repairs. He never returned. Staff Sergeant Tews came aboard next until he was wounded and evacuated during Operation Thor. His replacement was Staff Sergeant Waggle, whom I only met briefly before I moved up to be Alpha Company's XO.

I rotated back to "the world" in September 1968 and served the remainder of my active-duty obligation as a tank company commander at Camp Lejeune, North Carolina. One day, while walking over to confer with the CO of the tank company next door, I bumped into Corporal "Charlie" Brown, who snapped to attention when I passed him in the hallway. I put him "at ease" and asked him what was going on. He related that he had gotten himself in some trouble and was waiting to appear before his captain for a disciplinary hearing. I then entered the captain's office and, behind closed doors, expressed what an outstanding field Marine Brown was and that I would be proud to have him in my company. Brown's CO decided not only to dismiss the charges against him but also to keep Brown in his company.

O

Regarding the jinxed label placed on 1/9 (a.k.a. "The Walking Dead"), in retrospect it seems unfair, even cruel, to describe fellow Marines in that light, but that was the attitude many of us shared at the time. We were as sure of 1/9's ill fortune as we were certain the sun would rise tomorrow. A commonly accepted "fact" among those who operated with the Ninth Marines was that if anything could go wrong, it would happen to 1/9. And, periodically, the word would go around: "1/9 stepped into the shit again." Those within earshot invariably exchanged knowing glances, nodding their heads in unison, perhaps voicing a silent prayer thanking God they weren't assigned to 1/9. Those periodic rumors only reinforced our mutual convictions.

Undoubtedly, many outstanding, dedicated officers, NCOs, and enlisted men served in 1/9 during the time frame covered herein. But the stigma was there. It was real to us at the time; therefore, to portray accurately the US Marine experience at Con Thien, I found it necessary to bring out the "jinxed" label 1/9 wore in Vietnam. In no way is there any intention in this book to dishonor those Marines who served with 1/9, either living or dead, who saw their duty and performed it as professionally as any other Marine Corps unit that saw combat in Vietnam.

Also, in retrospect, the reader must understand that the unfairly harsh words directed toward the members of the press by us Marines were fueled by having to sit there and endure prolonged enemy shelling, day after day, and not be able to directly confront our nemesis, the North Vietnamese Army. We vented our anger instead on civilian members of the press. We never considered that they were risking their own lives to tell the world what we were enduring at Con Thien. We should have been thanking them.

O

I was honorably discharged from active duty in 1970. While on inactive reserve status in 1971, I was promoted to captain, USMCR. Con Thien and Vietnam were fading memories. I happily resumed the life of a civilian, secure in the knowledge that no matter how unpopular the war had become, I had served my country honorably and witnessed nothing in my thirteen-month overseas tour of duty that I felt compelled to protest. The Marine Corps had been given a difficult mission; we performed it well.

The US Marines conducted six major operations in the Con Thien/Leatherneck Square area of the DMZ from 1967 to 1969. In that two-year period, the NVA lost 11,627 dead and at least twice that number wounded, all in the Con Thien/Leatherneck Square area. We paid a heavy price to defeat the North Vietnamese there: 1,681 dead and 9,629 wounded.[1]

One can appreciate the shock and outrage that I and thousands of other Marine Corps veterans of the DMZ fighting experienced in the spring of 1972, when the South Vietnamese defenders of Con Thien and similar outposts below the DMZ were unceremoniously routed from their positions in one massive thrust by our former antagonists, the North Vietnamese Army. They carried all the way into and beyond the capital of Quang Tri Province, Quang Tri City. How in God's name, we asked, could such a disastrous debacle have occurred?

On April 30, 1975, Saigon fell to the invading North Vietnamese conquerors. So much for "peace with honor." The war was over. We lost, or should I say, gave it away. Perhaps it was never ours to win. But I ask myself, "How could we lose the war when we won most of the major battles?" I also ask myself almost every day, "Was it all worth it?" Then, I remember my friends Ted Christian, Ed Jory, Tom Dineen, Paul Marken, Dan Kent, Ed Lia, and Jim Muir. What would they have to say about the sacrifices we Marines made to secure Con Thien and the DMZ area? But we shall never know, because their lips were sealed forever when they forfeited all of their tomorrows trying to achieve that goal.

Appendix A

First Platoon, Alpha Company, at Con Thien

September 10, 1967	September 15, 1967	October 14, 1967
A-11 Sgt Guivara*	2ndLt Coan	2ndLt Coan
Cpl Hubert	Sgt Howard	Sgt Davis
Cpl Graham	Cpl Irizarry	Cpl Hodge
LCpl DuBose	LCpl DuBose	PFC Minch
A-12 2ndLt Coan	Sgt Carter	Sgt Carter
Cpl Sanders	Cpl Sanders	Cpl Irizarry
Cpl Johnson*	Cpl Crist	PFC Clark
LCpl Trevail	LCpl Trevail	LCpl Trevail
A-13 Cpl Aranda*	Sgt Osborne	Sgt Howard
PFC Sudduth*	PFC Minch	Cpl Baker
Pvt Burnett	PFC Burnett	PFC Bishop
LCpl Bores	LCpl Bores+	LCpl Coggins
A-14 Sgt Weicak+	Sgt Weicak	Sgt Weicak
Cpl Holmes	Cpl Holmes	LCpl Brown
Sgt Shands	Sgt Shands	LCpl Mims
LCpl Woodall	LCpl Woodall	PFC Palazzari
A-15 GySgt Hopkins	GySgt Hopkins	GySgt Hopkins
Cpl Martin*	LCpl Murphy+	Cpl Jordan
LCpl Apodaca*	LCpl Workman	LCpl Workman
LCpl Augustine*	PFC Birkholtz	PFC Berkholtz

*Short-timers rotated back to Dong Ha on September 15.
+WIA. Note that replacement crewmen Private Manchego and Lance Corporal Murphy arrived at Con Thien on September 15 and were wounded and evacuated less than two weeks later. Other replacements temporarily assigned to First Platoon were Sergeant Osborne, Corporal Crist, Private First Class Glass, and Lance Corporal Blum.

On October 14, the First Platoon's "time in the barrel" was over. Lieutenant Brignon and Gunnery Sergeant English brought up the Fifth Platoon of Alpha Company to replace First Platoon.

Appendix B

Vietnam Diary

(Written by the author during his thirteen-month tour in Vietnam)

29 Aug 67
I received news today that saddens me deeply. My TBS friend, Tom Dineen, was listed as KIA in the "Stars & Stripes" mag. He was a married man with a baby who volunteered to come over here. Our nickname for him at TBS was "Spanky." What a tragedy.

01 Sept 67
Vietnam is fascinating to me. The people are warm and laugh often, but I can't get used to people, male and female, who hoist up their pants leg and urinate at the side of the road or out in a field in full view. Naked little boys run around in the street. The people are wiry, yet fragile looking. It's not unusual to see men and boys (brothers?) walk hand in hand.

02 Sept 67
I led a patrol yesterday afternoon to try and locate an abandoned village about 2 miles from our base at Gia Le where the VC might be hiding out or storing rice, maybe weapons. About 20 of us from the base reaction force went, all loaded for bear with a machine gun, grenade launchers, etc. All we got out of it was soaking wet from sweat and a sunburn. We found the village which was at a stream junction located between two hills in a little green valley. It was a lovely, peaceful place, but long-ago deserted. A fierce battle must have been fought there once. Shrapnel and shell holes were all over the hills, plus old C-rat cans and expended cartridges. I even found the tail section of a U.S. helicopter that had crashed and burned. The country was similar to the Tucson mountains where I went hunting once in a while when I was home. The only thing missing was the cactus!

03 Sept 67
I've only been shot at once. It happened when I went with the colonel to visit our two tank platoons near the DMZ. While at Gio Linh, I heard a distant boom sound and then a crackling whizzz, which I knew was somebody firing artillery at us from close range. I beat the colonel into the nearest bunker just as the round exploded about 100 meters from us. Not close, but I was happy to leave there. The base has a tower for the FO's to climb up in and be able to spot enemy positions to the north. I would not want to be one of those arty folks and have to do that.

04 Sept 67

I was wound up tight today for some reason. A Vietnamese barber gave me a haircut and massage. Quite an experience for only 50 piasters (forty cents). He used hand clippers because there's no electricity. He then bathes you in after-shave lotion and cracks your neck.

Something is still bothering me. I heard a rumor that Ed (Duke) Jory was killed recently. I knew him from OCS. He was married and had a little baby girl. I met his wife on the beach at Oceanside while I was at tank school at Camp Pendleton. I hope and pray it's just a rumor.

07 Sept 67

We had something unusual today. A Marine patrol reported that they'd apprehended several Vietnamese women acting suspicious outside of our perimeter wire. They were blindfolded and brought in to our compound to be questioned by an ARVN interpreter. Even though blindfolded, I could see they were scared to death. For all they knew, we might beat them or who knew what else. They didn't have ID cards with them, which caused the suspicion. Turns out they all had ID cards, but left them home when they went out to gather firewood for their evening meal. One can't be too careful because both men and women sometimes work for the Viet Cong, planting booby traps, etc.

These women were all in their twenties, I think, but looked to be about 40. As peasant women, they worked in the fields and labored through broiling sun and drenching monsoons for most of their lives. One woman sitting near me was built real thin, but her hands were almost as big as mine. Not an ounce of fat on her. Her teeth were blackened in places through lack of dental care. The fingernails were stained black under the nails similar to a garage mechanic. Her bare feet were crusted with callouses as thick as leather.

23 Sept 67

Much water has gone under the bridge (literally) since I last wrote in my diary. On 10 September, I was sent up to Con Thien, which is an artillery firebase about two miles south of the DMZ. I took over a platoon of five tanks there. My first command. I can't be too optimistic though, because Con Thien is a real "hell hole." We get incoming mortars, rockets, and artillery all day into the night. I've had several close calls so far. We were on the northern perimeter one night when the NVA attacked us. We fired back at them with six 90mm HE and 3,000 rounds of .30-cal. Saw some bad things like a culvert that washed away while Marines were crossing and one Navy corpsman drowned. I saw some dead Marines today for the first time—a horrible sight I won't go into, but I'll never forget what I saw when an incoming medevac helicopter blew the blankets off those former human beings.

Sure wish I could write home and let you all know what I'm doing over here.

I'll just have to wait until I've been here a while and then let you know I'm not in Okinawa, that I'm actually in Vietnam. I don't wish to worry you all.

26 Sept 67

Yesterday, we underwent the heaviest barrage yet at Con Thien. I was told they threw in over 1,000 rounds of rockets, mortars, and artillery at us. Some of the artillery rounds are 152mm and each round weighs 107 pounds. Believe me, they make one hell of a scream coming down, and they blow a hole in the earth as big as a large Cadillac. We have a battalion of Marines holding the hill. All of us are scared stiff. I have six tanks around the perimeter and we spend all the time we can inside of them lately because they are the safest place to be. Con Thien had over a hundred casualties, killed and wounded, this past week. The medevac choppers are really shuttling in and out. The main supply route got flooded out, so we are totally dependent on helicopters for our casualty removal and resupply.

The damned mud is always with us. Some places the mud is knee deep, churned into a chocolate morass by tanks, amtracs, and other vehicles. I saw a Marine step into some deep mud yesterday and it took two men to pull him free.

Three of my men—Bores, Manchego, and Murphy—have been wounded by incoming and evacuated. Weicak got some shrapnel in the face, but was not medevaced. I've had a few close calls, myself. My bunker got a direct hit by an 82mm mortar while I was outside huddled in a ditch. Two more incoming rounds bracketed the ditch and I was praying hard that the third one would not land on top of me. Thank God it didn't. I'm lately a very religious and superstitious person, whereas before Con Thien, I was neither.

My first experience with rats has left me dreading them. The nervy, scummy creatures disgust me no end with their skittering around in our bunker and squeaking at night. They jump on you and run across you at night, looking for bits of food. I can't sleep knowing there are hungry rats crawling around on the floor, so I prefer to go sleep in my tank, even if it is crowded in there.

I understand the siege of Con Thien has attracted nation-wide news coverage. I hope my picture doesn't get put in Life Magazine. Someone might recognize me. I'm supposed to be in Okinawa, Ha! Ha!

18 Oct 67

We finally got pulled off of Con Thien for a rest. Thank God! I had to leave one of my tanks behind because the driver got his rear sprocket hopelessly entangled in concertina wire as he was attempting to come down from OP-3 and join us by the south gate. We also got a new company commander—Captain Baker. I hope he's a better CO than our last one. We are now at the Marine base known as C-2, about 4 miles south of Con Thien. For the first time in about 40 days, I can relax a little.

05 Nov 67

I've seen so many shocking things lately. Since I can't write home and trouble my family, I'll unload these thoughts on paper and maybe someone will care to read them some day. Where I am now at Charlie 2, getting wounded or killed is a 24-hour possibility. It hangs heavily on my mind that I could cease to exist in the world in one split second of violent destruction from an enemy mortar or rocket. I keep telling myself that God put me here and can just as easily take me if he wants.

Anyway, Con Thien captured all the headlines during the month of September, and my platoon of tanks was right in the thick of the shelling that still goes on up there, but not as bad as those terrible days in September when 1,000 rounds of incoming fell on us one day. What I saw and felt on that "artillery scarred Marine outpost," as Time Magazine called us, has changed my outlook on life. I shall never be the same as my innocent pre-war years.

Death is ugly and obscene when a young, healthy boy with years of full living ahead of him has it snatched away in one violent explosion or fatal bullet. I saw death in its most horrible and grotesque forms on Con Thien. One can never escape the feelings of fear and dread when seeing limp, nameless arms dangling from stretchers—some bloody, some hairy, some black, some muddy. Death is instantly recognizable to the most casual observer. The blue-gray cast to the face becomes more pronounced the longer they lay there. The facial expression of violent death is not a peaceful one.

08 Nov 67

Con Thien saw 140 U.S. Marines killed and over a thousand wounded during the 40-day siege by the North Vietnamese. It was weird sitting in my bunker knowing that, as soon as I walked outside, a silent mortar round could blast me into oblivion. Or, a screaming rocket might crash into my bunker while I was gone, killing or maiming everyone inside, but me, because I was elsewhere. It was Hell, but I feel some pride for having gotten all my men off The Hill without any being killed.

The enemy really tried hard to knock us off The Hill. They failed, because of the courage of every Marine and corpsman up there. I'll never forget the daily heroism of the artillerymen who must stand out in their open gun pits when they have a fire mission, regardless of how much incoming shrapnel is flying around, wearing only a helmet and flak jacket. When one man falls wounded, another takes his place and keeps on carrying out their fire mission, loading and firing their gun until the mission is over. Those Marines had to be terrified, yet they never faltered. How do you draw the line between duty and heroism?

I saw corpsmen run from cover to aid wounded Marines while incoming shells were still impacting around them. That's their job, but, again, where does one draw the line between duty and heroism. When my friend from Basic

School, Ted Christian, was killed at Con Thien, the word went out for all available corpsmen and stretcher bearers to respond. Again, without hesitation, several corpsmen jumped up, grabbed stretchers, and ran to aid their fallen comrades, knowing full well that death could rain from the sky at any moment.

10 Nov 67

Today, we celebrated the Marine Corps Birthday. The captain and first sergeant brought out a cake for us and read the birthday salute aloud from the Commandant. It's raining out and Gunny Hopkins and I are sitting on clean cots in our warm, dry, snug bunker at C-2. As I write this, the gunny is writing his wife. We have a portable radio that picks up the armed forces station, plus we have light by a kerosene lamp and candles. Gunny loves it when our radio picks up some country music. He knows all the words and sings along. Lucky for me, he can carry a tune. We also have an ice box of sorts to keep cokes, juice, etc., chilled, but the only drawback is we must use blocks of ice and it melts so darned fast. Gunny has a friend in the mess tent, so we get ice whenever we want it. Life is more tolerable now.

The whole area is overrun by rats! I've caught three so far and so has Sgt. Howard in his bunker. We're having a contest called "The Rat Race" to see who can catch the most in our traps. We use pieces of pork roast as bait. Every morning, we hang up our catches by their tails outside our bunker entrances. Whoever caught the most wins an extra meal of C-rats (pun intended).

Found out that our tank platoon has been selected for a Presidential Unit Citation as a result of Con Thien. Thanksgiving will be here soon, then Christmas. I pray that things stay quiet for a while longer.

16 Nov 67

My tanks are laid in with the artillery battery here at C-2. When they want us to carry out a fire mission, they call us on the land line phone and we put the data into our tank gun computers and blast away. Our tank 90mm cannons can reach out 18,000 meters, far beyond what the 105mm howitzers can do.

I almost bought the farm yesterday morning. One of my tanks parked behind my bunker was assigned to carry out a fire mission directed by the artillery battery. Right after this tank fired a 90mm round, I walked outside of my bunker to get a breath of fresh air, when WHOOM!! A blast of air socked me in the back. The glowing tracer element on a tank cannon projectile flew right over my head, exploding out beyond the C-2 minefield. The culpable tank commander had previously been in amtracs and was new to tanks. He'd only been with my platoon for a week. At the conclusion of the artillery fire mission, he'd lowered the main gun tube so the gunner could climb out of his seat. But the tank commander failed to ensure that the loader put the safety on after reloading the cannon. Thus, when the gunner was climbing out of his seat, he accidentally bumped the main gun firing pin with his knee. That combination of errors almost got me killed! I relieved the shook up tank commander on the spot and sent him back to the rear for some retraining in how to command a tank!

25 Nov 67

Well, time's going right along. I'll be starting my fifth month over here before too many days have passed. We have now been moved out of our comfy bunkers at C-2 to a place about two miles to the north to help guard a vital bridge position on the MSR to Con Thien. We have a "hairy" spot to defend. Two tanks are on one side of the bridge and the other two are on the west side. The enemy already tried to overrun the position on 14 October, but without success. It cost 21 Marines their lives in exchange for 155 NVA who lost their lives in that futile attack. I heard that one Marine got the Medal of Honor. My big worry is that the NVA could try again, only this time we are stretched so thin we would be overrun.

08 Dec 67

We've been moved across to the other side of the bridge. First it was called the Washout Bridge, then Bastard's Bridge, and now officially C-2 Bridge. All four of my tanks are together on the west side. Another platoon of five tanks joined us on the east side. The reason is that our intelligence folks suspected that a regimental-sized attack on the bridge was supposed to happen sometime this month. So far, all we've seen are a few snipers at night who crawl up to the edge of the tree line and "shoot and scoot." One night, a gook snuck into the abandoned tank retriever a hundred meters outside of our perimeter and started sniping at us. Sgt. Howard's tank put a 90mm armor piercing round into it and that gook never knew what hit him.

14 Dec 67

Some things I see here and take for granted, because they occur every day. But folks back home could never understand or know what I know. I can recognize in an instant what type of helicopter is overhead without looking up, just by the sound of the engine and rotor blades. I live with mud, that damned ever-present chocolate clay. It's up to my ankles and the same color as melted Hershey bars. The rains chill us night and day, never quite letting us dry off or warm up.

I know the thrill of watching glowing red tracer bullets fly through the night sky. There's the stabbing clutch in my gut at any unexpected blast or whooshing whine, such as a jet plane soaring by. And not being able to bathe but once every week or ten days, and then only in freezing creek water. Your head, armpits, and crotch itch constantly, and all you can do is scratch or douse foot powder on the itchy spots. I'd give a month's pay for a warm shower or bath right now.

Dawn is the most welcome time of the day. We've survived another night of mud, mosquitoes, rats, and chilling drizzle. We shave in cold water, eat boring C-rats day after day. We search in vain for the sun to come out, but all we see are more layers of thick, gray clouds and overcast. Christmas will be here soon. I don't feel too bad about being here, despite the hardships. I've finally realized how precious life is, and I plan to go home and live it to the fullest, if I ever survive this place.

24 Dec 67

My platoon came back up to Con Thien today, Christmas Eve. There's supposed to be a 24-hour cease fire starting tonight. We'll see if it actually lasts till morning. We have a little Christmas tree in our bunker, decorated with bits of colored paper and plastic. Someone made a gold paper star on top. Some big shots came in by chopper at dusk and then left. I think they were generals. It's strange, but I don't feel bad about being here on Christmas Eve. I think because I'm so glad to be alive.

25 Dec 67

It was quite a sight last night. I was standing watch on my tank atop OP-3 at around midnight when all the Marine firebases we could see from Con Thien were lit up with red, green and white pop-up flares at the same time. Then, the grunts on our perimeter joined in and started shooting up flares. The lifers were going nuts yelling at them to stop. They might as well have tried to stop the ocean tide from coming in. It seemed like Christmas everywhere one looked. Today, a single-engine plane circled overhead playing Christmas carols. Then, the captain and company gunny brought out cokes, beer, and cookies for us. We sure did appreciate it.

19 Jan 68

It's almost time to leave Con Thien and return to our old home at C-2 (now called Camp Leach). We haven't had much action here this time. I only had to duck into a trench or bunker a few times to avoid incoming mortars. Once again, I've received tragic news. Lt. Paul Marken, a friend from tank school, was killed while responding to an ambush over by Route 1. He took two bullets in the forehead. We called him "Pig Pen" at tank school because he seemed to be a grease magnet. He was always the dirtiest one of us at the end of a day working on the tanks. It seems you can be here one day, laughing and smiling and talking, and be dead the next. I wonder if I will ever see my mother's smiling face again and hear her welcoming me home. Why should I make it home? I certainly don't have any great destiny awaiting me. Oh, well, time will tell if I'll ever bask in the warm Tucson sun again.

24 Jan 68

Seen some pretty gruesome things in the past few days. The day before my platoon pulled off of Con Thien, an artillery round landed on a mortar pit behind my tank position and killed the infantry company gunnery sergeant. Another corporal was literally blown to bits. Rumor has it that it was friendly fire—an errant U.S. artillery round that should have cleared Con Thien—not hit us!

My platoon is now at Camp Leach (C-2) undergoing quarterly engine tune-ups. Today, I was ordered to take two tanks and a squad of Marines out the south gate to check out the scene where two Marine jeeps driving on the MSR from Cam Lo to C-2 were ambushed. I was standing near the gate when a lone jeep careened through, nearly knocking down the gate sentry. The driver was yelling at the top of his lungs that he'd been in an ambush back down the road. When we got there, a jeep was tipped over, on fire, lying atop two men trapped underneath. It was too late to do anything but call for corpsmen to cart off the corpses. I still have the stench of burnt flesh and hair in my nostrils. I wish this lousy war was over so no more boys have to die like that.

Read the 57th Psalm of David tonight in Exodus. I'm going to memorize it to comfort me at times like this, because I feel, lately, like I may not make it home alive.

11 Feb 68

I made First Lieutenant today. I should feel elated, but it's just one more hurdle to pass on the way to getting out of here. Those new silver bars do look good, though, and it means an extra $100 a month. Three of my tanks went out to help some Marines ambushed near Cam Vu. They fired 47 main gun rounds into the village where the enemy fire originated. I hope there were no innocent civilians or children in the line of fire.

21 Feb 68

Something unusual happened yesterday. Sgt. Howard came up to me and asked me to step outside my bunker. Seems one of Howard's new replacements had received a "Dear John" letter from his wife back home. "Joe" was sitting on the ground behind his bunker, holding his loaded .45 pistol in one hand, a crumpled letter in his other hand, and rocking back and forth, sobbing. Howard and I moved slowly towards him, me on one side and Howard on the other. We sat down slowly on either side of Joe, and Howard very carefully disarmed him. I'll never forget the look of pure agony on Joe's face. We got him calmed down enough to get up and go lay down on his cot. I radioed my CO and told him we were sending the distraught corporal back to Dong Ha. Sgt. Howard walked the man to the LZ and rode next to him on the chopper flight back to Dong Ha. Howard and another Marine spent the night in the tent keeping an eye on Joe, then made sure he got on the morning flight to Da Nang, where he'll be flown back to the States on an emergency furlough.

03 Mar 68

My .45 pistol got swiped out of my bunker at C-2 today. It sure pissed me off. Apparently, some truck drivers ran into my bunker for protection when their convoy got shelled as they were coming thru the south gate. My pistol was in my shoulder holster hanging from a hook over my cot while I had gone to use the head. Now, I've got to pay for it, which puts me out about $50. There's an old saying that you can trust a Marine with your life, but not with your lunch!

11 Mar 68

We're back at the Washout Bridge, living in an old bunker that Gunny English used to have. One company from the 1st Bn., 4th Marines is here with us. I'm certain we'll be rotated back to Con Thien again soon, probably for 60 days this time.

I've had thoughts lately after my last close call at C-2, that through sheer good luck or maybe fate, I'm lucky to still be alive. Still got five months more to go here. I've had at least four close calls so far where afterwards my knees and hands shook. This latest one was four days ago. We had a wounded infantry lieutenant on the back of our tank. After dropping him off at the C-2 aid station, I was sitting atop the cupola, my legs dangling down inside the turret, when I heard and FELT a tremendous, numbing blast right behind me. The wind was knocked out of me and my ears rang as I was knocked down into the turret. I looked out the vision blocks to my rear and saw nothing but a black, swirling cloud of dust and smoke. A huge 122mm rocket had impacted right behind my tank, leaving a huge crater. I never heard it come in. They say you never hear the one that gets you and I can attest to that!

27 Mar 68

I'm really going stir crazy around here at the Washout Bridge, just sitting around doing nothing but the same routine day after day. Some intellectual stimulation is coming from reading Steinbeck's "East of Eden" and "Grapes of Wrath." Also, thankfully, Trevail is nearby with his chess board. He usually wins, but it breaks up the monotony.

04 Apr 68

This day finds my platoon back at Con Thien again, this time for a minimum of 60 days. Things are real quiet here compared to what it was like in the past. We even have electricity in our huge Dyemarker bunker! The bunker has wooden floors and a reinforced roof that can withstand a direct hit by all but the largest NVA artillery and rockets. There's even a sandbag-protected shower built nearby—cold water only, but better than nothing. I feel much uplifted morale-wise, because I'm busy all the time and the infantry battalion here, 1/4, is an outstanding unit.

I went on a helicopter recon of the area today in preparation for a possible two-day operation into Leatherneck Square. I was stunned by the sight of thousands of bomb and artillery craters around Con Thien. It looked like the surface of the moon from the air. The enemy must have paid a terrible price that we can never know.

23 Apr 68

Just received the worst news of my entire tour in RVN. Capt. Sale just radioed me that I was being transferred to the 1st Amtrac Bn., over on the Qua Viet River. They're short of experienced platoon leaders and I was picked. I have no doubt my name came up because the new XO of Alpha Company and I have been at odds ever since he moved into that job last month. He's a former enlisted Mustang who likes to throw his weight around—a bully. But, we both know he's afraid to come out into the field where I'm at. He tried to pull rank on me last week, but since we are both first lieutenants, he couldn't. I challenged him to come up to Con Thien and talk with me man-to-man, rather than chew me out over the radio about some incorrect entries in one of my tank's record books. He never came out—no surprise there. I surely hate to lose my platoon after all we've been through for the past seven months. Hope everything will work out for the best.

03 May 68

A lot has happened lately!! I packed up all my gear, said my good-byes, and went to Battalion Headquarters in Quang Tri for three days. The 3rd Tank Bn. personnel officer asked me if I wanted to transfer to amtracs. I said, "No, sir. I'd prefer to stay with my tank platoon at Con Thien." He said, "Okay, you can go on back to your tanks." When I showed back up at Dong Ha, Alpha's XO looked really pissed. Ha! Rumor has it that my platoon sergeant, company gunny, and company first sergeant pitched a gripe about the unfairness of me being pulled out like that, and it went all the way up the chain to the battalion sergeant major, who spoke with the colonel about it, and he intervened on my behalf.

11 May 68

I finally wrote home and told my mom and family I had been in Vietnam this whole time, that I didn't want them to worry about me. Only I wrote that I'm being pulled out of the field and transferred to a "safe" place in the rear. Actually, though, I'm expecting to get the word any day that my days of getting shot at are over, especially since you can see by my handwriting that I got wounded in the right wrist by a piece of shrapnel from an NVA mortar. It hurts like hell, especially when I try to bend my wrist. My hand is all swollen. The Navy doctor here probed it real deep, but couldn't find the piece of shrapnel. He stopped because he said he didn't want to possibly cause permanent damage by probing any further.

I saw an F-8 Crusader jet (Navy) above Leatherneck Square making a dive bombing run and get hit by ground fire and crash in a huge fireball of aviation fuel and ammunition. His wingman circled the scene once slowly and waggled his wings in salute as he flew away. I felt like crying.

28 May 68
Here I am again up at Con Thien after going on R&R to Hawaii. I'd been trying to go to Australia, but kept getting bumped, so when Hawaii came available, I jumped on it. Everyone on the plane but me was married, going to meet their wives. It was a wonderful change of scenery.

I practically spent the entire first day in a hot shower at my hotel. My clogged pores are clean again!! My family thinks I've got a desk job in the rear, but I'm still up here getting shot at. Only 90 more days to go. A friend from college, Jim Muir, was an infantry officer with 1/4 who got killed west of Con Thien while I was gone on R&R. Jim was student body vice president at the U of A in 1965–66.

09 Jun 68
Finally getting to be a short-timer. Only about 75 more to go. Found out that I'll go to Camp Lejeune, North Carolina after leaving Nam. I'm kind of bummed out about it, because I wanted to be stationed on the West Coast and be nearer my family. Got to stay positive, though. Anywhere is better than here.

17 Jun 68
My new platoon sergeant took an ailing tank back to Dong Ha and never returned. He took a rear area job at company headquarters. I suspect he wanted out of Con Thien and jumped at the chance to go elsewhere. He was the fourth platoon sergeant I've had since taking over the platoon nine months ago. Also, the fourth company commander and the fourth XO have come and gone. Here I am, still out in the field and old as water. My replacement can't get here soon enough.

23 Jun 68
Yesterday, I took two tanks out east of Con Thien, along with a company of grunts, to search for some NVA bunkers and destroy them. We carried 500 pounds of explosives and three flame throwers (which made the flame thrower teams happy that they would not have to tote them). We were out all day in the hot sun. A short round from one of our 81mm mortars on Con Thien landed near some Marines, wounding one. We had to wait for a medevac chopper to land and fly off with him. We located the bunker system, but it was deserted. The engineers blew the bunkers up. Later, another "friendly" short round landed on us, wounding three Marines this time. The grunt CO was really pissed off, screaming and cursing into his radio handset at someone back at Con Thien.

A few days ago, the ammo and fuel dumps at Dong Ha went up in flames and smoke. The NVA got a lucky hit with their 130mm artillery. We are ten miles away, but we could feel the ground trembling and hear the rumbling of all that fuel and ammunition blowing up. Fireballs reached up hundreds of feet in the air at times, and the sky over Dong Ha was filled with black, oily smoke. It was something I won't ever forget.

22 Jul 68

Here I am at Dong Ha as the Alpha Company XO (finally!). The company commander, Capt. Patterson, said he was listening in on my radio talk with the other tank commanders during Operation Thor, and he "liked my leadership ability," whatever that means.

July 15 was my birthday. There were times when I thought I'd never see another birthday. But, lo and behold, I got the best present I'd ever gotten—a replacement. That's right!! A lieutenant named Frank Blakemore got off a helicopter by our position in Leatherneck Square and walked over to my tank. The most beautiful words I ever heard were: "Lieutenant Coan, I'm your replacement." I had one minute to grab my gear, say good-byes, and hop aboard the chopper. If I make it home alive, it'll be because of that birthday present.

17 Aug 68

In another week, I can start preparing to head home. I'm scheduled to fly out of Da Nang AFB on 26 Aug. These are really tense times right now, especially when thinking that something tragic could occur and deprive me of my goal of reaching home in one piece—ALIVE—after all these many months of hoping, praying, and dreaming I'd made it this long. So many friends died over here that I know we are never safe anywhere in Vietnam. At last count, 16 of my friends and TBS class mates died and twice that number were wounded.

On the 15th, ten tanks from Alpha and Bravo Companies went on a joint USMC/ARVN operation up to the Ben Hai River. The Alpha Company tanks were my old 1st Platoon. They caught a battalion of NVA cooking breakfast in the sand dunes. The Marine tanks and ARVN together killed over 400 NVA without suffering a single casualty. An overjoyed South Vietnamese general awarded everyone, including me, the Vietnamese Cross of Gallantry w/Palm. I would have been out there with the tanks, but I'm considered too close to going home to go on any more operations, which is okay with me, because I've had enough thrills to last me forever.

Glossary of Terms and Abbreviations

A-4 Skyhawk. Single-seat, lightweight, jet attack bomber used by US Navy and Marine Corps, built by Douglas.

Amtrac. Amphibious tractor used for hauling personnel, ammunition, and supplies inland. In ship-to-shore operations, they carry combat-loaded Marines ashore.

Arc Light. Code name for B-52 bomb strikes conducted in Vietnam.

Arty. Military shorthand for artillery.

ARVN. Army of the Republic of Vietnam; the South Vietnamese Regular Army.

B-52 Stratofortress. USAF eight-engine, swept-wing, heavy jet bomber built by Boeing.

Bangalore torpedo. An explosive device employed for clearing barbed wire obstacles and/or blowing a path through minefields. Explosives are stuffed into a long, hollow pole or pipe that is placed over or under an obstacle and detonated.

BAS. Battalion Aid Station. The battalion surgeon's location where casualties are treated in the field and more serious casualties are stabilized prior to medevac.

Battery. An artillery unit usually consisting of six 105mm howitzers.

Bird Dog. O-1 Cessna single-engine, tandem-seat, propeller-driven observation aircraft.

BLT. US Marine Battalion Landing Team that is aboard ships.

Bracketed. Incoming mortars or artillery landing over and short; the target being in between.

C-4. Plastic, putty-textured explosive.

"Charlie." Nickname for Viet Cong. In our military alphabet, VC is Victor Charlie.

Claymore. Directional, antipersonnel land mine, command detonated, deployed in front of infantry lines facing the most likely enemy avenue of approach.

CO. Commanding officer.

CP. Command post; unit headquarters and primary communications center.

Com-helmet. Hard-shell helmet used by tank crewmen; can transmit and receive radio communications.

Commo. Communication.

"Duster." Lightly armored US Army tracked vehicle; mounts twin 40mm antiaircraft guns in an open turret; often employed as an infantry support weapon.

Dyemarker. Code name for the Strong Point Obstacle System situated below the DMZ.

F-4B Phantom II. US Marine and Navy twin-engine, two-seat, supersonic jet fighter/attack bomber; built by McDonnell Douglas.

FAC. Forward Air Control; a Marine pilot on temporary assignment with a USMC ground unit.

FO. A forward observer trained to direct artillery and mortar fire.

Gear, 782. When Marines are issued equipment, they sign a Form 782.

Gook. Derogatory term for the enemy; derived from the Korean word for "person."

Grease gun. US, M3A1 .45-caliber submachine gun, 30-round, carried by USMC tank personnel.

Gun, 130mm, M-46. Soviet-built, towed artillery cannon; maximum range of 31,000 meters, which far outranged the US 105mm and 155mm guns (see Howitzer).

Gun, 175mm, M107. US, self-propelled gun; 32,800 meters maximum range.

Gunny. USMC gunnery sergeant.

Gypsy rack. Steel bar assembly welded to the rear of a tank turret to carry extra gear.

Hand grenade. Fragmentation, M-26; hand-thrown bomb weighing one pound; effective casualty range of 40 meters.

HE. High explosive.

HEAT. High Explosive Anti-tank round designed to penetrate armor.

Helicopter, CH-46D Sea Knight. Medium transport, tandem rotors; average payload 4,800 pounds; carries crew of three plus twenty-five combat troops or fifteen litters; built by Boeing.

Helicopter, CH-53A Sea Stallion. Single-rotor, heavy assault transport; carries a crew of three and thirty-eight combat troops or twenty-four litters; average payload of 12,800 pounds; built by Sikorsky.

Helicopter, UH-34D Sea Horse. Single-engine, medium transport; carries crew of three and eighteen combat troops or eight litters; average payload is 5,000 pounds. Built by Sikorsky.

H&I Fire. Harassment and interdiction artillery fired at suspected likely enemy locations.

Howitzer, 105mm, M101A1. Towed light artillery piece; maximum range of 11,155 meters.

"Huey." Popular name for UH-1 Bell light attack helicopter.

KIA. Killed in action.

Leatherneck Square. A six-mile by eight-mile area of northern I Corps just south of the DMZ, delineated by Marine bases at Con Thien, Gio Linh, Dong Ha, and Cam Lo.

LZ. Landing zone.

M-48A3 tank. USMC and US Army medium tank; fifty-two tons; 90mm main cannon; .30-caliber; coaxially mounted machine gun; .50-caliber commander's cupola mounted machine gun; crew of four.

Machine gun, .30-caliber, M-37. Tank weapon; air-cooled, disintegrating link, belt-fed; weighs 31 pounds; cyclic rate of fire 450 rounds per minute; effective range 800 meters.

Machine gun, .50-caliber. Cupola-mounted, belt-fed, recoil-operated, air-cooled; weighs 80 pounds; cyclic rate of fire 400 rounds per minute; effective range 1,450 meters.

Medevac. Evacuation of wounded via helicopter to a medical facility.

Meters. One meter equals 39.37 inches; 1,000 meters equals 1,093 yards.

Mortar, 4.2-in., M-2. 107mm rifled, muzzle-loaded; weighs 330 pounds, 4 feet tall; maximum range 4,000 meters; called "four-deuce" by Marines.

Mortar, 60mm, M-19. Muzzle-loaded, single-shot, high-angle-of-fire infantry weapon; assembled weight 45 pounds; maximum effective range 2,000 meters.

Mortar, 81mm, M-29. Assembled weight 115 pounds; maximum effective range 2200–3650 meters.

MOS. Military occupational specialty.

MSR. Main supply route. Route 561 from Cam Lo to Con Thien was the MSR.

NCO. Noncommissioned officer.

NVA. North Vietnamese Army.

Ontos M-50. Lightly armored tracked vehicle mounting six 106mm recoilless rifles with a .50-caliber target spotting rifle; originally designed as antitank weapon; three crewmen.

Otter. USMC light amphibious vehicle for transporting personnel and equipment.

Pistol, caliber .45, M1911A1. Standard sidearm of US military; weight 4 pounds with a full seven-round magazine; effective range 50 meters.

PM. Preventive maintenance on equipment.

Quad-fifty. US Army antiaircraft weapon carried aboard trucks; mounts four .50-caliber machine guns firing in concert.

Radio, AN/PRC-25. Short-range, portable; provides two-way communication in the 30–75.95 megacycle band.

Rifle, AK-47, Kalashnikov. Soviet-designed, Chinese-built 7.62mm assault rifle; semiautomatic or full automatic; weighs 10.5 pounds; cyclic rate of fire 600 rounds per minute; effective range 350 meters.

Rifle, M-16. Magazine-fed, 5.56mm, semiautomatic or full automatic; weight 7.6 pounds loaded; cyclic rate of fire 700–900 rounds per minute; effective range 460 meters.

Rocket, 122mm. Soviet-built, fin-stabilized, 9 feet long; weight 125 pounds; maximum range is 17,000 meters; fired from a launcher tube with tripod support.

RPG. The RPG-2 is a Chinese-built antitank rocket; muzzle loaded, shoulder-fired recoilless weapon with a 40mm spin-stabilized HEAT rocket; effective range 100 meters. The RPG-7 is Soviet-built, larger than an RPG-2; effective range 500 meters; can penetrate 12 inches of armor plate.

Sappers. Engineer troops highly trained in breaching wire obstacles and minefields.

Seabees. US Naval construction battalion.

Snake-eye bombs. Used for low-altitude aircraft support bombing missions; equipped with pop-up braking fins to slow the bombs' descent so jet aircraft will avoid damage from their own exploding bombs.

Trace. Official term used to describe the bulldozed 600-meter-wide strip between Con Thien and Gio Linh, 6 miles apart.

TPQ. AN/TPQ-10 ground-based radar system for guiding jet aircraft on bombing missions during inclement weather or darkness.

VT fuse. Variable timed fuse for an explosive projectile that causes an airburst.

WIA. Wounded in action.

Willie Peter. Any explosive or shell containing white phosphorus—a chemical agent that burns white hot in contact with oxygen.

XO. Executive officer.

Notes

The epigraph to this book is drawn from James Bradley and Ron Powers, *Flags of Our Fathers* (New York: Bantam Books, 2000), 247.

Preface

1. This article was originally published in the *American Enterprise Magazine*, August 2000, and subsequently reprinted in the *Proud Warrior, Newsletter of the 1/9 Network* (Winter 2000–1): 10–12. The author, James Webb, was an infantry platoon leader and rifle company commander with the Fifth Marine Regiment in the An Hoa basin, southwest of Da Nang. During his Vietnam service, he was awarded the Navy Cross, Silver Star, two Bronze Stars, and two Purple Hearts. His first novel, *Fields of Fire*, is one of the best books of that genre. He subsequently served as secretary of the navy and later as a US senator from Virginia.

Introduction

1. Gary L. Telfer, Lane Rogers, and V. Keith Fleming, *U.S. Marines in Vietnam: Fighting the North Vietnamese 1967* (Washington, DC: Headquarters USMC, 1984), 104.

Chapter 1

The chapter 1 epigraph is drawn from "Human Nature on the Rack—Aftermath of the Battle of Antietam," *musingwithclio* (blog), September 20, 2012, https://musingwithclio.wordpress.com/2012/09/20/human-nature-on-the-rackaftermath-of-the-battle-of-antietam/.

1. Moyers S. Shore II, *The Battle for Khe Sanh* (Washington, DC: Historical Branch, G-3 Division, Headquarters USMC, 1969), 21.

2. Edwin H. Simmons, *Marine Corps Operations in Vietnam, 1954–1973: An Anthology and Annotated Bibliography* (Washington, DC: History and Museums Division, Headquarters USMC, 1974), 74–75.

3. Several months after the siege of Con Thien was over, the author returned there again with his tank platoon to provide support for the First Battalion, Fourth Marines. A lieutenant from that outfit named Larry Campbell described what happened on May 8, 1967. He was awarded a Bronze Star for his heroism that night in his initial exposure to combat.

4. "Bloody Trial," *Newsweek*, May 22, 1967, 46.

5. James S. Santelli, *A Brief History of the 4th Marines* (Washington, DC: Historical Division, Headquarters USMC, 1970), 48.

6. Simmons, *Marine Corps Operations in Vietnam*, 82.

7. Simmons, *Marine Corps Operations in Vietnam*, 82–83.

Chapter 2

1. Eric Hammel, *Ambush Valley: I Corps, Vietnam 1967* (Novato, CA: Presidio Press, 1990). On September 10, 3/26 engaged and defeated an estimated NVA regiment at Nui Ho Khe. In retrospect, 3/26 likely blunted a planned attack on Con Thien by the NVA 324B Division's 812th Regiment.

2. Hammel, *Ambush Valley*, 207–12. One of the tanks lost was an M-48A3 gun tank, and the other was an M-67 flame tank. Both were hit by RPG antitank rockets.

3. James P. Coan, *Con Thien: The Hill of Angels* (Tuscaloosa: University of Alabama Press, 2004), 177–78. On September 4, I/3/4 was patrolling one-half mile southwest of Con Thien near the abandoned village of Thon An Nha when they came under heavy attack. The Battalion CO, Lieutenant Colonel Bendell, led a reaction force from Mike Company, along with two of Second Lieutenant Barry's tanks, that routed the NVA.

4. Coan, *Con Thien*, 240–41.

5. Coan, *Con Thien*, 241.

Chapter 3

1. J. W. Hammond Jr., "Combat Journal, Part I," *Marine Corps Gazette* 52 (July 1968): 24. The author states that 2/9 was at the Rocky Ford (later Washout) on the morning of September 15, and 2/4 was directly east of the Rocky Ford, preparing to move up into position southeast of Con Thien.

2. Personal communication with Lieutenant Robert McIntosh from L/3/4, July 2002. The morning of September 16, the supply officer for 2/9 near Yankee Station had requested a resupply of food and ammunition. Several Marine tracked amphibious vehicles called Otters were obtained and loaded at C-2. Lieutenant McIntosh was aboard the first Otter that entered the turbulent, muddy washout, and it capsized ten feet from the bank. All personnel escaped by grabbing on to overhanging tree branches and were saved from drowning, but the Otter was washed downstream and submerged with all of its cargo. From then on, until the washout could be repaired, all resupply had to be done by helicopter.

3. Tim O'Brien, *The Things They Carried* (New York: Mariner Books, 2009), 20.

4. Coan, *Con Thien*, 230. The Third Marine Division Headquarters in Dong Ha reported that northern Quang Tri Province received 17.39 inches of rainfall in twenty-four hours.

5. Third Tank Battalion, 3DMARDIV Command Chronology, September 1967. When Third Division Headquarters learned of our situation that night, the captain was ordered to abandon all of his armored vehicles and return to C-2. The following morning, the captain intended to return to the Washout and retrieve his abandoned vehicles, but he was prevented from undertaking this task because a series of B-52 Arc Light bombing raids was scheduled to occur near the Washout sometime within a twenty-

four-hour period commencing that morning.

6. Vietnam Helicopter Pilots Association website, www.whpa.org. The UH-34D Sikorsky Sea Horse medium helicopters belonging to HMM-163 all had the slanted eyes painted on their noses. The purpose for those painted eyes was that, according to legend, Asians believed the angry slanted eyes represented evil.

Chapter 4

1. Coan, *Con Thien*, 244. A lieutenant from Second Battalion, Twelfth Marines, was killed in his sleep one night by a direct hit on his bunker atop OP-2. His replacement and another artillery officer landed at Con Thien the next afternoon and ambled off the chopper, gawking at the surroundings as they went. Totally ignorant of the enemy's propensity for shelling the LZ during helicopter arrivals, they were both killed instantly when a salvo of incoming artillery shells hit the LZ.

2. Third Tank Battalion Command Chronology, September 1967, unclassified S-4 Report. When the vehicle recovery team from Headquarters Company, Third Tank Battalion, located the three tanks and the tank retriever at the Washout several days later, they found that A-11, A-13, and the Fifth Platoon tank had been used for target practice by the NVA, who fired several RPGs into them. They were recoverable, however, and were towed back to the rear for repairs. The burned-out tank retriever was declared a total loss and abandoned in place, a permanent reminder of the "Washout fiasco."

3. Hammond, "Combat Journal, Part I," 24. The CO of Second Battalion, Fourth Marines, Lieutenant Colonel Hammond, described the battle at Phu Oc as follows: "On the morning of September 21, companies E, F, and G came under heavy mortar and artillery fire from the DMZ while attempting to attack and envelop a large enemy bunker complex east of Con Thien. Our artillery, fixed-wing air, and helicopter gunships were called in to attack large groups of NVA reinforcements moving in from the north and southeast." Colonel Hammond had requested tanks, and they would have helped save the day for 2/4, but the soggy, saturated earth would not support armored vehicles. The fierce fight put up by 2/4 that day likely prevented a major attack at a later date on Con Thien.

4. Dennis Warner, "Bearing the Brunt at Con Thien," *The Reporter*, September 29, 1967, 21. According to Warner, in the three days from September 19 to 21, Marines on or near Con Thien lost 23 dead and 317 wounded. The 2/4 battle at Phu Oc accounted for most of those casualties.

5. Coan, *Con Thien*, 249.

6. Lieutenant Colonel David Douglas Duncan was a retired Marine officer and highly regarded as a published military historian.

Chapter 5

1. Coan, *Con Thien*, 109–36. Also, refer to Keith W. Nolan, *Operation Buffalo: USMC Fight for the DMZ* (Novato, CA: Presidio Press, 1991), 44–134. One of the worst defeats suffered by US Marines at the hands of the North Vietnamese Army occurred

on July 2, 1967, during Operation Buffalo. Two companies from 1/9, Alpha and Bravo, were conducting a routine sweep near an area called the "Marketplace," 2,500 meters northeast of Con Thien, when Bravo was caught in the middle of a multi-battalion NVA ambush. A combined reaction force of tanks and infantry from Con Thien was finally able to reach the decimated remnants of Bravo and rescue them. Only twenty-six Bravo Company Marines walked out unaided. Two days later, a relief force of tanks and infantry made it back to the Marketplace to retrieve Bravo Company's dead, which they had been forced to leave behind. Bravo Company ceased to be a viable combat unit after that disastrous encounter at the Marketplace; it had to be refilled almost completely with new replacements. Many superstitious Marines serving with attached units on Con Thien were not happy that 1/9 was next in line to serve their "time in the barrel" with them.

2. Richard B. Smith, "Leatherneck Square," *Marine Corps Gazette* (August 1969): 37.

3. David D. Duncan, *War Without Heroes* (New York: Harper and Row, 1970), 59–145. Lieutenant Colonel Duncan spent several days during the siege living with Marines from Mike Company atop OP-1. Several of the photos that Lieutenant Colonel Duncan took at Con Thien and included in his book are on permanent display at Headquarters Marine Corps.

Chapter 6

Regarding the chapter 6 epigraph, Colonel Duncan heard this said by a Marine to his comrades one night.

1. J. W. Hammond Jr., "Combat Journal, Conclusion," *Marine Corps Gazette* 52 (August 1968): 47–48.

2. Hammond, "Combat Journal, Conclusion," 47–51. Second Battalion, Fourth Marines, the same infantry battalion that tangled with and defeated the entrenched NVA at Phu Oc on September 21, assumed responsibility for defending the newly completed Washout bridge, which opened up the MSR, Route 561, to vehicular traffic, including tanks. Early in the morning of October 14, 2/4 repelled an attack on the bridge by NVA sappers. Again, 2/4 (a.k.a. "Magnificent Bastards") had prevented the NVA from carrying out their plans to attack Con Thien. One Marine, Sergeant Paul Foster, received the Medal of Honor for his heroism at that battle. In honor of the ferocious fight put up by 2/4, it was initially named "Bastards Bridge."

Epilogue

1. Simmons, *Marine Corps Operations in Vietnam*, 73–128. The total casualty figures were obtained by compiling the casualty figures listed from various operations within that article that related to the defense of Con Thien and the eastern DMZ area.

Bibliography

"Ambush at Con Thien." *Newsweek*, July 17, 1967, 45.

"Barring the Way: McNamara's Line." *Newsweek*, September 18, 1967, 29.

"Bloody Trial." *Newsweek*, May 22, 1967, 46.

Buckley, Tom. "Monsoon Rains Cut Off Marines Near Buffer Zone." *New York Times*, September 19, 1967.

Caulfield, M. P. "India Six." *Marine Corps Gazette* 53 (July 1969): 28–29.

Coan, James P. *Con Thien: The Hill of Angels*. Tuscaloosa: University of Alabama Press, 2004.

Command Chronology, Third Tank Battalion declassified document; September 1967.

"Demilitarizing the Zone." *Time*, May 26, 1967, 24–25.

Duncan, David Douglas. "Con Thien: Inside the Cone of Fire." *Life*, October 27, 1967, 23–42.

———. *War Without Heroes*. New York: Harper and Row, 1970.

Edelman, Bernard. *Dear America: Letters Home from Vietnam*. New York: Norton, 1985.

Eigen, Daryl J. *A Hellish Place of Angels: Con Thien—One Man's Journey*. Bloomington, IN: iUniverse, 2012.

Gilbert, Oscar E. *Marine Corps Tank Battles in Vietnam*. Philadelphia: Casemate Publishers, 2007.

Hammel, Eric M. *Ambush Valley: I Corps, Vietnam, 1967*. Novato, CA: Presidio Press, 1990.

Hammond, J. W., Jr. "Combat Journal, Part I." *Marine Corps Gazette* 52 (July 1968): 20–29.

———. "Combat Journal, Conclusion." *Marine Corps Gazette* 52 (August 1968): 46–51.

Hemingway, Al. "A Place of Angels." *Vietnam* (February 1991): 27–32.

Herr, Michael. *Dispatches*. New York: Alfred A. Knopf, 1978.

Horn, Derl. *Blood, Sweat & Honor: Memoir of a Walking Dead Marine in Vietnam*. Self-published, Createspace, 2015.

Long, Joseph C. *Hill of Angels: U.S. Marines and the Battle for Con Thien*. Quantico, VA: History Division, Marine Corps University, 2016.

Martin, Bruce. "Time in the Barrel." *Leatherneck* 54 (November 1971): 71–75.

Murphy, Edward F. *Semper Fi—Vietnam*. Novato, CA: Presidio Press, 2000.

Nolan, Keith W. *The Magnificent Bastards*. Novato, CA: Presidio Press, 1994.

———. *Operation Buffalo: USMC Fight for the DMZ*. Novato, CA: Presidio Press, 1991.

North, Don. "A Little Piece of Hell." *New York Times*, July 4, 2017; http://www.nytimes.com/2017/07/04/opinion/vietnam-war-con-thien.html.

O'Brien, Tim. *The Things They Carried*. New York: Mariner Books, 2009.

Santelli, James S. *A Brief History of the 4th Marines*. Washington, DC: Historical Division, Headquarters, US Marine Corps, 1970.

Shore, Moyers S. *The Battle for Khe Sanh*. Washington, DC: Historical Branch, G-3 Division, Headquarters US Marine Corps, 1969.

Simmons, Edwin H. *Marine Corps Operations in Vietnam, 1954–1973: An Anthology and Annotated Bibliography*. Washington, DC: History and Museums Division, Headquarters, US Marine Corps, 1974.

Smith, Richard B. "Leatherneck Square." *Marine Corps Gazette*, August 1969, 34–42.

Steele, Richard. "Siege at Con Thien." *Newsweek*, October 9, 1967, 49–50.

Sturkey, Marion F. *Bonnie-Sue: A Marine Corps Helicopter Squadron in Vietnam*. Plum Branch, SC: Heritage Press International, 1996.

Telfer, Gary L., Lane Rogers, and V. Keith Fleming. *U.S. Marines in Vietnam: Fighting the North Vietnamese, 1967*. Washington, DC: History and Museums Division, Headquarters, US Marine Corps, 1984.

Walt, Lewis W. *Strange War, Strange Strategy*. New York: Funk and Wagnalls, 1970.

Warner, Dennis. "Bearing the Brunt at Con Thien." *The Reporter*, September 19, 1967, 21.

Webb, James H. "Heroes of the Vietnam Generation." *The Proud Warrior, Newsletter of the 1/9 Network* (Winter 2001–2): 10–12.

Index

A-4 Skyhawk (jet): Marine close air support, 71, 168
A-6 Intruder (jet), 177. *See also* TPQ strike
AC-47 ("Puff, the Magic Dragon"), 192
Alpha Company, 3rd Tank Battalion: abandoned tanks, 89–90, 92–93, 96, 101; and attack on Con Thien, 4–5; Dong Ha headquarters of, 9, 13, 34, 59, 86; 5th Platoon, 82; platoon rotation policy, 199; recovery of 1st Platoon's abandoned tanks, 225n2 (chap. 4); 2nd Platoon, 85–87. *See also* Marine Corps units: 3rd Tank Battalion
Amtracs. *See* Marine Corps units: 1st Amphibian Tractor Battalion
Aranda, Cpl., 35
Arizona Army National Guard: and rationale for joining, 17; service obligation completed, 20
Army of the Republic of Vietnam (ARVN). *See* South Vietnamese Army (ARVN)

B-52 bombers, 32, 60–61, 152, 168; and Arc Lights, 46; mission scheduled for Washout vicinity, 111–12, 224n5 (chap. 3)
Baker, Capt., 209
Baker, Cpl.: courage during NVA rocket attack, 191
Bangalore torpedo, 4, 72, 153–54, 162
Barney, 1st Lt. Douglas, 100–101, 120
Barry, 2d Lt. Thomas C., 9–12, 21–23, 30, 60, 97, 101, 164, 171, 201, 224n3 (chap. 2); and reason for being replaced, 42–43
Basic School, The (TBS), 12, 51–52, 170, 176; number of classmates lost, 218.

See also Quantico, Virginia
Bendell, Lt. Col. Lee R., 30, 224n3 (chap. 2)
Ben Hai River, 1, 2, 32, 54, 121, 218. *See also* Demilitarized Zone (DMZ)
Bird Dog (spotter plane), 57, 154–55
Blakemore, 2d Lt. Frank, 218
Bores, Lance Cpl. Kenneth, 73, 83–84, 86, 91, 104, 107, 110; and mine-damaged tank, 93; reunited with, 201–2; wounded and medevaced, 156–57, 209
Brown, Lance Cpl. "Charlie," 88–90, 151, 202
Burnett, PFC, 86, 107

C-123 Provider (transport aircraft), 120
C-130 Hercules (transport aircraft), 53, 55, 120
C-2 Bridge. *See* Washout Bridge
Ca Lu, 12
Cam Lo, 2; black market, 90; bridge, 14; firebase, 54, 71, 147, 167, 214; resettlement village, 6
Cam Lo River, 12, 88, 90
Camp Carroll (firebase), 2, 3, 12, 54–55, 71, 147, 167
Camp Con Thien (US Army Special Forces base), 3, 4, 24
Camp Leach. *See* Charlie-Two
Camp Lejeune, North Carolina, 202, 217
Camp Pendleton, California: tank school, 52–53, 170, 208
Cam Vu: tank attack, 214
Carter, Sgt. Paul, 75, 101, 127, 149, 196, 201; survived an NVA ambush, 103–4
casualties, 209–10; from friendly fire, 13, 213, 217; in Leatherneck Square, 203. *See also* TPQ strike
CH-53 Sea Stallion (helicopter), 72, 107–

Sale, Capt., 216
Sanders, Cpl., 28, 33, 43, 57, 62–64, 70,
    148; departure of, 149
Seabees. *See* Navy, US, Mobile Construc-
    tion Battalion
South China Sea, 1–2, 33, 154
South Vietnamese Army (ARVN), 2, 4, 6,
    24; interpreters, 208. *See also* Opera-
    tion Lam Son 250
SPOS. *See* Strong Point Obstacle System
Steppe, 2d Lt. Dean, 102–3, 123, 126–27,
    129–31, 162–64; and anger toward
    news reporters, 153; departure of,
    166–67
Strong Point Obstacle System (SPOS),
    6; origin of, 2–3. *See also* McNamara,
    Secretary of Defense Robert S.
Sword of Damocles Syndrome, 42, 76,
    143

Tews, Staff Sgt., 202
Thatcher, Sgt. Charles: Navy Cross
    awarded, 5
Thomason, Gunnery Sgt.: wounded and
    medevaced, 199, 202
TPQ strike, 62; and errant bombing of
    Con Thien, 177–80
Trace, the, 2–3, 29, 127, 200. *See also*
    Strong Point Obstacle System (SPOS)
Trevail, Lance Cpl. Albert, 27–30, 32–33,
    43–44, 57, 61–62, 67, 75, 125, 201, 215;
    saved another Marine's life, 46
Tucson, Arizona, 113, 207; author's per-
    sonal history, 16–20

UH-34D Sea Horse (helicopter), 39, 59;
    and slanted eyes, 109, 225n6 (chap. 3)

Viet Cong, 120, 208
Viet Minh, 4. *See also* Dien Bien Phu
Vo Nguyen Giap (general), 5–6

Waggle, Staff Sgt., 202
Washout, the: abandoned tanks at,
    96–98, 101, 112, 121; attempt to ford,
    92–93; fiasco, 124–25, 127–28, 134,
    177, 182–83, 200; MSR culvert col-

lapse at, 83–84, 90
Washout Bridge, 198, 200, 215; attacked,
    192–93; constructed by US Marines
    and Navy Seabees, 181, 187; named
    Bastard's Bridge, then later C-2
    Bridge, 212
Wayne, John: childhood hero, 16, 178;
    and taking unnecessary combat risks,
    87, 166
Webb, James H., xi, 223n1 (preface)
Weicak, Sgt., 35, 77, 149–51, 209; casu-
    alty, 68, 156; and TPQ near miss, 179
Westmoreland, General William, 2–4, 92
Woodard, Staff Sgt., 202

Yankee Station, 78, 81–82, 85, 100, 102,
    104, 122, 165, 167–68, 183, 196–97;
    distance from Con Thien, 45; 2/9 loca-
    tion at, 94. *See also* Washout, the